15th Blue Book

Dolls & Values®

by Jan Foulke
Photographs by Howard Foulke

Antique Section — Pages 21 to 206.
Modern Section — Pages 207 to 311.

Published by Hobby House Press, Inc.
Grantsville, Maryland
www.hobbyhouse.com

Front Cover Illustrations: Top Right: 23in (58cm) Simon & Halbig 719 child. *H & J Foulke, Inc.* Bottom Left: 14in (36cm) Alexander hard plastic *Little Women "Amy,"* all original. *H & J Foulke, Inc.* Bottom Left: 15in (38cm) Effanbee black composition *Baby Grumpy*, all original. *H & J Foulke, Inc.*

Back Cover Illustration: *Dramatic New Living Skipper.* For additional information, see page 238. *McMasters Premiere Doll Auctions.*

Title Page Illustration: 20in (51cm) Gebrüder Heubach 7246 character girl. For additional information, see pag 102. *Richard Saxman.*

Additional copies of this book may be purchased at
$19.95 (plus postage and handling) from
Hobby House Press, Inc.
1 Corporate Drive
Grantsville, MD 21536
1-800-554-1447
www.hobbyhouse.com

© 2001 by Jan and Howard Foulke

Printed in the United States of America

ISBN: 0-87588-614-0

Using This Book

Welcome to the Doll Collecting World! If you have any interest in dolls, whether you are new to dolls, or an old hand at them, the *Blue Book of Dolls & Values* was written for you. It can help you identify and learn more about your dolls or dolls you are thinking of purchasing. It can help you evaluate or appraise your dolls or guide you on prices for future additions to your collection. It puts, right at your fingertips, in a well-organized easy-to-use format, a great amount of information that you will need to know in order to build your doll collection. The great success of the *Blue Book of Dolls & Values,* through 15 revisions since 1974, speaks for itself as it fills the needs of doll lovers, collectors, dealers,

appraisers and estate executors who return to buy the latest editions.

For convenience in locating a doll more quickly, the *Blue Book* is divided into two color-coded sections: *Antique & Vintage Dolls* in the blue section; *Modern & Collectible Dolls* in the pink section. Generally, the dolls in the *Antique Section* are the older dolls made from wood, wax, papier-mâché, china, bisque and cloth. Most of the dolls in the *Modern Section* are made of composition, hard plastic and vinyl, although there is some unavoidable overlapping. Where certain dolls, such as *Raggedy Ann* and *Kewpie*, were made over very long periods, the modern examples are included with the main entry in the *Antique Section*

Georgene Averill *Allie Dog*. For additional information, see page 40. *Connie & Jay Lowe.*

4

Maud Tousey Fangel
Sweets. For additional
information, see page
41. *H & J Foulke, Inc.*

in order to keep the whole production history of a doll in one place. An extensive index of doll names and manufacturers and an index of mold numbers of bisque and china heads are included at the back of the **Blue Book** to help you find dolls more quickly. Information aids provided are a bibliography of books suggested for in-depth study and a glossary of doll terms.

Within their sections, the dolls presented in the **Blue Book** are listed alphabetically by maker, material or, sometimes, trade name. For the most part, dolls are arranged in chronological order by date within a main entry. For each doll, we have included historical information, physical description, marks and labels, and the retail selling price. Photographs are shown for as many dolls as possible, but since every doll cannot be shown in each edition, you should consult previous **Blue Books** for additional photographs.

As for the doll sizes listed for most of the antique dolls, sizes priced are chosen at random, so do not assume that they are only made in the sizes listed. It just is not possible for us to list all sizes of a doll which can range from 6in (15cm) to 42in (106cm). If we do not list your doll's size, you will need to use a little common sense to interpolate a price.

Some of the historical information given for dolls was compiled

17in (43cm) 30B6 bisque shoulder head, so-called *American Schoolboy*. For additional information, see page 50. *H & J Foulke, Inc.*

from original research already published by Dorothy S., Elizabeth A. and Evelyn J. Coleman; Johana G. Anderton; Jürgen and Marianne Cieslik; and Pam and Polly Judd. The Colemans allowed some of the doll marks to be reproduced from their book *The Collector's Encyclopedia of Dolls.*

We gathered the data for compiling the retail prices during 2000 and 2001. We checked prices at antique shops and shows, auctions (including the internet), doll shops and shows, dealers' web sites, advertisements in collectors' periodicals, lists from doll dealers and purchases and sales reported by both collectors and dealers. This information, along with our own valuations and judgments, was computed into the range of prices shown in the **Blue Book**. When we could not find a sufficient number of dolls to be sure of giving a reliable range, we marked those prices with two asterisks (**).

The international market continues to be important in the antique doll world. Though trade is not as brisk as it once was, still a large number of dolls are leaving the United States for Europe. Of particular interest to the Europeans are the German bisque dolls, particularly those of Kestner, Kämmer & Reinhardt, Handwerck and Simon & Halbig; Käthe Kruse dolls; and German celluloid dolls. This international interest continues to keep prices in these categories relatively strong.

The price range for a doll listed in the **Blue Book** is the retail value of the doll if purchased from a dealer in the condition as noted in the description. Fine examples, especially those which are all original or boxed with original tags or never played with, can bring a premium of at least 50 percent more than the prices quoted. Sometimes a specific example will bring a premium price because it is particularly cute, sweet, pretty or visually appealing, having an outstanding appearance. There is just no way to factor this aspect into a price guide.

All prices given in the **Blue Book** for antique dolls are for those of good quality and condition, but showing some normal wear and aging. Dolls should be appropriately dressed in old clothing or

20in (51cm) early Martha Chase cloth child. For additional information, see page 68. *Nancy A. Smith Collection.*

12in (31cm) mask-faced googly. For additional information, see page 94. *Connie & Jay Lowe.*

new clothing made from old fabrics. Bisque or china heads should not be cracked, broken or repaired, but may have slight manufacturing imperfections such as speckling, surface lines, darkened mold lines or uneven coloring. Bodies may have repairs but should be old and appropriate to the head. A doll with its original old dress, shoes and wig will generally be valued higher than the quoted prices because these items are in scarce supply and can easily cost more than $85 each, if purchased separately.

Prices given for composition dolls are for those in overall good to excellent condition with original hair and clothing, unless noted otherwise. Composition may be lightly crazed, but should be colorful. Hard plastic and vinyl dolls must be perfect with hair in its original set and crisp original clothes. A never-played-with doll in original box with labels would bring a premium price.

When you use the ***Blue Book***, please keep in mind that no price guide is the final word about a doll. It cannot provide an absolute answer as to what to pay. It should be used only as an aid to you in purchasing and evaluating a doll. The final decision of whether to buy and what to pay, must be yours personally, for only you are on the scene actually examining the specific doll in question. Also, please remember that no book can take the place of actual field experience. Before you buy, do a lot of looking. Ask lots of questions. You will find most dealers and collectors are glad to talk about their dolls and pleased to share their information.

Happy Dolling!
Jan Foulke
June 2001

Acknowledgements

Many friends, customers, fellow dealers and doll collectors around the world contributed to the *15th Blue Book of Dolls & Values*. We would like to express our appreciation to H & J Foulke, Inc.; Becky & Andy Ourant; Nancy A. Smith, Mary Barnes Kelley, Connie & Jay Lowe, Richard Wright Antiques, Terri & Kathy's Dolls; Dorothy Hunt & Jeremy (Sweetbriar); Linda Kellerman; Keifer Collection; Floyd Jones; Carmel Doll Shop; Geri Gentile; Kay & Wayne Jensen; Richard Saxman; Lesley Hurford; Betty Harms; Ann Lloyd; Elliott Zirlin; Rae-Ellen Koenig (The Doll Express); Sidney Jeffrey; McMasters Premier Doll Auctions; Rosemary Kanizer; Emma Vann; Helen Hargett; George Humphrey; Miriam Blankman; Susan Babkowski; June & Norman Verro; and several collectors who wished to remain anonymous.

Also, thanks to Gary Ruddell of Hobby House Press, Inc. with whom we have worked for 27 years and Virginia Ann Heyerdahl for editorial assistance.

All of these people helped make this book possible.

Jan & Howard Foulke
June 2001

Investing In Dolls

Collectors talk about a doll collection being an investment, and it can be a very good one. Unfortunately, there is no guarantee that any particular doll will appreciate consistently year after year. I never advise people to collect dolls strictly as an investment. I think you should collect dolls because you like them and enjoy the hobby. If the doll appreciates in value, consider that as a bonus. We like to think that 20 or 30 years down the road when we get ready to sell our dolls, we will get more for them than we paid and, in general, I think this is true if we have bought wisely. The track record for vintage or antique dolls over 40 years old has been fairly good. Collectible dolls of the past 30 years or so are a more risky market. Most of them bring, on the secondary market, only 25 to 50 percent of their original cost.

Since assembling a doll collection can be rather costly in today's market and most of you have only a limited amount of money to allocate to it, you must be sure that you are spending your dollars to the best advantage. In this chapter, I will provide some suggestions about what to look for and what to consider before buying a doll. My basic tenet is, if you do not have the knowledge to be sure about the doll you are buying, do be sure you are buying it from someone you trust to give you the correct information about it.

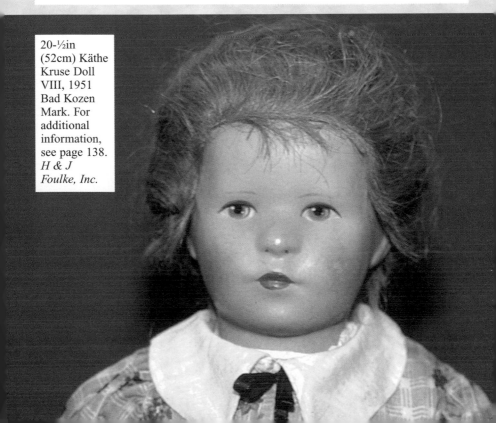

20-½in (52cm) Käthe Kruse Doll VIII, 1951 Bad Kozen Mark. For additional information, see page 138. *H & J Foulke, Inc.*

Marks

Fortunately, most of the antique bisque, some of the papier-mâché, cloth and other types of antique dolls are marked or labeled. Marks and labels give you confidence because they identify the trade name, the maker, the country of origin, the style or mold number, or perhaps even the patent date.

Most composition and modern dolls are marked with the maker's name and sometimes also the trade name of the doll and the date. Some dolls have tags sewn on or into their clothing to identify them; many still retain original hangtags.

Of course, many dolls are unmarked, but after you have seen quite a few dolls, you begin to notice their individual characteristics and can often determine what a doll possibly is. When you have had some experience buying dolls, you begin to recognize an unusual face or an especially fine quality doll, and the lack of a mark may be less important. The doll has to speak for itself, and the price must be based upon your frame of doll reference. That is, you must relate the face and quality to those of a known doll maker and make price judgments from that point.

Quality

The mark does not tell you everything about a doll. Two examples from the same mold could look entirely different and carry vastly different prices because of the quality of the work done on the doll, which can vary from head to head, even with dolls made from the same mold by one firm. To command top price, a bisque doll should have lovely bisque, decoration, eyes and hair. Before purchasing a doll, you should determine whether the example is the best available of that type. Even the molding of one head can be much sharper with more delineation of such details as dimples or locks of hair. The molding detail is especially

25in (64cm) cloth boudoir doll marked "Rose White Doll Co. Chehalis Wa, Pat. Jan 1920." For additional information, see **14th Blue Book,** page 243. *Ray Jensen Antique Dolls.*

14in (36cm)
François
Gaultier *poupée.*
For additional
information, see
page 87. *H & J
Foulke, Inc.*

important to notice when purchasing dolls with character faces or molded hair.

The quality of the bisque should be smooth; dolls with bisque which is pimply, peppered with tiny black specks or unevenly colored, or which has noticeable firing lines on the face, would be second choices at a lower price. However, collectors must keep in mind that porcelain factories sold many heads with small manufacturing defects because companies were in business for profit and were producing expendable play items, not works of art. Small manufacturing defects do not devalue a doll. It is perfectly acceptable to have light speckling, light surface lines, firing lines in inconspicuous places, darkened mold lines, a few black specks, or cheek rubs. The absolutely perfect bisque head is a rarity.

Since doll heads are hand-painted, you should examine the artistry of the decoration. The tinting of the complexion should be subdued and even, not harsh and splotchy. Artistic skill should be evident in the portrayal of the expression on the face and in details such as the lips, eyebrows and eyelashes, and particularly in the eyes, which should show highlights and shading when they are painted. On a doll with molded hair, individual brush marks to give the hair a more realistic look would be a desirable detail.

If a doll has a wig, the hair should be appropriate if not old. Dynel or synthetic wigs are not appropriate for antique dolls; a human hair or good quality mohair wig should be used. If a doll has glass eyes, they should be old with natural color and threading in the irises to give a lifelike appearance.

If a doll does not meet all of these standards, if should be priced lower than one that does. Furthermore, an especially fine example will bring a premium over an ordinary but nice model.

Condition

Another important factor when pricing a doll is the condition. A bisque doll with a crack on the face or extensive professional repair involving the face would sell for one-quarter or less than a doll with only normal wear. An inconspicuous hairline would decrease the value somewhat, but in a rare doll it would not be as great a detriment as in a common doll. As the so-called better dolls are becoming more difficult to find, a hairline is more acceptable to collectors if there is a price adjustment. The same is true for a doll which has a spectacular face — a hairline would be less important to price in that doll than in one with an ordinary face.

Sometimes a head will have a factory flaw which occurred in the making, such as a firing crack, scratch, piece of kiln debris, dark specks, small bubbles, a ridge not smoothed out or light surface lines. Since the factory was producing toys for a profit and not creating works of art, heads with slight flaws were not all discarded, especially if flaws were inconspicuous or could be covered. If factory defects are not detracting, they have little or no effect on the value of a doll.

It is to be expected that an old doll will show some wear. Perhaps there is a rub on the nose or cheek, a few small "wig pulls" or maybe a chipped earring hole; a Schoenhut doll or a Käthe Kruse may have some scuffs; an old papier-mâché may have a few age cracks; a china head may show wear on the hair; an old composition body may have scuffed toes or missing fingers. This wear is to be expected and does not necessarily affect the value of a doll. However, a doll in exceptional condition will bring more than "book" price.

Unless an antique doll is rare or you particularly want that specific doll, do not pay top price for a doll that needs extensive work: restringing, setting eyes, repairing fingers, replacing body parts, new wig or dressing. All of these repairs add up to a

28in (71cm) *Morning Glory* china. For additional information, see page 73. *Connie & Jay Lowe.*

considerable sum at the doll hospital, possibly making the total cost of the doll more than it is really worth.

Composition dolls in perfect condition are becoming harder to find. Because their material is so susceptible to the atmosphere, their condition can deteriorate literally overnight. Even in excellent condition, a composition doll nearly always has some fine crazing or slight fading. It is very difficult to find a composition doll in mint condition and even harder to be sure that it will stay that way. However, in order for a composition doll to bring "book" price, there should be a minimum of crazing, very good coloring, original uncombed hair and original clothes in very good condition. Pay less for a doll that does not have original clothes and hair or that is all original but shows extensive play wear. Pay even less for one with heavy crazing and cracking or other damages. For composition dolls that are all original, unplayed with, in original boxes and with little or no crazing, allow a premium of about 50 percent over "book" price.

Hard plastic and vinyl dolls must be in excellent condition if they are at "book" price. The hair should be perfect, in the original set; clothes should be completely original, fresh and unfaded. Skin tones should be natural with good cheek color. Add a premium of 25 to 50 percent for mint dolls never removed from their original boxes.

Body

In order to command top price, an old doll must have the original or an appropriate old body in good condition. If a doll does not have the correct type of body, you end up not with a complete doll but with parts that may not be worth as much as one whole doll. As dolls are becoming more difficult to find, more are turning up with "put together" bodies. Many dolls are now entering the market from old collections assem-

22in (56cm) 1860s china with youthful face. For additional information, see page 72. *H & J Foulke, Inc.*

23in (58cm) Kämmer & Reinhardt 117n character girl with flirty eyes. For additional information, see page 119. *H & J Foulke, Inc.*

bled years ago. Some of these contain dolls which were "put together" before there was much information available about correct heads and bodies. Therefore, the body should be checked to make sure it is appropriate to the head, and all parts of the body should be checked to make sure that they are appropriate to each other. A body with mixed parts from several makers or types of bodies is not worth as much as one with correct parts.

Minor damage or repair to an old body does not affect the value of an antique doll. An original body carefully repaired, recovered or even, if necessary, completely repainted is preferable to a new one. An antique head on a new body would be worth only the value of its parts, whatever the price of the head and new body, not the full price of an antique doll. A rule of thumb is that an antique head is generally worth about 40 to 50 percent of the price of the complete doll. A very rare head could be worth up to 80 percent. If there is a choice

of body types for the same bisque head, a good quality ball-jointed composition body is more desirable than a crudely made five-piece body or stick-type body with only pieces of turned wood for upper arms and legs. Collectors prefer jointed composition bodies over kid ones for dolly-faced dolls, and pay more for the same face on a composition body.

Occasionally, the body adds value to the doll. In the case of bisque heads, a small doll with a completely jointed body, a French fashion-type with a wood-jointed body, a *Tête Jumeau* head on an adult body or a character baby head on a jointed toddler-type body would all be higher in price because of their special bodies.

As for the later modern dolls, a composition doll on the wrong body or with a body that is cracked, peeling and in poor condition would have a greatly reduced value. The same is true of a vinyl doll with replaced parts, body stains or chewed-off fingers.

Clothing

It is becoming increasingly difficult to find dolls in old clothing because, as the years go by, fabrics continue to deteriorate. Consequently, collectors are paying more than "book" price for an antique doll if it has original old clothes, shoes and hair. Even faded, somewhat worn or carefully mended original or appropriate old clothes are preferable to new ones. As collectors become more sophisticated and selective, they realize the value of old doll clothing and accessories. Some dealers are now specializing in these areas. Good old leather doll shoes will bring more than $85 per pair; a lovely Victorian white-work doll dress can easily cost $95; an old dress for a French fashion lady, $300 and more. Good old doll wigs can bring from $25 to $250.

However, when clothing must be replaced and appropriate old clothing cannot be obtained, new clothes should be authentically styled for the age of the doll and constructed of fabrics that would have been available when the doll was produced. There are many reference books and catalog reprints showing dolls in original clothing, and doll supply companies offer patterns for dressing old dolls.

To bring top price, a modern doll must have original clothes. It is usually fairly simple to determine whether or not the clothing is original and factory made. Some makers even placed tags in the doll's clothing. Replaced clothing greatly reduces the price of modern dolls. Without the original clothing, it is often impossible to identify a modern doll because so many were made using the same face mold.

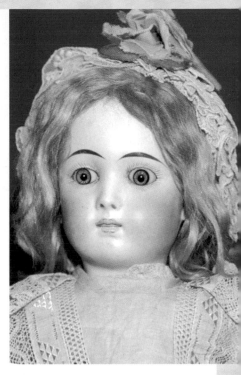

19in (48cm) 137 Belton with French style face. For additional information, see page 46. *Richard Saxman.*

Total Originality

Today totally original antique dolls are becoming rare. It is often difficult to determine whether the head and body and all other parts of a doll, including wig, eyes and clothes, have always been together. Many parts of a doll may have been changed and clothing and accessories could have been added over the years. Many dolls labeled "all original" are simply wearing contemporary clothing and wigs. Some collectors and dealers are "embellishing" more expensive dolls by taking original clothing and wigs from cheaper dolls to further enhance the value of the most costly ones.

Dolls with trunks of clothing should be examined to determine whether or not the clothes actually go with the doll or are an assembled wardrobe. A little common sense goes a long way in deciding whether the clothes are of the proper fit, fabric and style for the dolls. The same is true for accessories.

Boxed sets of dolls and accessories should be examined very carefully as some very charming sets of newly assembled old items are being offered as totally original for very, very high prices. Of course, when these ensembles are genuine, they are the ultimate in doll collecting.

Age

The oldest dolls do not necessarily command the highest prices. A lovely old china head with exquisite decoration and a very unusual hairdo would bring a price of several thousand dollars but not as much as a 20th century German bisque character child. Many desirable composition dolls of the 1930s and *BARBIE®* dolls of the 1960s are selling at prices higher than older bisque dolls of 1890 to 1920. So, in determining price, the age of the doll may or may not be significant.

Size

The size of a doll is usually taken into account when determining a price. Generally, the size and price for a certain doll are related: a smaller size is lower, a larger size is higher. However, there are a few exceptions. The 11in (28cm) *Shirley Temple* and tiny German dolly-faced dolls on fully-jointed bodies are examples of small dolls that bring higher prices than their larger counterparts.

Availability

The price of a doll is directly related to its availability in most cases. The harder a doll is to find, the higher its price will be. Each year

20in (25cm) Vogue *Little Imp*, all original. For additional information, see page 311. *Rosemary Kanizer*.

19in (48cm) Ideal 1957 *Shirley Temple,* all original. For additional information, see page 302. *H & J. Foulke, Inc.*

brings more new doll collectors than newly discovered, desirable old dolls; hence, the supply of old dolls is diminished. As long as the demand for certain antique and collectible dolls is greater than the supply, prices will rise. This explains the great increase in prices of less common dolls, such as the Kämmer & Reinhardt and other German character children, early china heads and papier-mâchés, composition personality dolls, *Sasha* dolls and some Alexander dolls that were made for only a limited period of time. Dolls that are fairly common, primarily the German dolly faces and the later china head dolls made over a long period of production, show a more gentle increase in price.

the early Jumeaus, all-bisques, German character children, *Patsy* family dolls, *Shirley Temples,* early *BARBIE®* dolls, composition personality dolls, hard plastic dolls of the 1950s, vinyl fashion dolls and Nancy Ann storybook dolls. Some dolls are popular enough to tempt collectors to pay prices higher than the availability factor warrants. Although *Shirley Temples, Tête Jumeaus, Bye-Lo Babies, Hildas,* Kämmer & Reinhardt 117 and some plastic Alexander dolls are not rare, the high prices they bring are due to their popularity. American cloth dolls, Schoenhuts, Heubachs, Greiners and closed-mouth shoulder head dolls are in a soft period, so many bargains can be found in these categories.

Popularity

There are fads in dolls just as in clothes, food and other aspects of life. Dolls that have recently risen in price because of their popularity include

Desirability

Some very rare dolls do not bring a high price because they are not particularly desirable. There are not many collectors looking for them.

Falling into this category are the dolls with shoulder heads made of rubber or rawhide and the Springfield jointed wood dolls. While an especially outstanding example will bring a high price, most examples bring very low prices in relationship to their rarity.

Uniqueness

Sometimes the uniqueness of a doll makes price determination very difficult. If you have never seen a doll exactly like it before, and it is not cited in a price guide or even shown in any books, deciding what to pay can be a problem. In this case, you have to use all available knowledge as a frame of reference for the unknown doll. Perhaps a doll marked "A.M. 2000" or "S & H 1289" has been found, and the asking price is 25 percent higher than for the more commonly found numbers by that maker. Or perhaps a black *Kamkins* is offered for twice the price of a white one, or a French fashion lady with original wardrobe is offered at 60 percent more than a re-dressed one. In cases such as these, you must use your own expertise and judgment to determine what the doll is worth.

Visual Appeal

Perhaps the most elusive aspect in pricing a doll is its visual appeal. Sometimes, particularly at auction, we have seen dolls bring well over their "book" value simply because of their look. Often this is nothing more than the handiwork of someone who had the ability to choose just the right wig, clothing and accessories to enhance the doll's visual appeal and make it look particularly cute, stunning, beautiful or otherwise especially outstanding.

Sometimes, though, the visual appeal comes from the face of the doll itself. It may be the way the teeth are put in, the placement of the eyes, the tinting on the face or the sharpness of the molding. Or it may not be any of these specific things; it may just be what some collectors refer to as the "presence" of the doll, an elusive indefinable quality which makes it the best example known!

14in (36cm) vinyl *Roberta Ann*, all original. *Rosemary Kanizer.*

Selling A Doll

So many times we are asked, "How do I go about selling a doll?," that it seems a few paragraphs on the topic are in order. The first logical step is to look through the **Blue Book** to identify the doll and to ascertain a retail price. Work from there to decide what you might ask for your doll. It is very difficult for a private person to get a retail or "book" price for a doll.

Be realistic about the condition. If you have a marked 18in (46cm) *Shirley Temple* doll with combed hair, no clothing, faded face with crazing and a piece off of her nose, do not expect to get the "book" price of $1,000 for her because that would be a retail price for an excellent doll, all original, in pristine unplayed-with condition, if purchased from a dealer. Your very used doll is probably worth only $50 to $75 because it will have to be purchased by someone who wants to restore it.

If you have an antique doll with a perfect bisque head but no wig, no clothes and unstrung, but with all of its body parts, you can probably expect to get about half of its retail value depending upon how desirable the particular doll is. If your doll has a perfect bisque head with original wig, clothing and shoes, you can probably get up to 75 percent of its retail value.

As for actually selling the doll, there are several possibilities. Possibly the easiest is to advertise in your local paper. You may not think there are any doll collectors in your area, but there probably are. You might also check your local paper to see if anyone is advertising to purchase dolls; many dealers and collectors do so. Check the paper to

20in (51cm) Effanbee Composition *Honey*, all original and very rare. *Rosemary Kanizer.*

find out about antique shows in your area. If a dealer has dolls, ask if he would be interested in buying your doll. Also, you could inquire at antique shops in your area for dealers who specialize in dolls. You will probably get a higher price from a specialist than a general antique dealer because the former are more familiar with the market for specific dolls. A roster of doll specialists is available from The National Antique Doll Dealers Association, Inc., through their web site at www.nadda.org.

You could consign your doll to an auction. If it is a common doll, it will probably do quite well at a local sale. If it is a more rare doll, consider sending it to one of the auction houses that specializes in selling dolls; most of them will accept one doll if it is a good one, and they will probably get the best price for you.

If you are on-line, you can try selling your doll on one of the auction services, such as eBay™. You will need to have a digital camera or scanner to provide photographs, which are very important to on-line selling. You should decide on a minimum price you will accept, otherwise known as a reserve price, just in case it is a slow auction week. Of course, you will have to ship the doll. If it has a bisque head with glass or sleep eyes, you will have to stuff the head to protect the eyes. Improper packing of the head is the most common cause of damage during shipping.

It would probably be worth your while to purchase a doll magazine from your local book store, doll shop or newsstand; most doll magazines include ads from auction houses, doll shows and leading dealers. You could advertise in doll magazines, but you might have to ship the doll and guarantee return privileges if the buyer does not like it.

If you cannot find your doll in the **Blue Book**, it might be a good idea to have it professionally appraised. This will involve your paying a fee to have the doll evaluated. We provide this service and can be contacted through the publisher. Many museums and auction houses also appraise dolls.

For more detailed information about collecting and selling dolls, consult my book *Doll Buying and Selling,* available from Hobby House Press.

14in (36cm) Alexander *Alice in Wonderland*, all original. For additional information, see page 213. *Rosemary Kanizer.*

Antique & Vintage Dolls

Dolls in this section are listed alphabetically by maker, by material or sometimes by trade name. Dolls are arranged in chronological order by date within a main entry.

Values given in this section are retail prices for clean dolls in very good overall condition with no cracks, chips or repairs in porcelain heads and with proper bodies and appropriate wigs and clothes. Naked, wigless, dirty, unstrung "attic dolls" are worth 35 to 60 percent, depending upon the rarity of the doll.

19in (48cm) Simon & Halbig 1009 brown bisque child, all original. For additional information, see page 56. *H & J Foulke, Inc.*

Alabama

Early Alabama Indestructible Doll: All-cloth painted with oils, tab-jointed shoulders and hips, flat derriere for sitting; painted hair with circular seam on head, molded face with painted facial features; applied ears; painted stockings and shoes (a few with bare feet); appropriate clothes; all in good condition, some wear acceptable, no repaint or touch up.

11-15in (28-38cm)	**$1,400-$1,600**
21-24in (53-61cm)	**$2,500-$3,000**
Black: 14-19in (36-48cm)	**$6,600****
Wigged: 24in (61cm)	**$3,000-$3,500****

Later doll, molded ears, bobbed hair-do:

14-15in (36-38cm)	**$1,000-$1,200**
21-24in (53-61cm)	**$2,000-$2,500**
Black: 14-19in (36-48cm)	**$3,000**

**Not enough price samples to compute a reliable range.

FACTS

Ella Smith Doll Co., Roanoke, AL, 1899-1925.

Mark: Various stamps, including:

PAT. NOV. 9, 1912

NO. 2

ELLA SMITH DOLL CO.

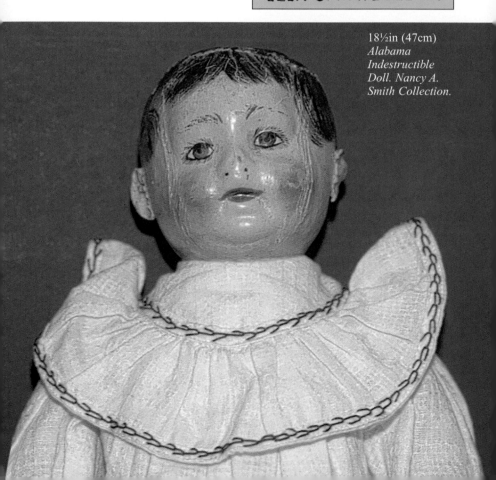

18½in (47cm) *Alabama Indestructible Doll. Nancy A. Smith Collection.*

Alexandre

H.A. Bébé: 1889-1891. Perfect bisque socket head, closed mouth, paperweight eyes; jointed composition and wood body; lovely clothes; all in good condition.
Mark: H ᗺ A

17-19in (43-48cm) **$5,800-$6,800****

Bébé Phénix: 1889-1900. As above; composition body sometimes with one-piece arms and legs.
Mark: Red Stamp:

Incised: PHENIX ★95

17-18in (43-46cm)	**$3,800-$4,200**
22-23in (56-58cm)	**$4,700-$5,200**
Open mouth:	
17-19in (43-48cm)	**$2,300-$2,500**

**Not enough price samples to compute a reliable range.

FACTS
Henri Alexandre, Paris, France, 1888-1892; Tourrel, 1892-1895; Jules Steiner and successors, 1895-1901.
Designer: Henri Alexandre.
Trademark: Bébé Phénix.

All-Bisque
(So-called French)

All-Bisque French Doll: Ca. 1880. Jointed at shoulders and hips, swivel neck, slender arms and legs; solid dome head, good wig, glass eyes, closed mouth; molded shoes or boots and stockings; appropriately dressed; all in good condition, with proper parts.

5¼in (13cm)	**$1,650-$1,850***
5¾in (15cm)	**$2,250-$2,500***
7½in (19cm)	**$4,300**
8in (20cm)	**$5,000-$6,000****
9¼in (24cm) at auction	
	$8,800-$9,240

*Allow extra for original clothes.
**Not enough price samples to compute a reliable range.

FACTS
Various French and/or German firms. Ca. 1880-on. Smiling-faced dolls made by Simon & Halbig for the French trade.
Mark: None, sometimes numbers.

17in(43cm) *H.A. Bébé.*
Private Collection.

With bare feet:

5in (13cm)	**$2,250-$2,500***
6in (15cm)	**$2,650-$2,850***
7in (18cm) at auction	**$5280**

With jointed elbows and knees:

5½in (14cm)	**$5,500-$6,500****

With jointed elbows:

5½in (14cm)	**$5,000-$5,500***
Oriental: 5½in (14cm)	**$1,800-$2,000**
Black: 5½in (14cm)	**$1,800-$2,000**

Painted eyes:

4-4½in (10-12cm), all original	**$850-$1,000**
2½in (6cm), blue boots, all original	**$225-$275**

Later French Dolls: 1910-1920
S.F.B.J., long tan stockings, swivel neck, glass eyes: 6in (15cm) **$575-$675**
J.V., tall black boots, swivel neck, glass eyes: 6in (15cm) **$450-$500**

*Allow extra for original clothes.
**Not enough price samples to compute a reliable range.

5½in (14cm) French all-bisque with smiling face. *H & J Foulke, Inc.*

Left: 5½in (14cm) French all-bisque with jointed elbows and bare feet, all original. *H & J Foulke, Inc.*

All-Bisque Dolls (German)

All-Bisque with molded clothes: Ca: 1890-on. Good quality work; all in good condition, with proper parts.

3½-4in (9-10cm)	$115-$150
5-6in (13-15cm)	$200-$250
7in (18cm)	$275-$325

All-Bisque Slender Dolls: Ca. 1900-on. Stationary neck, slender arms and legs, glass eyes, molded shoes or boots and stockings; many in regional costumes; all in good condition, with proper parts.

3¾-4in (9-10cm)	$165-$185*
5-6in (13-15cm)	$275

*Allow extra for original child clothes.

Swivel neck:

4in (10cm) 10a or 39/11	$250-$300
5½in (14cm) 13a	$450-$500

Black or Mulatto:

4-4½in (10-12cm)	$350-$400
Swivel neck: 5in (13cm)	$550

Round face: swivel neck, two-strap heeled shoes, pegged shoulders and hips:

4½-5½in (11-14cm)

re-dressed	$375-$425
original clothes	$500-$550

FACTS
Various firms including Hertwig & Co.; Alt, Beck & Gottschalck; Kestner; Kling; Simon & Halbig; Hertel, Schwab & Co.; Bähr & Pröschild; Limbach; Ca. 1880-on. **Mark:** Some with "Germany" and/or numbers; some with paper labels on stomachs.

4¼ (10cm) Hertwig & Co. all-bisque sailor with molded clothes. *H & J Foulke, Inc.*

All-Bisque with painted eyes: Ca. 1880-1910. Stationary neck, painted eyes, molded and painted shoes and stockings; fine quality work; all in good condition, with proper parts.

1¼in (3cm) crocheted clothes	$85-$110
1½-2in (4-5cm)	$75-$85
4-5in (10-13cm)	$175-$225
6-7in (15-18cm)	$250-$300

Swivel neck:

4-5in (10-13cm)	$250-$300

Early style, bootines, yellow or blue boots or shirred hose:

4-5in (10-13cm)	$300-$350
6-6½in (15-16cm)	$400-$450
8in (20cm)	$750-$850

5in (13cm) all-bisque with painted eyes, black stockings and tan slippers. *H & J Foulke, Inc.*

Long black or brown stockings, tan slippers:

4¼in (11cm)	$375
5in (13cm)	$425
6in (15cm)	$500

All-Bisque with glass eyes: Ca. 1890-1910. Stationary neck, glass eyes, molded and painted shoes and stockings; all in good condition, with proper parts, fine quality.

3in (8cm)	$275-325*
4½-5in (11-13cm)	$275-$350*
6in (15cm)	$375-$400*
7in (18cm)	$450-$500*
8in (20cm)	$600-$650*
9in (23cm)	$800-$900
10in (25cm)	$1,000-$1,200
12in (31cm)	$1,400-$1,600

Early style model, stiff hips, shirred hose or bootines:

3in (8cm)	$325
4½in (11cm)	$325-$350
6in (15cm)	$550
7in (18cm)	$650-$750
8½in (21cm)	$1,000-$1,200

Long black or white stockings, tan shoes:

5in (13cm)	$575-$675
7½in (19cm)	$900-$950

*Allow $50 - $150 extra for yellow boots or unusual footwear and/or especially fine quality.

All-Bisque with swivel neck and glass eyes: Ca. 1880-1910. Swivel neck, glass eyes, molded and painted shoes or boots and stockings; all in good condition, with proper parts, fine quality.

3¼in (8cm)	$350-$375*
4-5in (10-13cm)	$450-$550*
6in (15cm)	$650-$750*
7in (18cm)	$750-$850*
8in (20cm)	$1,100-$1,250*
9in (23cm)	$1,400-$1,650*
10in (25cm)	$1,800-$2,000

Early Kestner or Simon & Halbig-type:

4½-5in (12-13cm)	$1,850-$2,000
6in (15cm)	$1,850-$2000
7in (18cm)	$2,150-$2,250
8in (20cm)	$2,500-$2,750
10in (25cm)	$3,200-$3,500

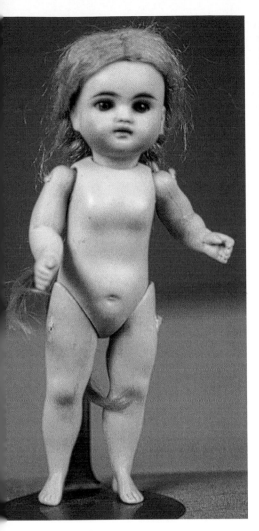

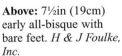

Above: 7½in (19cm) early all-bisque with bare feet. *H & J Foulke, Inc.*

Top Right: 6¼ (15cm) all-bisque with glass eyes, round face and bootines. *H & J Foulke, Inc.*

Right: 8in (20cm) early all-bisque Kestner with jointed knees. *H & J Foulke, Inc.*

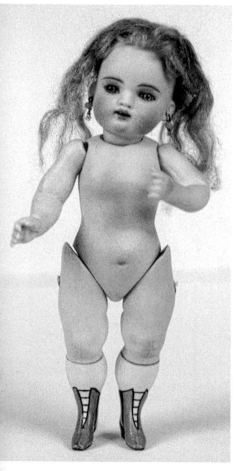 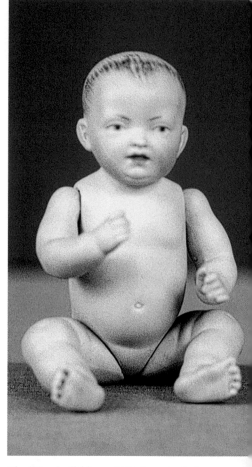

8½in (22cm) early all-bisque Kestner 102, so-called *Wrestler. H & J Foulke, Inc.*

7in (18cm) all-bisque 830 character baby. *H & J Foulke, Inc.*

With swivel waist:
   7in (18cm) at auction   **$17,600**
With jointed knees:
   6in (15cm)   **$3,500-$4,000**
   8in (20cm)   **$5,500-$6,500**
#102 (so-called *Wrestler*):
   5½ (14cm)   **$1,000-$2,200**
   8½-9in (22-23cm)   **$3,500-$4,000**
#120 (Bru-type face): 8½in (22cm)
       $4,250**
Bare feet:
   5½-6in (14-15cm)   **$2,250-$2,500**
   8in (20cm)   **$3,800-$4,200**
   12in (31cm)   **$6,000****

Round face, bootines:
   6in (15cm)   **$1,350-$1,500**
   8in (20cm)   **$2,200-$2,400**
Long black stockings, tan slippers:
   7½in (19cm)   **$1,250**

*Allow $100 - $150 extra for yellow boots or unusual footwear.
**Not enough sample prices to compute a reliable range.

Simon & Halbig **886** and **890**: See page 185.

All-Bisque Baby: Ca. 1900-on. Jointed at shoulders and hips, curved arms and legs; molded hair, painted features; all in good condition, with proper parts.

2½-3½in (6-9cm)	**$75-$95**
4-5in (10-13cm)	**$125-$175**

Fine early quality, blonde molded hair:

3½-4½in (9-11cm)	**$160-$185**
6-7in (15-18cm)	**$250-$300**
13in (33cm)	**$900-$1,000**
Immobile: 5-6in (13-15cm)	
	$160-$195

All-Bisque Character Baby: Ca. 1910. Jointed at shoulders and hips, curved arms and legs, molded hair, painted eyes; all in good condition, with proper parts, very good quality.

3½in (9cm)	**$95-$110**

4½-5½in (11-14cm)	**$175-$225**
7in (18cm)	**$325-$375**
8in (20cm)	**$425-$475**

Molded white shift: 6in (15cm)   **$300**

#830, #391 and others with glass eyes:

4-5in (10-13cm)	**$275-$325**
6in (15cm)	**$400-$450**
8in (20cm)	**$600-$650**
11in (28cm)	**$850-$950**

Swivel neck, glass eyes:

6in (15cm)	**$625-$675**
8in (20cm)	**$800-$850**
10in (25cm)	**$1,000-$1,100**

Swivel neck, painted eyes:

5-6in (13-15cm)	**$325-$375**
8in (20cm)	**$575-$625**
11in (28cm)	**$800-$900**

Mildred, the Prize Baby:

5in (13cm) at auction	**$4,600**

Baby Darling #497: 6in (15cm)   **$850**

9in (23cm) all-bisque 150 character girl, probably by Kestner. *H & J Foulke, Inc.*

8in (20cm) all-bisque 156 character girl, probably by Kestner. *H & J Foulke, Inc.*

Limbach (clover mark):

4-5in (10-13cm)	**$55-$85**
7in (18cm)	**$110-$135**
11-12in (28-31cm) fine quality	**$550-$650**

All-Bisque Character Dolls with Glass Eyes: Ca. 1910. Excellent quality with proper parts.

#150, 155:

5-6in (13-15cm)	**$400-$500**
7in (18cm)	**$650**

#156:

5-6in (13-15cm)	**$400-$500**
7in (18cm)	**$850**

#602, swivel neck:

5½-6in (14-15cm)	**$550-$650**

#79, pierced nose: 4½in (12cm)   **$500**
#609, 22: 4½in (12cm)   **$425-$450**

All-Bisque Character Dolls: 1913-on. Painted eyes; all in good condition with proper parts.

Pink bisque:

2-3in (5-8cm)	**$55-$65**
5in (13cm)	**$100-$110**
Glass eyes, wig: 2¾in (7cm)	**$85-$95**

Thumbsucker: 3in (8cm)   **$225-$250**

Girl with molded hair bow loop:

2½in (6cm)	**$75**

Chubby:

4½in (11cm)	**$210-$240**
6in (15cm)	**$325-$375**

HEbee, SHEbee:

5in (13cm)	**$650**
7in (18cm)	**$850**
Boxed	**$950**

Peterkin: 5-6in (13-15cm) **$275-$375**
Little Imp: 5in (13cm)   **$150**

Orsini girls, 5in (13cm):

Glass eyes	**$2200-$2500**
Painted eyes	**$1,100-$1,300**

Happifats: 4in (10cm) boy and girl
$500-$600 pair

Happifats Baby:

3¾in (10cm)	**$275-$300**

Wide Awake: 5in (13cm)   **$225**

Little Annie Rooney:

4in (10cm)	**$300**

September Morn, Grace Drayton:

4in (10cm)	**$2,500**
7in (18cm) at auction	**$4,000**

Max & Moritz:

3¾in (9cm)	**$2,000 pair**
4-1/2in (11cm) molded clothes	**$2,500 pair**

#222 Our Fairy, glass eyes:

5in (13cm)	**$650-$700**
8½in (22cm)	**$875-$900**
11in (28cm)	**$1,800**

Cupid or Sister: 5½in (14cm) **$100**

Snowflake (Oscar Hitt):

2½in (6cm)	**$250**

#790, 791, 792:

5½-6in (14-15cm)	**$450-$500**

#150, 160, 165:

3¾in (10cm)	**$225**
5½-6in (14-15cm)	**$300-$350**

5in (13cm) all-bisque 222 *Our Fairy.*
H & J Foulke, Inc.

Later All-Bisque with painted eyes:
Ca. 1920. Many by Limbach (clover mark) and & Co.; some of pretinted bisque; mohair wig or molded hair, molded and painted one-strap shoes and white stockings; all in good condition, with proper parts.

3½in (9cm)	**$70-$80**
4½-5in (12-13cm)	**$100-$110**
6in (15cm)	**$160-$185**
7-8in (18-20cm)	**$225-$250**

All-Bisque "Flapper" (tinted bisque):
Ca. 1920. Molded bobbed hair with loop for bow, painted features; long yellow stockings, one-strap shoes with heels; all in good condition, with proper parts, very good quality.

5in (13cm)	**$325-$350**
6-7in (15-18cm)	**$450-$500**
Standard quality:	
4-5in (10-13cm)	**$135-$165**

All-Bisque Baby: Ca. 1920. Pink bisque, curved arms and legs; all in good condition, with proper parts.
"Candy Baby," original factory

clothes: 2½in-3in (6-8cm)	**$95-$110**
Two-face, swivel neck:	
4in (10cm)	**$150-$175**

All-Bisque "Flapper:" Ca. 1920. Pink bisque with molded bobbed hair; original factory clothes, all in good condition, with proper parts.

3in (8cm)	**$95-$125**
Molded hat	**$250**
Molded bunny ears cap	**$350**
Aviatrix	**$225-$250**
Swivel Waist, 3½in (9cm)	**$350**
Wigged, 3½ (9cm)	**$95-$125**
Adult, 5¾in (14cm)	**$300-$350**

All-Bisque Nodder Characters: Ca. 1920-on. Many made by Hertwig & Co. Nodding heads, elastic strung, molded clothes; all in good condition.

3-4in (8-10cm)	**$35-$50**
Comic characters	**$45 up***
Dressed Animals	**$150-$175**
Dressed Teddy Bears	**$200-$225**
Santa	**$200-$225**
Dutch Girl, 6in (15cm)	**$150-$165**

All-Bisque Immobiles: Ca. 1920. Molded clothes, in good condition. Adults and children:

1½in-2¼in (4-6cm)	**$35-$45**
Children: 3¼in (8cm)	**$55-$65**
Santa: 3in (8cm)	**$125-$135**
Children with animals on string:	
3in (8cm)	**$165-$185**

Jointed Animals: Ca. 1910-on. All-bisque animals, wire-jointed shoulders and hips; original crocheted clothes, in good condition.

Rabbit: 2-2¾in (5-7cm)	**$475-$525**
Bear: 2-2½in (5-6cm)	**$450-$500**
Frog, Monkey, Pig	**$600-$700**
Bear on all fours:	
3¼in (8cm)	**$225-$275**

*Depending on rarity.

5¾ (14cm) all-bisque doll house mother and father, all original. *H & J Foulke, Inc.*

All-Bisque Dolls (Made in Japan)

Baby:
  White: 4in (10cm)   **$30-$33**
  All original elaborate outfit **$50-$65**
  Two-face, crying and sleeping
                 $150-$175
  Black: 4-5in (10-13cm)   **$55-$65**
  Bye-Lo Baby: 6in (15cm)   **$125**
Betty Boop-type:
  4-5in (10-13cm)   **$25-$30**
  6-7in (15-18cm)   **$38-$42**
Black Character Girl:
  Molded hair bow loop:
  4½in (12cm)   **$40-$50**
Bride & Groom: boxed set:
  4in (10cm)   **$70-$75**
Buster Brown: 2¾in (7cm)   **$40**
Child:
  4-5in (10-13cm)   **$32-$35**
  6-7in (15-18cm)   **$40-$50**

With animal on string:
  4½in (12cm)   **$38-$42**
Stiff with molded clothes:
  3-4in (8-10cm)   **$10-$15**
  6-7in (15-18cm)   **$35-$40**
Cho-Cho San: 4½in (12cm)   **$70-80**
Circus Set: boxed, 11 pieces
                 $150-$175
Comic Characters:
  3-4in (8-10cm)   **$30 up***
Mickey Mouse   **$175-$225**
"Nippon" Characters:
  4-5in (10-13cm)   **$85-$95**
Nodders: 4in (10cm)   **$25-$35**
Old Woman in Shoe: boxed set
                 $225-$250
Orientals: 3-4in (8-10cm)   **$20-$25**
Queue San: 4in (10cm)   **$70-$80**
Shirley Temple: 5in (13cm) **$100-$125**
Skippy: 5½in (14cm)   **$95-$110**
Snow White: boxed set
                 $400-$600
Teddy Bear: 3in (8cm)
                 $40-$50
Three Bears: boxed set
                 $250-$300
Three Little Pigs
                $40-$50 each
Wedding Set: boxed, three
pieces,
  4½in (13cm)   **$125-$135**

*Depending upon rarity

> **FACTS**
> Various Japanese firms. Ca.
> 1915-on.
> **Mark:** "Made in Japan" or
> "NIPPON."

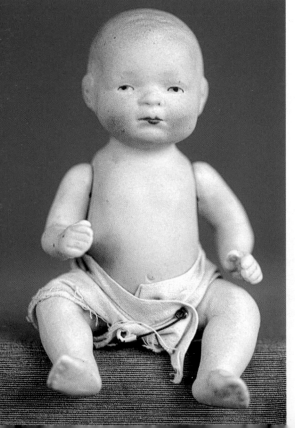

6in (15cm) "Made in Japan" all-bisque *Bye-Lo Baby. H & J Foulke, Inc.*

Alt, Beck & Gottschalck

China Shoulder Heads: Ca. 1880. Black or blonde-haired china head; old cloth body with china limbs; dressed; all in good condition. Mold numbers such as 784, 1000, 1008, 1028, 1046, 1142, 1210 and others.

Mark: *1008 X 9*

16-18in (41-46cm)	**$350-$400**
22-24in (56-61cm)	**$500-$550**
28in (71cm)	**$700-$750**

Bisque Shoulder Head: Ca. 1880. Molded hair, closed mouth; cloth body with bisque lower limbs; dressed; all in good condition. Mold numbers such as 890, 990, 1000, 1008, 1028, 1064, 1142, 1254, 1288, 1304.

Painted eyes:

15-17in (38-43cm)	**$425-$475**
22-23in (56-58cm)	**$575-$625**

Glass eyes:

9in (23cm)	**$300-$325***
14-16in (36-41cm)	**$600-$700***
22in (56cm)	**$1,100***

#926, molded pink and white scarf on head: 16in (41cm) **$2,000****
#990, pink mob cap, #998, white mob cap: 20in (51cm) **$850-$950**
#894, blue scarf, glass eyes:
21in (52cm) **$1,650-$1,750****
#1024, molded orange bonnet:
17½in (44cm) **$2,100****
#1022, short blonde curly hair, molded blue hairband, molded necklace with orange pendant, glass eyes:
22in (56cm) **$1,650****

*Allow extra for unusual or elaborate hairdo or molded hat.
**Not enough sample prices to compute a reliable range.

20in (51cm) 1880s china shoulder head child. *H & J Foulke, Inc.*

16in (41cm) unmarked bisque shoulder head of the type made by Alt, Beck & Gottschalck. *H & J Foulke, Inc.*

FACTS
Alt, Beck & Gottschalck, porcelain factory, Nauendorf near Ohrdruf, Thüringia, Germany. 1854-on.

20in (51cm) turned bisque shoulder head with glass eyes. *H & J Foulke, Inc.*

29in (74cm) 1362 *Sweet Nell. H & J Foulke, Inc.*

Bisque Shoulder Head: Ca. 1885-on. Turned shoulder head, wig, glass eyes, closed mouth; kid or cloth body; dressed; all in good condition. Mold numbers, such as 639, 698, 870, 1032, 1123, 1235.
Mark: 639 ✕ 6

with "DEP" after 1888

17-19in (43-48cm)	**$750-$850**
23-25in (58-64cm)	**$1,100-$1,200**
With open mouth:	
16-18in (41-46cm)	**$475-$525**
21-23in (53-58cm)	**$600-$675**

#911, 916, swivel neck, closed mouth:
20-23in (51-58cm)	**$1,500-$1,650**

#912:
21-23in (53-58cm)	**$1,400-$1,500**

Child Doll: Perfect bisque head, open mouth; ball-jointed body in good condition; appropriate clothes.
Mark: 2 ½

A B & G
Made in Germany

#1362 Sweet Nell:
14-16in (36-41cm)	**$425-$475**
19-21in (43-53cm)	**$525-$550**
23-25in (58-64cm)	**$650-$750**
29-30in (74-76cm)	**$1,000-$1,100**
36in (91cm)	**$1,600-$1,700**

#630, closed mouth:
   23in (58cm)   **$1,900-$2,200**
#911, closed mouth:
   16in (41cm)   **$1,500-$1,600**
#938, closed mouth:
   22in (56cm) at auction   **$4,100**
#989, closed mouth:
   23in (58cm)   **$4,500****

All-Bisque Girl: 1911, Chubby body, molded white stockings, blue garters, black Mary Janes.
Mold #83 over #100, 125, 150 or 225:
   5-6in (13-15cm)   **$225-$275***
   7in (18cm)   **$325-$350***
   8in (20cm)   **$475-$525***

All-Bisque Baby:
   8½in (21cm) swivel neck, closed mouth   **$900-$1,000****
#29-14, character baby, glass eyes, swivel neck:
   6in (15cm)   **$650-$700****

*Allow extra for real eyelashes.
**Not enough price examples to computer a reliable range.

Character: Ca. 1910-on. Perfect bisque head, good wig, sleep eyes, open mouth; some with open nostrils; composition body; all in good condition; suitable clothes.
Mark:

#1322, 1352, 1361:
   10-12in (25-31cm) **$400-$450***
   16-18in (41-46cm) **$575-$625***
   22-23in (56-58cm) **$850-$900***

Toddler:
   10in (25cm) five-piece body
              $750-$800
   14-16in (36-41cm)   **$900-$1,000**
#1329, 1321: 17-18in (43-46cm)
toddler, at auction   **$2,300-$2,400**
#1357:
   16-18in (41-46cm)   **$1,250-$1,500**
#1407 Baby Bo Kaye:
   8in (20cm)   **$1,350-$1,500**
#1431 Orsini, earthenware baby:
   24in (61cm)   **$900-$1,100**
#1450, smiling girl:
   14in (36cm)   **$14,000-$15,000**

*Allow $50 extra for flirty eyes.

7in (18cm) all-bisque 150. *H & J Foulke, Inc.*

Louis Amberg & Son

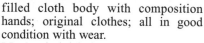

Newborn Babe, Bottle Babe, My Playmate: Ca. 1914-on. Perfect bisque head, painted hair, sleep eyes; soft cloth body; appropriate clothes; all in good condition. Mold **886** by Recknagel. Mold **371** with open mouth by Marseille.

Mark: L·A·&·S·
371·3/0 D·R·G·M·
Germany

THE ORIGINAL
NEWBORN BABE
(C) Jan. 9th, 1914 — No. G 45520
AMBERG DOLLS
The World Standard

Length:
9-10in (23-25cm)	**$375-$425**
13-14in (33-36cm)	**$500-$600**
17in (43cm)	**$700-$750**

Charlie Chaplin: 1915. Composition portrait head, molded mustache; straw-filled cloth body with composition hands; original clothes; all in good condition with wear.

Mark: cloth label on sleeve
14in (36cm)	**$600-$650**

Mibs: 1921. Composition shoulder head designed by Hazel Drucker with wistful expression, molded blonde or reddish hair; cloth body with composition arms and legs with painted shoes and socks; appropriate old clothes; all in good condition. (See photograph on page 37.)

Mark: None on doll; paper label only:

"Amberg Dolls
Please Love Me
I'm Mibs"

16in (41cm)	**$950-$1,050**

Mibs: 1921. Bisque shoulder head only, at auction **$650**

Baby Peggy: 1923. Composition head, molded brown bobbed hair, smiling closed mouth; appropriately dressed; all in good condition.
20in (51cm)	**$650-$750****

Baby Peggy: 1924. Perfect bisque head by Armand Marseille with character face, brown bobbed mohair wig, brown sleep eyes, closed mouth; composition or kid body, fully-jointed; dressed or undressed; all in very good condition.

Mark: "19 © 24"
LA & S NY
Germany
—50—
982/2"

**Not enough price samples to compute a reliable range.

13in (33cm) long *Newborn Babe. H & J Foulke, Inc.*

#982 or 983 shoulder head:
20in (51cm)   **$1,800-$2,000**
#972 or 973 socket head:
18-22in (46-56cm) **$2,200-$2,500**

All-Bisque Character Children:
1920s. Made by a German porcelain factory, probably Hertwig & Co.; pink pretinted bisque.
4in (10cm)   **$125**
5-6in (13-15cm)   **$160-$185**
Girl with molded bow:
6in (15cm)   **$375-$425**
Girl with downward gaze, glass eyes, wig:
5½in (14cm)   **$475-$525**
7in (18cm)   **$600-$650**

Mibs:
3in (8cm)   **$275**
4¾in (12cm)   **$425-$450**
6in (15cm)   **$575**
Baby Peggy:
3in (8cm)   **$325-$350**
5½in (14cm)   **$500-$550**
4½in (12cm) wigged   **$475-$525**
Mibs-type girl: molded flowers in hair:
4¾in (12cm)   **$225**

FACTS
Louis Amberg & Son,
New York, NY, U.S.A.
1907-on.

6in (15cm) all-bisque *Mibs. H & J Foulke, Inc.*

4½in (11cm) all-bisque wigged *Baby Peggy. H & J Foulke, Inc.*

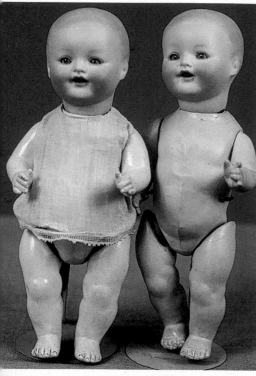

Left: 10in (25cm) *Vanta Baby* twins. *H & J Foulke, Inc.*

Vanta Baby: 1927. A tie-in with Vanta baby garments. Composition or bisque head with molded and painted hair, sleep eyes, open mouth with two teeth; suitably dressed; all in good condition.
Mark: Bisque Head

> Vanta Baby
> L A&S · 3/0 D·R·G·M·
> Germany.

Bisque head:
  10in (25cm) $600-$650
  20-22in (51-56cm)
                              $1,100-$1,250
Composition head:
  18-20in (46-51cm) $325-$375

Sue, Edwina or It: 1928. All-composition with round ball joint at waist, appropriate clothes.
  14in (36cm) $475-$525

Tiny Tots Body Twists: 1928. All-composition with large round ball joint at the waist.
  8in (20cm) $165-$195
  Little Amby, all original with
    paper label, at auction $300

Sunny Orange Maid: 1924. Composition/cloth. Molded "orange" hat; orange dress.
  14in (36cm), at auction $1,100

Left: 14in (36cm) composition *Edwina* with swivel waist. *Mary Barnes Kelley Collection.*

Georgene Averill
(Madame Hendren & Georgene Novelties, Inc.)

Bonnie Babe: 1926. Bisque heads by Alt, Beck & Gottschalck; cloth bodies by K & K Toy Co.; distributed by George Borgfeldt & Co., New York. Perfect bisque head with smiling face, open mouth with two lower teeth; cloth body with composition arms (sometimes celluloid) and legs often of poor quality; all in good condition. Mold #1386 or 1402.

Mark: *Copr. by Georgene Averill Germany 1005/3652 1386*

Length:

12-13in (31-33cm)	**$1,000-$1,100**
16-18in (41-46cm)	**$1,400-$1,600**
22-23in (56-58cm)	**$1,800-$1,900**

Composition body:

8in (20cm) tall	**$1,250**

Celluloid head:

16in (41cm) tall	**$550-$650**

All-Bisque Bonnie Babe: 1926.

5in (13cm)	**$850-$950**
7in (18cm)	**$1,200-$1,350**

Rag or Tag: All-bisque dog or cat with swivel neck, glass eyes; molded booties, crocheted yarn tail.
Mark: Incised "RAG TRADE MARK Copr. By Georgene Averill 890 Germany." Tag is mold 891.

5in (13cm)	**$3,500**
Boxed, at auction	**$4,725**

**Not enough price samples to compute a reliable range.

FACTS
Averill Mfg. Co. and Georgene Novelties, Inc., New York, NY, U.S.A. 1915-on.
Designer: Georgene Averill.
Trademarks: Madame Hendren, Georgene Novelties.

15½in (39cm) *Bonnie Babe. H & J Foulke, Inc.*

5in (13cm) all-bisque cat 891 *Tag. Richard Wright Antiques.*

Allie Dog: Bisque dog head by Alt, Beck & Gottschalck, glass eyes, smiling open mouth with teeth and tongue; cloth or fur body. See photograph on page 3.
Mark: "ALLIE DOG Copr. By Georgene Averill Germany 1405."
    12-15in (31-38cm)   **$7,500-$8,000**

Sunny Boy and Girl: Ca. 1927. Celluloid "turtle" mark head; stuffed body with composition arms and legs; appropriate or original clothes; all in good condition.
    15in (38cm)   **$350-$450**

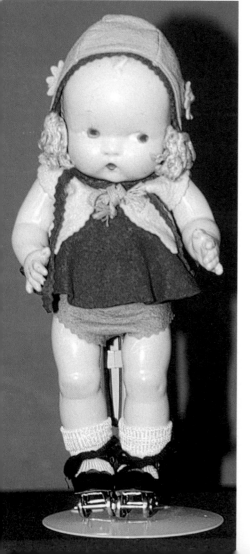

Composition Dolls: All appropriately dressed in good condition.
Mme. Hendren Character: Ca. 1915-on. Original tagged felt costume, including Dutch children, Indians, cowboys, sailors:
    10-14in (25-36cm)   **$150-$200**
Mama and Baby Dolls: Ca. 1918-on. Composition with cloth bodies; names such as *Baby Hendren* and *Baby Georgene:*
    15-18in (38-46cm)   **$250-$300**
    22-24in (56-61cm)   **$400-$450**
Dolly Reckord: 1922. Record-playing mechanism in torso, with records:
    26in (66cm)   **$600-$700**
Grace G. Drayton: 1920s.
    Chocolate Drop with yarn pigtails:
    14in (36cm)   **$575**
    Bobby: 14in (36cm)   **$400-$425**
Whistling Doll: 1925-1929. Doll whistles when feet are pushed up or head is pushed down, 14-15in (36-38cm):
    Dan, sailor or cowboy: **$300-$350**
    Black Rufus or **Dolly Dingle**
    $450-$475
Little Brother and **Little Sister:** 1927. Grace Corry (Rockwell):
    14in (36cm)   **$450-$500**
Snookums: 1927.
    14in (36cm)   **$350-$375**
Body Twists: 1927. **Dimmie** and **Jimmie** with a large round ball joint at waist:
    14½in (37cm)   **$475-$525**
Patsy-type Girl: 1928.
    14in (36cm)   **$325-$350**
    17-18in (43-46cm)   **$400-$450**
Lenci-type Girl: Ca. 1930. Lenci-style, composition face (some flocked); original felt and organdy clothes, may have **Val-Encia** tag:
    19in (48cm)   **$400-$500**
Little Cherub: 1937. Designed by Harriet Flanders; original clothes.
    16in (41cm)   **$325-$425**
    12in (31cm) painted eyes
    $325-$425

10in (25cm) composition Harriet Flanders *Little Cherub*, all original. *Terri & Kathy's Dolls.*

15in (38cm)
Little Lulu, all
original.
Sweetbriar.

Cloth Dolls: Original clothes; all in excellent condition, clean with bright color.
Children or Babies:
12in (31cm) **$135-$165**
24-26in (61-66cm) **$225-$275**
Girl Scout or Brownie:
13½in (35cm) **$250-$275**
International and Costume Dolls:
12in (31cm) **$100-$110**
Mint-in-box with wrist tag **$135**
Becassine:
13-15in (33-38cm) **$600-$700**
Uncle Wiggily or Nurse Jane:
18-20in (46-51cm) **$650-$750**
Comic Characters:
Little Lulu, Nancy, Sluggo,
Tubby Tom, 14in (36cm) **$500-$600**
Topsy Turvy:
Topsy & Eva,
10in (25cm) **$175-$225**
Kris Kringle, vinyl face:
10in (25cm) boxed with tag **$145**

Maud Tousey Fangel, 1938. Snooks, Sweets, Peggy-Ann. Marked "M.T.F." Bright color, all original. See photograph on page 4.
12-14in (31-36cm) **$650-$750**
17in (43cm) **$850-$900**
22in (56cm) **$1,100-$1,250**
Grace G. Drayton: good clean condition, some wear acceptable.
Chocolate Drop, 1923. Brown cloth with three yarn pigtails:
11in (28cm) **$450-$500**
16in (41cm **$750-$850**
Dolly Dingle, 1923:
11in (28cm) **$400-$450**
16in (41cm) **$600-$650**
10in (25cm) double-faced
$750

Vinyl Dolls:
Baby Dawn, Ca. 1950. Vinyl and cloth, all original and excellent.
19in (48cm) **$350**

Baby Bo Kaye

Baby Bo Kaye: Perfect bisque head with flange neck (marked as shown), molded hair, glass eyes, open mouth with two lower teeth; cloth torso with composition limbs; dressed; all in good condition.

16-19in (41-48cm) **$2,400-$2,800**
Celluloid head: 16in (41cm) **$750**
#1407 (ABG) bisque head; composition body: 7½in (19cm) **$1,350-$1,500**

All-Bisque Baby Bo Kaye: Molded hair, glass sleep eyes, open mouth with two teeth; swivel neck, jointed shoulders and hips; molded pink or blue shoes and socks; unmarked but may have sticker on torso:

5in (13cm) **$1,500-$1,600**
6in (15cm) **$2,000**

FACTS
Bisque heads made in Germany by Alt, Beck & Gottschalck; bodies by K & K Toy Co., New York, NY, U.S.A. 1925.
Designer: J.L. Kallus.
Distributor: George Borgfeldt & Co., New York, NY
Mark: "Copr. by J.L. Kallus Germany 1394/30"

5in (13cm) all-bisque *Baby Bo Kaye*. H & J Foulke, Inc.

Babyland Rag

Babyland Rag: Cloth face with hand-painted features, sometimes mohair wig; cloth body jointed at shoulders and hips; original clothes.
Mark: None

Early face (hand-painted features):
13-15in (33-38cm):
Very good	**$750-$850**
Fair	**$400-$500**
22in (56cm):
Very good	**$1,000-$1,200**
Fair	**$550-$600**
30in (76cm) Very good
$2,000-$2,200

Topsy Turvy:
13-15in (33-38cm) Very good
$700-$800

Buster Brown:
30in (76cm) Very good **$2,200**
Black:
15in (38cm) Fair **$650-$700**
20-22in (51-56cm) Very good
$1,200-$1,400

Life-like face (printed features):
13-15in (33-38cm) Very good
$600-$650
Topsy Turvy: 14in (36cm) Good
$700-$800

Babyland Rag-type (lesser quality):
14in (36cm) White
Good **$375-$475**
Brückner Rag Doll: Stiffened mask face, cloth body, flexible shoulders and hips; appropriate clothes; all in good condition.
12-14in (31-36cm)
White	**$210-$235**
Black	**$300-$325**
Topsy Turvy	**$550-$600**
Dollypop and other dolls with printed faces: 12in (31cm) **$250**

Mark: PAT 'D. JULY 8ᵀᴴ 1901

FACTS
E. I. Horsman, New York, NY, U.S.A. Some dolls made for Horsman by Albert Brückner. 1901-on.

12in (31cm) Brückner cloth doll with painted face. *H & J Foulke, Inc.*

Bähr & Pröschild

Marked Belton-type Child Doll: Ca. 1880. Perfect bisque head, solid dome with flat top having two or three small holes, paperweight eyes, closed mouth with pierced ears; wood and composition jointed body with straight wrists; dressed; all in good condition. Mold numbers in **200** series.

Mark: 204

12-14in (30-36cm)	**$1,750-$2,000**
18-20in (46-51cm)	**$2,500-$2,800**
24in (61cm)	**$3,600**

Marked Child Doll: Ca. 1888-on. Perfect bisque socket head, good human hair or mohair wig, set or sleep eyes, open mouth with four or six upper teeth; jointed composition body (many of French-type); dressed; all in good condition. Mold numbers in **200** and **300** series.

Mark: 224
   dep

#204, 239, 273, 275, 277, 289, 297, 300, 325, 340, 379, 394 and other socket heads:

12-13in (30-33cm)	**$600-$650**
16-18in (41-46cm)	**$700-$800**
22-24in (56-61cm)	**$1,000-$1,150**

#204, square teeth: 10in (25cm) at auction, all original **$1,380**
#208, 209: 8-8½in (20-21cm) jointed body with molded shoes **$850-$950**
#224 (dimples):

14-16in (36-41cm)	**$875-$925**
22-24in (56-61cm)	**$1,250-$1,500**

#246, 309 and other shoulder heads on kid bodies:

16-18in (41-46cm)	**$500-$525**
22-24in (56-61cm)	**$625-$675**

#302, 325, swivel neck, kid body:

17in (43cm)	**$625-$650**
20in (51cm)	**$700-$750**

#513, possibly by B.P.:

22-26in (56-66cm)	**$750-$800**

All-Bisque Girl, yellow stockings (heart mark):

5in (13cm)	**$350-$400**
7in (18cm)	**$450-$500**

FACTS
Bähr & Pröschild, porcelain factory, Ohrdruf, Thüringia, Germany. Made heads for Bruno Schmidt, Heinrich Stier, Kley & Hahn and others. 1871-on.

14in (36cm) 204 Belton-type child with closed mouth. *H & J Foulke, Inc.*

Marked B.P. Character Baby: Ca. 1910-on. Perfect bisque socket head, solid dome or good wig, sleep eyes, open mouth; composition bent-limb baby body; dressed; all in good condition. Mold #585, 604, 624, 678, 619, 620 and 587.

Mark: 585
5

B & P

Germany

10-12in (25-31cm)	**$400-$450**
15-17in (36-43cm)	**$600-$700**
20-21in (51-53cm)	**$700-$800**
Toddler, fully-jointed body:	
12-13in (31-33cm)	**$1,000**
22in (56cm)	**$1,500**
Toddler, five-piece body:	
10-12in (25-31cm)	**$650**
14in (36cm)	**$750**
#425, All-bisque baby:	
5½-6in (13-15cm)	**$300-$350**
#642, Character child:	
17in (43cm) at auction	**$2,700**

Right: 14in (36cm) 224 child with open mouth. *H & J Foulke, Inc.*

Left: 12½ (32cm) 275 child with open mouth. *H & J Foulke, Inc.*

Belton-Type (So-called)

Belton-type Child Doll: Perfect bisque socket head, solid but flat top with two or three small holes for stringing, paperweight eyes, closed mouth, pierced ears; wood and composition ball-jointed body with straight wrists; dressed; all in good condition.

TR 809: 17in (43cm)   **$1,600-$1,650**

Bru-type face:
12-14in (30-35cm)   **$2,500-$3,000**

FACTS
Various German firms, such as Bähr &
Pröschild. 1875-on.
Mark: None,
except sometimes numbers.

French-type face, fine early quality (some mold **#137** or **#183**):

13-15in (33-38cm)	**$2,400-$2,700**
18-20in (46-51cm)	**$3,100-$3,400**
22-24in (56-61cm)	**$3,600-$4,000**

German-type face, good quality:

8-9in (20-23cm) five-piece body	**$850-$950**
12in (31cm)	**$1,250-$1,450**
15-17in (38-43cm)	**$1,600-$1,800**
20in (51cm)	**$2,200-$2,400**

N4 with bisque lower arms and legs:
13in (33cm)   **$2,400-$2,600****

#200 Series, see Bähr & Pröschild, page 44.

**Not enough price samples to compute a reliable range.

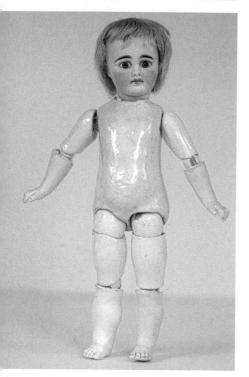

13in (33cm) N4 Belton-type child with German-style face and unusual bisque lower arms and legs. *H & J Foulke, Inc.*

10in (25cm) Belton-type child with French-style face. *H & J Foulke, Inc.*

C.M. Bergmann

Bergmann Child Doll: Ca. 1889-on. Marked bisque head, good wig, sleep or set eyes, open mouth; composition ball-jointed body; dressed; all in nice condition.

Heads by **A.M.** and unknown makers:

10in (25cm)	**$400**
14-16in (36-41cm)	**$375-$425**
20-22in (51-56cm)	**$475-$500**
25in (64cm)	**$525**
28-29in (71-74cm)	**$650-$700**
32-33in (81-84cm)	**$900-$1,000**
35-36in (89-91cm)	**$1,200-$1,400**
39-42in (99-111cm)	**$2,200-$2,400**

Heads by **Simon & Halbig:**

10in (25cm)	**$500-$600**
13-15in (33-38cm)	**$400-$450**
18-20in (46-51cm)	**$525-$575**
23-24in (58-61cm)	**$625-$675**
29-30in (81-91cm)	**$900-$1,000**
35-36in (81-91cm)	**$1,500-$1,650**
39in (99cm)	**$2,500**
Eleonore: 25in (64cm)	**$800-$900**

#612 Character Baby, open-closed mouth:

14-16in (36-41cm)	**$2,200-$2,400**

#134 Character Toddler:

12in (31cm)	**$950**

FACTS

C. M. Bergmann doll factory of Waltershausen, Thüringia, Germany; heads manufactured for this company by Armand Marseille; Simon & Halbig; Alt, Beck & Gottschalck and perhaps others. 1888-on.
Distributor: Louis Wolfe & Co., New York, NY
Trademarks: Cinderella Baby (1897), Columbia (1904), My Gold Star (1926).
Mark: CM BERGMANN
A - H i · M·
Made in Germany

C.M. Bergmann
Waftershausen
Germany
1916
6½ a

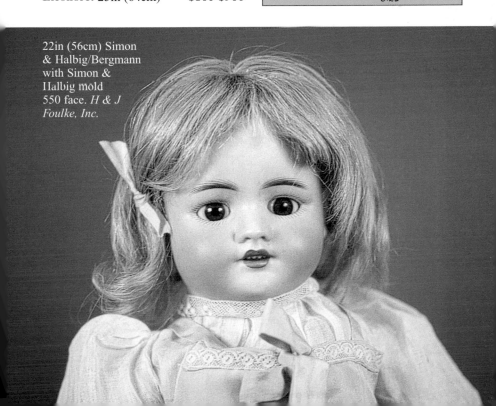

22in (56cm) Simon & Halbig/Bergmann with Simon & Halbig mold 550 face. *H & J Foulke, Inc.*

Bisque, French
(Unmarked or Unidentified Marks and Unlisted Small Factories)

Marked A.L. Bébé: Ca. 1875. Possibly Alexander Lefebvre & Cie. Perfect pressed bisque socket head, closed mouth, paperweight eyes; French wood and composition jointed body; appropriate clothing; all in good condition.

22in (56cm) at auction   **$35,000**

Marked B.M. Bébé: 1880-1895. Alexandre Mothereau. Perfect pressed bisque socket head, closed mouth, paperweight eyes; French wood and composition jointed body; appropriate clothing; all in good condition.

16in (41cm)   **$15,000-$18,000****
27-29in (69-74cm)   **$25,000****

Marked C.P. Bébé: Ca. 1875. Possibly Pannier. Perfect pressed bisque socket head, closed mouth, paperweight eyes; French wood and composition body; appropriate clothing; all in good condition.

20in (51cm) at auction   **$58,500**

Marked H Bébé: Ca. late 1870s. Possibly by A. Halopeau. Perfect pressed bisque socket head of fine quality, cork pate, good wig, paperweight eyes, pierced ears, closed mouth; French wood and composition jointed body with straight wrists; appropriate clothing; all in excellent condition.

Mark: 2 • H

Size:	
0 = 16½in (42cm)	
2 = 19in (48cm)	
3 = 21in (56cm)	
4 = 24in (61cm)	

21-24in (53-61cm) **$65,000-$75,000**

Huret Child: Ca. 1878. Maison Huret. Perfect bisque head; appropriate clothing; all in excellent condition. Gutta-percha body:

18in (46cm)   **$70,000-$80,000**
Wood body, 18in (46cm)   **$34,000**

Marked J. Bébé: Ca. 1880s. Joseph Louis Joanny. Perfect pressed bisque socket head, paperweight eyes, closed mouth; French wood and composition body; appropriate clothing; all in good condition.

15-16in (38-41cm)   **$5,000-$6,000**
22in (56cm)   **$7,500-$8,500**

Marked J.M. Bébé: Ca. 1880s. Perfect pressed bisque socket head, good wig, paperweight eyes, closed mouth, pierced ears; French composition and wood body; appropriate clothing; all in good condition.

Mark: 5

$$\mathcal{J} \, \mathcal{P} \, \mathcal{M}$$

13in (33cm) at auction   **$7,500**
19-21in (48-53cm)   **$20,000****

Marked M. Bébé: Mid 1890s. Perfect bisque socket head, good wig, closed mouth, paperweight eyes, pierced ears; French jointed composition and wood body; appropriate clothing; all in good

**Not enough price samples to compute a reliable range.

16in (41cm) B 4 M *Bébé Mothereau. Private Collection.*

19½in (50cm) M 6 French *bébé. H & J Foulke, Inc.*

condition. Some dolls with this mark may be Bébé Mascottes.

Mark:

M
4

18-21in (46-53cm) **$3,500-$4,000**

Marked Bébé Mascotte: 1890-1897, May Freres Cie; 1898-on, Jules Nicholas Steiner. Perfect bisque socket head, closed mouth, paperweight eyes, pierced ears; jointed composition and wood body; appropriate clothing; all in good condition.

11-12in (28-31cm)	**$2,250-$2,500**
17-19in (42-48cm)	**$3,800-$4,200**
24-26in (61-66cm)	**$5,500-$5,800**

Marked P.D. Bébé: 1878-1890. Petit & Dumontier, Paris. Perfect bisque head with good wig, paperweight eyes, closed mouth, pierced ears; jointed composition body (some with metal hands); appropriate clothes; all in good condition.

19-23in (48-58cm) **$16,500-$18,500**

Mark: P.2.D

Marked P.G. Bébé: Ca. 1880-1899. Pintel & Godchaux, Montreuil, France. Perfect bisque socket head, good wig, paperweight eyes, closed mouth; jointed French composition and wood body; appropriate clothing; all in good condition.

Trademark: Bébé Charmant

Mark: B   A
          P9G   P7G

20-22in (51-56cm)**$3,000-$3,200**
Open mouth:
  18-20in (46-51cm)**$1,600-$1,800**

Marked PAN Bébé: Ca. 1887. Henri Delcroix, Paris and Montreuil-sous-Bois (porcelain factory). Perfect bisque socket head, good wig, paperweight eyes, closed mouth, pierced ears; French composition and wood body; appropriate clothes; all in good condition.

Mark: PAN
              2

Size:	2 = 12in (31cm)
	10 = 27in (68cm)
	11 = 28½in (72cm)

12in (31cm)   **$6,000-$7,000****

Unmarked Bébé: Ca. 1880-1890. Perfect bisque socket head, paperweight eyes, closed mouth; jointed French composition and wood body; appropriate clothing; all in good condition.
Jumeau quality:

12-14in (31-36cm)	**$3,100-$3,400**
20-22in (51-56cm)	**$4,400-$4,600**

*For lady and fashion dolls *(poupées)* see pages 83 and 84.
**Not enough price samples to compute a reliable range.

22in (56cm) P. D. *bébé* with metal hands. *Linda Kellerman.*

Bisque, German
(Unmarked or Unidentified Marks and Unlisted Small Factories)

Shoulder head with molded hair: Ca. 1880. Tinted bisque shoulder head with beautifully molded hair (usually blonde), closed mouth; original kid or cloth body, bisque lower arms; appropriate clothes; all in good condition.

American Schoolboy:

12-14in (31-36cm)	$550-$650
17-20in (43-51cm)	$750-850
6in (15cm) head only	$290

Composition body:

11-12in (28-31cm)	$650-$750

Boy or girl, painted eyes:

14-16in (36-41cm)	$350-$400

Boy or girl, glass eyes:

16in (41cm)	$700-$750

Lady, painted eyes:

12-14in (31-36cm)	$325-$375

Hatted or Bonnet Doll: Ca. 1880-1920. Bisque shoulder head, molded bonnet; original cloth body with bisque arms and legs; good old clothes or nicely dressed; all in good condition.

Standard quality:

8-9in (20-23cm)	$210-$265
11-13in (28-33cm)	$325-$375
15in (38cm)	$450
18in (46cm)	$550-$600

Fine quality:

18-22in (46-56cm)	$1,000 up*

All-bisque:

4½in (12cm)	$175-$195*
7in (18cm)	$250-$300*

*Allow extra for unusual style.

FACTS
Various German firms. 1860s-on.
Mark: Some numbered, some "Germany," some both.

10½in (26cm) 104 hatted bisque. *H & J Foulke, Inc.*

Doll House Doll: Ca. 1890-1920. Man or lady bisque shoulder head; cloth body, bisque lower limbs; original clothes or suitably dressed; all in nice condition.

4½-7in (12-18cm):

Molded hair, glass eyes, ca. 1870 **$450-$500**

Girl with bangs, ca. 1880, all original **$210**

Victorian man with mustache **$200-$225**

Victorian lady, all original **$200**

Lady with glass eyes and wig **$350-$400**

Man with mustache, original military uniform **$800-$1,000**

Chauffeur with molded cap **$350-$400**

Black man **$650-$700**

Soldier, molded hat, goatee and mustache **$1,500-$1,600**

Maid, all original **$110-$135**

1920s man or lady **$100-$125**

1920s man with molded hat, all original **$225**

Child Doll with closed mouth: Ca. 1880-1890. Perfect bisque head, good wig, glass eyes; nicely dressed; all in good condition, excellent quality.

Kid or cloth body:

17-19in (43-48cm) **$750-$850***

23-25in (58-64cm) **$1,100-$1,200***

#50 shoulder head:

14-16in (35-41cm) **$1,100-$1,200**

22in (56cm) **$1,650**

#132, 120, 126 Bru-type face:

13-14in (33-36cm) **$2,500-$2,800**

19-21in (48-53cm) **$3,800-$4,000**

#51, swivel neck shoulder head:

17-19in (43-48cm) **$1,550-$1,750**

#86, Bru-type Nurser:

13in (33cm) at auction **$1,000**

*Allow 30 percent extra for swivel neck fashion-type model.

Above: Shoulder head 50/10 for 22½in (57cm) doll with kid or cloth body. *H & J Foulke, Inc.*

Right: 19in (48cm) 136 with closed mouth. *Private Collection.*

Composition body (German look):
11-13in (28-33cm)	**$1,450-$1,650**
16-19in (41-48cm)	**$1,950-$2,250**

#136 (French look):
12-15in (31-38cm)	**$2,200-$2,400**
19-21in (48-53cm)	**$2,800-$3,200**

E. G. (Ernst Grossman):
16in (41cm) at auction	**$2,600**

Child Doll with open mouth "Dolly Face": 1888-on. Perfect bisque head, good wig, glass eyes, open mouth; ball-jointed composition body or kid body with bisque lower arms; dressed; all in good condition. Very good quality; including dolls marked **G.B.**, and **K** inside **H, L.H.K., P.Sch., D&K.**
12-14in (31-35cm)	**$400-$450***
18-20in (46-51cm)	**$550-$600***
23-25in (58-64cm)	**$700-$800***
30-32in (76-81cm)	**$1,200-$1,300**

#50, 51, square teeth:
14-16in (36-41cm)	**$950-$1,050**

#444, 478, 422:
17in (43cm)	**$600-$650**
23-25in (58-64cm)	**$900**
35in (81cm)	**$1,800**

Standard quality; including **My Sweetheart, Princess, My Girlie, My Dearie, Pansy, Viola, G & S, MOA** and **A.W.:**
14-16in (35-41cm)	**$325-$375**

20-23in (51-58cm)	**$450-$500**
30-32in (76-81cm)	**$850-$950**

Small Child Doll: 1890 to World War I. Perfect bisque socket head, set or sleep eyes; five-piece composition body; cute clothes; all in good condition.
Very good quality (**Simon & Halbig**-type):
5-6in (13-15cm)	**$300-$350**
8-10in (20-25cm)	**$400-$450**

Fully-jointed body:
7-8in (18-20cm)	**$550-$600**

Closed mouth:
4½-5½in (12-14cm) all original	**$500**
8in (20cm)	**$750-$850**

Standard quality:
5-6in (13-15cm)	**$100-$125**
8-10in (20-25cm)	**$175-$225**

#39-13, five-piece mediocre body, original clothes:
5in (13cm) glass eyes	**$200-$225**
Painted eyes	**$90-$100**

Globe Baby: 1898. Carl Hartmann.
8in (20cm)	**$325-$375**
8in (20cm) all original clothes and wig	**$400-$450**
12in (31cm)	**$450-$550**

*Allow $150 to $250 extra for a jointed toddler body.

22in (56cm) *Viola* "dolly face." *H & J Foulke, Inc.*

Character Baby: Ca. 1910-on. Perfect bisque head, good wig or solid dome with painted hair, sleep eyes, open mouth; composition bent-limb baby body; suitably dressed; all in good condition. Including dolls marked **G.B., S&Q, Goebel** and **F.B.**

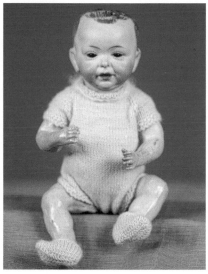

10in (25cm) unmarked character baby. *H & J Foulke, Inc.*

9-10in (23-25cm)	**$250-$300**
14-16in (35-41cm)	**$400-$450***
19-21in (48-53cm)	**$500-$550***
23-24in (58-61cm)	**$700-$750***

My Sweet Baby:
23in (58cm) toddler   **$1,000-$1,200**
#110, A. Wislizenus toddler:
   15in (38cm)   **$1,250-$1,350**

Character Child: Ca. 1910-on. Perfect bisque head, jointed composition body; dressed; all in good condition.
#101: 19in (48cm)   **$1,950**
#111: 18-20in (46-51cm   )**$20,000****
#125, smiling:
   13in (33cm) at auction   **$6,380**
#128: 18-20in (46-51cm)   **$25,000****
#129, wide smile with molded teeth:
   16in (41cm) at auction   **$9,250**
#159: 23in (58cm)   **$1,150**
#163: 14in (36cm)   **$750**
#214, Bawo & Dotter, socket head, glass eyes, closed mouth:
   15in (38cm) at auction   **$13,000**
#215, Bawo & Dotter, shoulder head lady: 20in (51cm) at auction   **$11,500**
#2-22, black molded hair:
   18in (46cm) at auction   **$2,400**
#500, G.H. Erste Steinbacher:
   15in (38cm) at auction   **$1,700**
#660, PR:
   23in (58cm) at auction   **$2,100**
#820, PM shoulder head:
   12in (31cm)   **$350**
N & T, shoulder head, molded hair, side-glancing eyes:
   13in (33cm) at auction   **$2,000**

Infant, unmarked or unidentified maker: Ca. 1924-on. Perfect bisque head; cloth body; dressed; all in good condition.
   10-12in (25-31cm) long   **$325**
   15-18in (38-46cm) long   **$525-$550**
#800: 11-12in (28-31cm)   **$550-$600**
HvB: 15in (38cm) long   **$450**
Gerling Baby:
   17in (43cm) long   **$550-$600**
#926, smiling: 16in (41cm)   **$2,200**
#697: 12in (31cm) at auction   **$1,200**

*Allow $150 - $250 extra for a jointed toddler body.
**Not enough price samples to compute a reliable range.

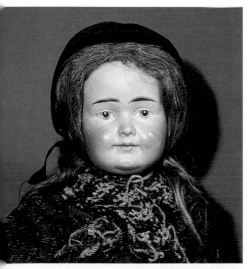

19in (48cm) 101 character child. *H & J Foulke, Inc.*

Bisque, Japanese
(Caucasian Dolls)

Character Baby: Perfect bisque socket head with solid dome or wig, glass eyes, open mouth with teeth, dimples; composition bent-limb baby body; dressed; all in good condition.

9-10in (23-25cm)	**$110-$125***
13-15in (33-38cm)	**$150-$200***
19-21in (48-53cm)	**$275***
24in (61cm)	**$300-$400***

Hilda look-alike:

19in (48cm)	**$750-$850***

Heubach Pouty look-alike, F.Y. Nippon 305:

17in (43cm)	**$650-$750**

Child Doll: Perfect bisque head, mohair wig, glass sleep eyes, open mouth; jointed composition or kid body; dressed; all in good condition.

14-16in (36-41cm)	**$200-$250**
20-22in (51-56cm)	**$300-$350**

*Do not pay as much for doll with inferior bisque head.

FACTS
Various Japanese firms; heads were imported by New York distributors such as Morimura Brothers, Yamato Importing Co. and others. 1915-on.
Marks:

F Y
NIPPON 501

M B
Japan 3

1 4 A

H
Nippon

All-Bisque Dolls: see page 32.

8in (20cm) 3-3/0 character baby. *H & J Foulke, Inc.*

Black Dolls*

Black Bisque Doll: Ca. 1880-on. Various French and German manufacturers from their regular molds or specially designed ones with Negroid features. Perfect bisque socket head either painted dark or with dark coloring mixed in the slip, running from light brown to very dark; composition or sometimes kid body in a matching color; cloth bodies on some baby dolls; appropriate clothing; all in good condition.

French Makers:
Bru, Circle Dot:
17in (43cm) **$30,000**
E.D., open mouth:
16in (41cm) **$2,200**
F. Gaultier:
Poupée, 12in (31cm) **$2,600**
Child, scroll mark,
18in (46cm) **$4,500-$5,000**

Jumeau:
Early **E. J.:**
19in (48cm) at auction **$31,000**
Bébé, open mouth:
17in (43cm) **$2,750-$3,000**
DEP, closed mouth:
17in (43cm) at auction **$4,100**
Déposé 8, closed mouth:
18in (46cm) at auction **$17,600**
Exhibition Doll (1876):
25in (64cm) at auction **$88,000**
All original with hairline, at
auction **$46,000**
Lanternier:
18-20in (46-51cm) **$950-$1,250**
Paris Bébé, closed mouth:
15½in (39cm) **$4,800-$5,000**
Poupée shoulder head, jointed wood body; original ethnic clothes **$13,000**
SFBJ, fully-jointed body:
11in (28cm) **$1,300**

*Also see entry for specific maker of doll or for material of doll.

Below: 12in (31cm) F. G. *Poupée. Private Collection.*

15in (38cm) Van Rozen character. *Private Collection.*

Steiner, Figure A:
8in (20cm) closed mouth in baby
walker, at auction   **$6,500**
21in (53cm) open mouth
    $4,000-$4,200
Van Rozen, all original:
15in (38cm) at auction   **$17,000**
With crack behind ear   **$5,100**

German Makers:
Bähr & Pröschild #277:
10in (25cm)   **$800**
12in (30cm)   **$1,000**
Belton-type 179: 14in (36cm)   **$3,000**
Gebrüder Heubach #7671:
18in (46cm)   **$3,500**
H. Handwerck:
12in (31cm)   **$1,000**
18in (46cm)   **$1,600-$1,800**
E. Heubach, #399, 414, 452:
7½in (19cm) toddler   **$425-$450**
10-12in (25-30cm)   **$500-$550**
#444, 13in (33cm)   **$650**
#463, 10-12in (25-30cm)   **$750**
#300, 6in (15cm)   **$450-$500**
#316, 18in (46cm)   **$1,925**
#418, 14in (38cm)   **$1,100**
Kämmer & Reinhardt:
Child, 16in (41cm)   **$1,500-$1,800**
#100 Baby:
11in (28cm)   **$900**
19in (48cm)   **$1,800**
#101:
13-14in (33-36cm)   **$4,000-$4,500**
#126, toddler:
8-9in (20-23cm)   **$1,250**
#192: 21in (53cm)   **$2,500-$2,650**
J. D. Kestner:
Child, 16in (41cm)   **$1,600-$1,900**
Hilda,
12-13in (31-33cm)   **$3,000-$3,200**
Kuhnlenz #34:
7-8in (18-20cm) fully-jointed   **$950**
8½in (21cm) five-piece body all
original Mammy with baby   **$750**
19-20in (48-53cm)   **$6,500**
Armand Marseille:
#341, cloth body:
10-12in (25-31cm)   **$400-$425**
#351, composition body:
8-12in (20-31cm)   **$500-$600**
14-16in (38-41cm)   **$650-$750**
21in (53cm)   **$1,000**

2¾in (6cm) all-bisque Hertwig characters, boxed. *H & J Foulke, Inc.*

#362, composition body:
15in (38cm)   **$900**
#1894:
10in (25cm) fully-jointed   **$600**
Recknagel #126 infant:
10½in (26cm)   **$400**
S PB H:
Hanna: 7-8in (18-20cm)   **$375-$425**
#1923 child:
19-20in (48-51cm)   **$900-$1,000**
Simon & Halbig:
#739: 19-22in (48-56cm)
    $2,900-$3,100
#949, open mouth:
16in (41cm)   **$2,600-$2,900**
#1009: 18in (46cm)   **$2,100-$2,200**
All original, French trade   **$4,250**
#1078, 1079
15in (38cm)   **$1,600**
20in (51cm)   **$2,000**
#1249: 20in (51cm)   **$1,900-$2,100**
#1349 Jutta: 13in (33cm)   **$1,750**
#1358: 19-20in (48-51cm)
    $8,000-$9,000
Franz Schmidt:
#1272: 22½in (57cm)   **$2,600**
#1297:
10in (25cm) at auction   **$950**
TR809: closed mouth;
19in (48cm)   **$1,500**
Unmarked Child:
10-13in (25-33cm) jointed body
    $400-$500

8-9in (20-23cm) 5-piece body
$300-$350
4-5in (10-14cm) S & H quality
$450-$500
All-Bisque:
Glass eyes, wig:
5in (14cm)   **$500-$550**
Kestner, swivel neck, bare feet:
6in (15cm)   **$1,650-$1,850**
Simon & Halbig 886:
4½in (11cm)   **$600**
7in (18cm)   **$1,200-$1,350**
G.K. 61, swivel neck:
3½in (9cm)   **$575**
5in (13cm)   **$900**
7in (18cm) mulatto   **$2,200**
Molded shorts:
5-6in (13-15cm)   **$500-$600**
Box character pair: 2¾in (6cm) **$450**

Cloth Black Doll*: Ca. 1880-on.
American-made cloth doll with black
face, painted, printed or embroidered
features; jointed arms and legs; original
clothes; all in good condition.
Primitive: painted or embroidered
face   **$1,000-$2,000+**
Stockinette (so-called Beecher-type):
20in (51cm)   **$3,200**
1930s Mammy:
18-20in (46-51cm)   **$350+**
WPA: molded cloth face,
22in (56cm)   **$1,100-$1,200**
Alabama-type:
24in (61cm)   **$2,500-$3,500**
Chase Mammy:
26in (66cm)   **$10,000****
Golliwogg: Ca. 1925-1930. English
cloth character; all original; very good
condition.
18in (46cm)   **$425-$525**
Ca. 1950,
16-18in (41-46cm)   **$225-$325**

Black Papier-mâché Doll: Ca. 1890.
By various German manufacturers.
Papier-mâché character face, arms and
legs, cloth body; glass eyes; original
or appropriate clothes; all in good
condition.
12-14in (31-36cm)   **$350-$450**
18-20in (46-51cm) character with
broad smile   **$1,200-$1,500**

Black Low-Fired Pottery: Ca. 1930.
English and German. Molded curly
hair.
16in (41cm)   **$850**
K & R: 24in (61cm) flirty eyes
$1,250

*Also check under manufacturer if
known.
**Not enough price samples to compute a
reliable range.
+Greatly depending on appeal.

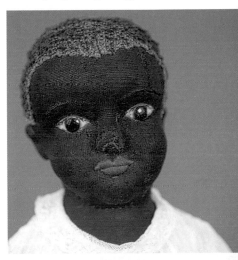

20in (51cm) stockinette character (so-
called Beecher-type). *H & J Foulke, Inc.*

Chase Mammy. *Keefer Collection.*

Bru

Poupée (Fashion Lady): Ca. 1866-on. Perfect bisque swivel head on shoulder plate, cork pate, appropriate old wig, closed mouth, paperweight eyes, pierced ears; gusseted kid lady body; original or appropriate clothes; all in good condition.

Smiling face, sizes **A** (11in, 28cm) to **O** (36in, 91cm):

14-16in (35-41cm)	**$3,500-$4,000***
19in (48cm) with original trousseau	**$11,250**
20-21in (51-53cm)	**$5,500-$6,000***

Wood arms:

16in (41cm)	**$4,900-$5,100***

Wood body, naked:

15-17in (38-43cm)	**$6,000-$6,800***
21in (53cm)	**$9,000***

Oval face, incised with numbers only. Shoulder plate sometimes marked "**B. Jne & Cie.**"

12-13in (31-33cm)	**$2,800-$3,000***
15-17in (38-43cm)	**$3,500-$3,800***
20-21in (51-53cm)	**$4,400-$4,900***

Wood body, naked: 16in (41cm) **$5,500**

Candy Container: 1867. Two faces (crying and smiling):

14in (36cm) at auction	**$8,000***

All-Bisque: 1867. Two faces:

9½in (24cm)	**$4,500-$5,500****

Marked Breveté Bébé: Ca. 1879-1880. Perfect bisque swivel head on shoulder plate, cork pate, skin wig, paperweight eyes with shading on upper lid, closed mouth with white space between lips, full cheeks, pierced ears; gusseted kid body pulled high on shoulder plate and straight cut with bisque lower arms

*Allow extra for original clothes.
**Not enough samples to compute a reliable range.

FACTS
Bru Jne. & Cie, Paris, and Montreuil-sous-Bois, France. 1866-1899.

17in (43cm) size F smiling Bru *poupée. H & J Foulke, Inc.*

19in (48cm) *Bébé Bru* with circle dot mark. *Floyd Jones.*

(no rivet joints); appropriate old clothes; all in good condition.
Mark: Size number only on head. Oval sticker on body: *BÉBÉ Breveté Sodo PARIS*

or rectangular sticker like Bébé Bru one, but with words "Bébé Breveté."

Size 5/0	= 10½in (27cm)
Size 2/0	= 14in (36cm)
Size 1	= 16in (41cm)
Size 2	= 18in (46cm)
Size 3	= 19in (48cm)

11in (28cm)	**$12,000-$14,000**
14-16in (35-41cm)	**$16,000-$18,000**
19-22in (48-56cm)	**$22,000-$23,000**

Bébé Modèle: Ca. 1880. Breveté face, wood body:
21in (31cm)   **$25,000****

Marked Crescent or Circle Dot Bébé: 1879-1884. Perfect bisque swivel head on a deep shoulder plate with molded breasts, cork pate, attractive wig, paperweight eyes, closed mouth with slightly parted lips, molded and painted teeth, plump cheeks, pierced ears; gusseted kid body with bisque lower arms (no rivet joints); appropriate old clothes; all in good condition.
Mark:

Sometimes with "BRU Jne"

Approximate size chart for Circle Dot and Bru Jne Bébés:

0	= 11in (28cm)
1	= 12in (31cm)
2	= 13in (33cm)
5	= 17in (43cm)
8	= 22in (56cm)
10	= 26in (66cm)
12	= 30in (76cm)
14	= 35in (89cm)

10½in (26cm)	**$12,000=$14,000**
13-14in (33-35cm)	**$15,000-$17,000**
18-19in (46-48cm)	**$20,000-$22,500**
24in (61cm)	**$26,500**

Marked Nursing Bru (Bébé Têteur):
Ca. 1878-1898. Perfect bisque head, shoulder plate, open mouth with hole for nipple, mechanism in head sucks up liquid, operates by turning key; nicely clothed; all in good condition.

Early model:
13-15in (33-38cm)   **$8,500-$9,500**
Later model:
13-15in (33-38cm)   **$5,500-$6,500**
Bébé Gourmand:
18in (46cm)   **$26,500****

Marked Bru Jne Bébé: Ca. 1884-1889. Perfect bisque swivel head on deep shoulder plate with molded breasts, cork pate, attractive wig, paperweight eyes, closed mouth, molded tongue, pierced ears; gusseted kid body with scalloped edge at shoulder plate, bisque lower arms with lovely hands,

**Not enough price samples to compute a reliable range.

Bébé Bru, size 5.
Gentile's Antique Dolls.

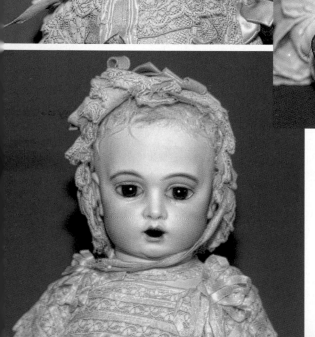

Above: Original *Bébé Gourmand* shoes showing "trap door." *Carmel Doll Shop.*

Left: 18in (46cm) *Bébé Gourmand. Carmel Doll Shop.*

kid over wood upper arms, hinged elbow, all kid or wood lower legs (sometimes on a jointed wood body); appropriate old clothes; all in good condition (for photograph, see *6th Blue Book,* page 79).

Mark: "BRU Jne"
Body Label:

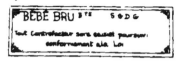

12-13in (31-33cm)
                $16,500-$18,500*
15-17in (38-43cm)
                $21,000-$23,000*
23-24in (58-61cm)**$23,000-$25,000**
27in (69cm)   **$27,500-$30,000***
Late model, no molded tongue:
  18-20in (46-51cm) **$12,500-$13,500**
  18in (46cm) jointed composition
  body   **$10,000**

Mannekin, wood body,
  46in (117cm) at auction   **$24,000**

Marked Bru Shoes   **$800-$900**

Bru factory dress and hat
                $1,700-$2,000

Marked Bru Jne R Bébé: Ca. 1889-1899. Perfect bisque head on a jointed composition body.
Mark: BRU J**ᴺᴱ** R
              1ſ

Body Stamp: "Bebe Bru" with size number.

Closed mouth:
  11-13in (28-33cm) **$2,200-$2,600**
  19-21in (48-53cm) **$6,000-$7,000**
  27in (69cm)   **$9,000**
Open mouth:
  12in (31cm)   **$1,500-$1,800**
  20-21in (51-53cm) **$3,000-$4,000**

*Allow extra for original clothes.

Bucherer

Saba Figures: Composition character head sometimes with molded hat; metal ball-jointed body with large composition hands and composition molded shoes; original clothes, often felt; all in good condition.
8in (20cm) average:
  Man and woman in provincial costumes **$200 each**
  Fireman, clown, black man, aviator, military, baseball player, Pinocchio, Mr. & Mrs. Peter Rabbit and others
                $275-$325
  Becassine   **$400**
Characters: *Mutt, Jeff, Muggie, Jlggs, Katzenjammers, Happy Hooligan, Charlie Chaplin, Aggie, Jimmy Dugan, Puddin' head* and others
                $400-$500

FACTS
A. Bucherer, Amriswil, Switzerland. 1921.
Mark: "MADE IN SWITZERLAND PATENTS APPLIED FOR"

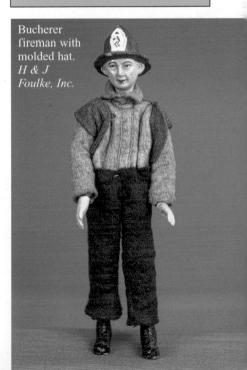

Bucherer fireman with molded hat. *H & J Foulke, Inc.*

Bye-Lo Baby

Bisque Head Bye-Lo Baby: Ca. 1923. Perfect bisque head, sleep eyes; cloth body with curved legs (sometimes with straight legs), composition or celluloid hands; dressed. Made in seven sizes, 9-20in (23-51cm). "Bye-Lo Baby" stamp on front of body. Sometimes Mold #1373 (ABG).

Mark: © 1923 by
Grace S. Putnam
MADE IN GERMANY

Head circumference:
7½-8in (19-20cm)	**$500-$525***
9-10in (23-25cm)	**$475-$500****
12-13in (31-33cm)	**$550-$600***
15in (38cm)	**$900***
17in (43cm)	**$1,100-$1,300***
18in (46cm)	**$1,400-$1,600***

Toddler with wardrobe:
12in (31cm) tall, at auction	**$2,500**
Tagged Bye-Lo gown	**$50**
Bye-Lo pin	**$95**
Bye-Lo blanket	**$40-$50**

#1369 (ABG) socket head on composition body, some marked "K&W:"
12-13in (30-33cm) long	**$700-$900**

Painted eyes:
12-13in (30-33cm) long	**$800**

#1415, smiling with painted eyes:
13-1/2in (34cm) h.c.	**$4,000****

Composition head, 1924:
12-13in (31-33cm) h.c., all original with tag	**$400-$425**
re-dressed	**$225-$275**

Celluloid head:
10in (25cm) h.c.	**$350-$375**

Painted bisque head, late 1920s:
12-13in (31-33cm) h.c.	**$325-$350**

Wooden head, (Schoenhut), 1925
	$1,700-$2,000**

Vinyl head, 1948:
16in (41cm)	**$150-$200**

Wax head, 1922:
16in (41cm)	**$700-$800**

*Allow extra for original tagged gown and button.
**Not enough price samples to compute a reliable range.

> **FACTS**
> **Bisque heads**—J.D. Kestner; Alt, Beck & Gottschalck; Kling & Co.; Hertel, Schwab & Co.; all of Thüringia, Germany.
> **Composition heads**— Cameo Doll Company, New York, NY
> **Celluloid heads**— Karl Standfuss, Saxony, Germany.
> **Wooden heads** (unauthorized)— Schoenhut of Philadelphia, PA
> **All-Bisque Baby**—J.D. Kestner.
> **Cloth Bodies and Assembly**— K & K Toy Co., New York, NY
> **Composition Bodies**— König & Wernicke, 1922-on.
> **Designer:** Grace Storey Putnam.
> **Distributor:** George Borgfeldt & Co., New York, NY, U.S.A.

12¾in (32cm) head circumference Bye-Lo Baby. H & J Foulke, Inc.

Baby Aero or **Fly-Lo Baby,** bisque head: #1418:

11in (28cm)	**$3,800-$4,200**

Composition head, original costume:

12in (31cm)	**$800-$900**

Marked All-Bisque Bye-Lo Baby: Ca. 1925-on. Solid head with molded hair and painted eyes; jointed shoulders and hips:

4-5in (10-13cm)	**$325-$425***
6in (15cm)	**$475-$525***
8in (20cm)	**$675-$725***

Solid head with swivel neck, glass eyes, jointed shoulders and hips:

4-5in (10-13cm)	**$550-$650***
6in (15cm)	**$750-$850***
8in (20cm)	**$1,200-$1,300***

Head with wig, glass eyes; jointed shoulders and hips:

4-5in (10-13cm)	**$700-$800**
6in (15cm)	**$900-$1,000**
8in (20cm)	**$1,450**

Action Bye-Lo Baby, immobile, in various positions, painted features:

3in (8cm)	**$400**

All-Celluloid: 4in (10cm)   **$250-$300**

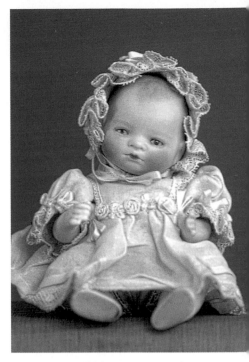

6½in (17cm) all-bisque *Bye-Lo Baby* with pink molded shoes. *H & J Foulke, Inc.*

*Allow extra for original clothes.

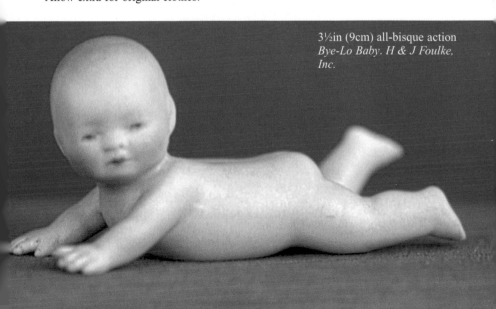

3½in (9cm) all-bisque action *Bye-Lo Baby. H & J Foulke, Inc.*

Catterfelder Puppenfabrik

C.P. Child Doll: Ca. 1902-on. Perfect bisque head, good wig, sleep eyes, open mouth with teeth; composition jointed body; dressed; all in good condition.
#264 (made by Kestner):

17-19in (43-48cm)	$700-$750
22-24in (56-61cm)	$850-$950

C.P. Character Child: Ca. 1910-on. Perfect bisque character face with wig, painted eyes; composition jointed body; dressed; all in good condition.
#207, 219: 15-16in (38-41cm)
$3,000-$4,000**
#217: 18in (46cm) $9,750**
#220: 14in (36cm) glass eyes $7,500**
#210: 14in (36cm) at auction $8,250**

C.P. Character Baby: Ca. 1910-on. Perfect bisque character face with wig or molded hair, painted or glass eyes; jointed baby body; dressed; all in good condition.
#200, 201, 208:

14-16in (36-41cm)	$450-$500
19-21in (48-53cm)	$700-$750

#201, toddler: 10in (25cm) $700-$800
#262, 263 (made by Kestner):

15-17in (38-43cm)	$525-$575
20-22in (51-56cm)	$750-$800

#262 toddler, five-piece body:
18-20in (46-51cm) $1,000

**Not enough price samples to compute a reliable range.

> **FACTS**
> Catterfelder Puppenfabrik, Catterfeld, Thüringia, Germany. Heads by J.D. Kestner and other porcelain makers. 1902-on. Bisque head; composition body. **Trademark:** My Sunshine. **Mark:**
>
> *C. P.*
> *208*
> *45*
> *N*

14½in (37cm) 264 child.
H & J Foulke, Inc.

Celluloid Dolls

Celluloid Shoulder Head Child Doll:
Ca. 1900-on. Cloth or kid body,
celluloid or composition arms; dressed;
all in good condition.
Painted eyes:
  16-18in (41-46cm)   **$160-$185**
Glass eyes:
  19-22in (48-56cm)   **$225-$250**
Original provincial costume:
  12-14in (30-36cm)   **$210-$235**
  Boy/girl pair   **$525-$550**

All-Celluloid Child Doll: Ca. 1900-on.
Jointed at neck, shoulders and hips; all
in good condition.
Painted eyes:
  4in (10cm)   **$55-$65***
  7-8in (18-20cm)   **$85-$100***
  10-12in (25-31cm)   **$125-$150***
  14-15in (36-38cm)   **$175-$225***
Googly: 5in (12cm)   **$175-$200**
French with original provincial
costume by **LeMinor, Poupées Magali**
and others:
  8in (20cm)   **$75-$85**
  12-14in (31-36cm)   **$160-$185**
  19in (48cm)   **$275-$325**
SNF pair with molded provincial
costumes: 9in (23cm)   **$250**
Tommy Tucker-type character:
  12-14in (31-36cm)   **$225-$250**

Glass eyes:
  12-13in (31-33cm)   **$200-$225***
  15-16in (38-41cm)   **$275-$300***
  18in (46cm)   **$375-$425***
  21in (53cm)   **$475-$500***
Turtle Mark Black Toddler:
  16in (41cm)   **$450-$500**
Marie-France, by Petitcollin, smiling
character, all original:
  18in (46cm)   **$350-$400**
  Boxed, in child's dress   **$565**
K & R 717 or 728:
  14-16in (36-41cm)   **$700-$750**

*Allow extra for unusual dolls.

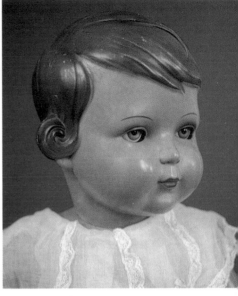

20in (51cm) all-celluloid girl with turtle
mark. *H & J Foulke, Inc.*

FACTS
Germany: Rheinische Gummi und
Celluloid Fabrik Co. (Turtle symbol);
Buschow & Beck, *Minerva* trademark
(Helmet symbol); E. Maar & Sohn,
Emasco trademark (3 M symbol);
Celba (Mermaid symbol).
Poland: P.R. Zask (ASK in triangle).
France: Petitcollin (Eagle symbol);
Société Nobel Française
(SNF in diamond);
Neumann & Mars (Dragon symbol);
Société Industrielle de Celluloid
(Sicoine).
United States: Parsons-Jackson Co.,
Cleveland, OH, and other companies
England: Cascelloid Ltd. (Palitoy).
1895-1940s.
Marks: Various as indicated above;
may also be in combination with the
marks of J.D. Kestner, Kämmer &
Reinhardt, Bruno Schmidt,
Käthe Kruse and König & Wernicke.

All-Celluloid Baby: Ca. 1910-on. All in good condition.

6-8in (15-20cm)	**$65-$85**
10-12in (25-31cm)	**$110-$135***
15in (38cm)	**$175-$200***
21in (53cm)	**$250-$300***

SNF black baby:

16-18in (41-46cm)	**$450-$500**

All-Celluloid, Made in Japan: Ca. 1920s. Molded clothes:

4-5in (10-12cm)	**$60-$80**
8-9in (20-23cm)	**$150-$175**

Child with pedestal legs, jointed arms:

3-4in (8-10cm)	**$15-$20**
6-7in (15-18cm)	**$25-$35**

Baby:

4-5in (10-13cm)	**$20-$30**
8-10in (20-25cm)	**$85-$110**
13in (33cm)	**$150-$175**
24in (61cm)	**$350-$400**

Occupied Japan, chubby toddler character: 6½in (17cm) **$85-$95**

16in (41cm) German celluloid head doll. *H & J Foulke, Inc.*

Parsons-Jackson, Stork Mark:

11½in (29cm) baby	**$165-$185****
14in (36cm) toddler	**$350****

Celluloid Head Infant: Ca. 1920s-on. Baby head with glass eyes; cloth body, appropriate clothes; all in good condition. 12-15in (31-38cm) **$175-$225**

Celluloid Socket Head Doll: Ca. 1910-on. Wig, glass eyes, sometimes flirty, open mouth with teeth; ball-jointed or bent-limb composition body; dressed; all in good condition.

K★R 701 child:

12-13in (31-33cm)	**$900-$1,100**

K★R 717 child, flapper body:

16-18in (41-46cm)	**$750-$800**
17in (43cm) with trunk and wardrobe	**$1,250**

K★R 700 baby:

14-15in (36-38cm)	**$325-$375**

K★R 728:

12-13in (31-33cm)	**$300-$350**
20in (51cm) toddler	**$550-$650**
18in (46cm) flapper	**$750-$850**

F.S. & Co. 1276:

20in (51cm) baby	**$550-$600**

*Allow $25 to $35 extra for glass eyes.
**Allow extra for molded shoes and socks.

10in (25cm) German celluloid character doll. *H & J Foulke, Inc.*

Chad Valley

Chad Valley Doll: All-cloth, usually felt face and velvet body, jointed neck, shoulders and hips; mohair wig, glass or painted eyes; original clothes; all in excellent condition, clean with good color.

Characters, painted eyes:
10-12in (25-31cm)	**$85-$115**

Characters, glass eyes:
17-20in (43-51cm)	**$1,000-$2,000***

Children, painted eyes:
9in (23cm)	**$135-$150**
13-14in (33-36cm)	**$375-$475**
16-18in (41-46cm)	**$550-$650**

Smiling face:
14-15in (36-38cm)	**$425-$475**

Children, glass eyes:
16-18in (41-46cm)	**$700-$800**

Royal Children, glass eyes:
16-18in (41-46cm)	**$1,250-$1,350**

Mabel Lucie Attwell, glass inset side-glancing eyes, smiling watermelon mouth:
15-17in (38-43cm)	**$750-$850**

Snow White Set:
Dwarfs, 10in (25cm)
	$250-$275 each

Snow White, 16in (41cm)
	$500-$600
Complete set	**$2,500-$3,000**

*Depending on rarity.

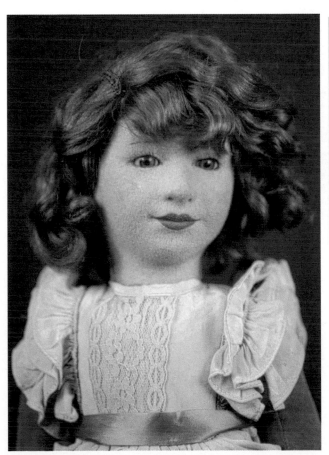

FACTS
Chad Valley Co. (formerly Johnson Bros., Ltd.), Birmingham, England. 1917-on. **Mark:** Cloth label usually on foot: "HYGIENIC TOYS Made in England by CHAD VALLEY CO. LTD."

16in (41cm) *Princess Elizabeth.* all original. *H & J Foulke, Inc.*

Martha Chase

Chase Doll: Head and limbs of stockinette, treated and painted with oils, large painted eyes with thick upper eyelashes, rough-stroked hair to provide texture, cloth bodies jointed at shoulders, hips, elbows and knees, later ones only at shoulders and hips; some bodies completely treated; appropriate clothing; showing wear, but no repaint.

Baby:
9in (23cm)	**$6,000****
13-15in (33-38cm)	**$575-$675***
17-20in (43-51cm)	**$750***
24-26in (61-66cm)	**$850***

Hospital Baby:
19-20in (49-51cm)	**$750**

Child, molded bobbed hair:
12-15in (31-38cm)	**$1,000-$1,200**
20in (51cm)	**$1,500-$$1,600**

Boy with side part and side curl:
15-16in (38-41cm)	**$3,000**

Lady:
13-15in (33-38cm)	**$1,500-$1,600**

Man: 15-16in (38-41cm)   **$3,000****

Black, Mammy or **child**   **$10,000****

Hospital Lady:
64in (163cm)	**$900-$1,200**

Alice in Wonderland character set:
Six dolls	**$67,000**

George Washington:
24in (61cm) at auction	**$6,250**

*Allow extra for a doll in excellent condition or with original clothes.

**Not enough price samples to compute a reliable range.

FACTS
Martha Jenks Chase,
Pawtucket, RI, U.S.A. 1889-on.
Designer: Martha Jenks Chase.
Mark: "Chase Stockinet Doll"
stamp on left leg or under left arm,
paper label on back (usually gone).

PAWTUCKET, R.I
MADE IN U.S.A.

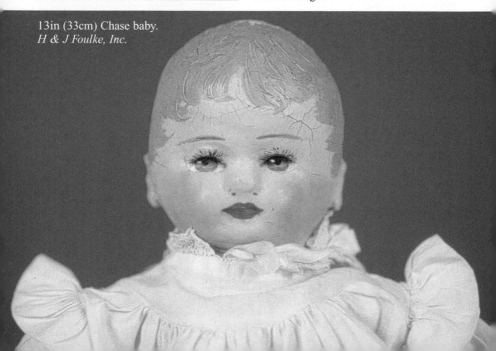

13in (33cm) Chase baby.
H & J Foulke, Inc.

China Heads, French

French China Head Fashion-type Doll: China shoulder head, open crown, cork pate, good wig, glass or beautifully painted eyes, painted eyelashes, feathered eyebrows, closed mouth; shapely kid fashion body (may have china arms curved to above elbow); appropriately dressed; all in good condition.

12-14in (31-36cm)	**$2,800-$3,300**
16-17in (41-43cm), naked	**$3,600-$4,000**
Child, 28in (71cm), with lever eyes, at auction	**$5,830**

Rohmer *poupée:*
15-16in (38-41cm)	**$4,500-$5,500**

Huret *poupée:*
17in (43cm)	**$8,500-$9,500**
With gutta percha body	**$15,000-$17,000**

FACTS

Various French doll firms; some heads sold through French firms may have been made in Germany. 1850s.
Mark: None.

Blampoix *poupée:*
12in (31cm) pair with original Watteau-type costumes, at auction	**$3,750**
28in (71cm)	**$6,500**

Painted black hair:
9-11in (23-28cm)	**$850-$950**
16in (41cm)	**$2,500**

Jacob Petit, head only, wigged:
4½in (11cm)	**$1,500**

English

English China Doll: Possibly Rockingham area, Ca. 1840-1860. Flesh-tinted shoulder head with bald head (some with molded slit for inserting wig), human hair wig, painted features, closed mouth; cloth torso and upper arms and legs, china lower limbs with holes to attach them to cloth, bare feet; appropriately dressed; all in good condition.

19-22in (48-56cm)	**$2,500-$3,000**
without china limbs	**$1,200**

13in (33cm) French china *poupée. Private Collection.*

22in (56cm) English pink-tinted china. *Private Collection.*

China Heads, German

1840s Hairstyles: China shoulder head with black molded hair; may have pink tint complexion; old cloth body; (may have china arms); appropriate old clothes; all in good condition.

Hair swept back into bun:

5in (13cm)	**$600**
13-15in (33-38cm)	**$2,000-$2,600**
18-21in (46-53cm)	**$3,200-$4,200**

Fancy braided bun:

22-24in (56-61cm)	**$5,000-$6,000**

Long curls, early face:

21in (53cm)	**$3,400**

K.P.M.:

Brown hair with bun:

16-18in (41-46cm)	**$6,000**

Long curls:

17in (43cm) at auction	**$9,250**

Young man, brown hair:

16-18in (41-46cm)	**$4,500**
22-23in (56-58cm)	**$7,000-$7,500**

Kinderkopf (child head):

10½in (27cm)	**$800-$900**
18-22in (46-56cm)	**$2,200-$2,800**

Wood jointed body, china lower limbs:

5-6in (13-15cm)	**$1,600-$1,800**
11in (28cm)	**$3,500-$4,500**

1850s Hairstyles: China shoulder head (some with pink tint), molded black hair (except bald), painted eyes; old cloth body with leather or china arms; appropriate old clothes; all in good condition.

Bald head, some with black areas on top, proper wig. Allow extra for original human hair wig in fancy style.

Fine quality:

12in (31cm)	**$700-$750**
15-17in (38-43cm)	**$1,000-$1,200**
22-24in (56-61cm)	**$1,700-$1,900**

Left: 16in (41cm) pink-tinted complexion china with bun. *H & J Foulke, Inc.*

Right: China with molded bun. *Private Collection.*

18½in (47cm) china lady with molded head band and snood. *H & J Foulke, Inc.*

20in (51cm) china lady with Greiner-style hairdo and brown eyes. *H & J Foulke, Inc.*

Standard quality:

13in (33cm)	**$500-$550**
16-17in (41-43cm)	**$750-$800**
20-22in (51-56cm)	**$900-$1,000**

Covered wagon with blue eyes:

5-7in (13-18cm)	**$325-$350**
17-20in (43-51cm)	**$800-$900**
24-26in (61-66cm)	**$1,250-$1,350**
Wood body, 9in (23cm)	**$1,350**

Covered wagon with brown eyes:

20-22in (51-56cm)	**$1,400-$1,500**

Greiner-style with brown eyes:

14-15in (36-38cm)	**$1,000-$1,200**
19-22in (48-56cm)	**$,1700-$2,000**
26in (66cm) at auction	**$3,410**

Greiner-style with glass eyes:

15-16in (38-41cm)	**$3,850****
22in (56cm)	**$4,800****

Waves, framing face, brown eyes:

20-21in (51-53cm)	**$1,700-$2,000**

With glass eyes:

18-21in (46-53cm)	**$3,000-$3,500**

Alice Hairdo, with molded headband:

22-24in (56-61cm)$	**950-$1,150**

Braided Coronet with bow:

13½in (34cm) at auction	**$2,200**

Sophia Smith, long curls, brown eyes:

15in (38cm) at auction	**$1,705**

Child or Baby, flange swivel neck; taüfling body with china or papier-mâché shoulder plate and hips, china lower limbs; cloth midsection (may have voice box) and upper limbs.

6½in (16cm) hairline	**$2,500**
10in (25cm)	**$3,000-$4,000**

Child with Alice Hairstyle:

8-11in (20-28cm)	**$4,000-$5,000**
17in (43cm) plate repaired, line on face, at auction	**$5,200**

**Not enough price samples to compute a reliable range.

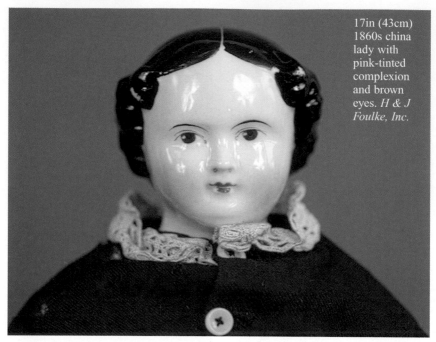

17in (43cm) 1860s china lady with pink-tinted complexion and brown eyes. *H & J Foulke, Inc.*

1860s and 1870s Hairstyles: China shoulder head with black molded hair (a few blondes); old cloth body may have leather arms or china lower arms and legs; appropriate old clothes; all in good condition.
Plain style with center part (so-called flat top and high brow):

6-7in (15-18cm)	**$165-$185***
14-16in (36-41cm)	**$275-$325***
19-22in (48-56cm)	**$400-$450***
24-26in (61-66cm)	**$450-$550***
28in (71cm)	**$750-$850***
34-35in (86-89cm)	**$1,000-$1,100**

Molded necklace:

22-24in (56-61cm)	**$700-$800**

Blonde hair: 18in (46cm)   **$475-$525**
Brown eyes:

20-22in (51-56cm)	**$600-$700**

Swivel neck: 15½in (40cm)   **$1,500**
Child face: 22in (56cm)   **$600-$650**

All-china Child, jointed shoulders and hips: 9in (23cm)   **$3,800-$4,000**

Mary Todd Lincoln, with snood:

18-21in (46-53cm)	**$1,000-$1,100**

Blonde hair, fancy snood:

20-21in (51-53cm)	**$1,500**

Conta and Boehme:

19in (48cm)	**$700-$800**

Molded bonnet, applied flowers, poor quality: 20in (51cm)   **$500**
Young Man: 16in (41cm) **$900-$1,100**
Dolley Madison, with molded bow:

14-16in (36-41cm)	**$425-$475**
21-24in (53-61cm)	**$625-$700**

Blonde hair, pierced ears:

22in (56cm)	**$750-$800**

Adelina Patti:

13-15in (33-38cm)	**$425-$475**
19-22in (48-56cm)	**$650-$725**

14in (36cm) original body and limbs
$600

Dagmar-type: 18in (46cm)   **$800**
Jenny Lind:

12in (31cm)	**$850**
21-24in (53-61cm)	**$1,600-$1,800**

Currier & Ives, long hair on shoulders:

15in (38cm)	**$600**

Curly Top:

14in (36cm) black hair	**$600**
19in (48cm) tan hair	**$900**

Grape Lady:

18in (46cm)	**$2,200-$2,500**

*Allow more for all original body and clothes.

Spill Curl:
19-22in (48-56cm)   **$900-$1,100**

Morning Glory:
21in (53cm)   **$7,500-$8,500****
24in (61cm) at auction   **$10,250**

Fancy blonde hairdo with headband and pierced ears:
17in (43cm) at auction   **$2,530**

Fancy long curls with molded comb and pierced ears:
26in (66cm) at auction   **$2,200**

Hair pulled back into cascading curls, brown eyes:
22in (56cm)   **$2,000**

Braid across top of head and braided coiled bun in back:
23in (58cm)   **$2,700**

Fancy hairdo with molded gold beads:
21in (53cm)   **$2,500**

Overall short pin curls:
22in (56cm) at auction   **$2,200**

1880s Hairstyles: China shoulder head with black or blonde molded hair; appropriate old clothes; all in good condition. Many made by Alt, Beck & Gottschalck or Kling & Co.

6in (15cm) all original	**$165-$185**
14-16in (36-41cm)	**$325-$375**
21-23in (53-58cm)	**$500-$550**
28in (71cm)	**$700-$750**
Head only, 5in (13cm)	**$175-$225**

**Not enough price samples to compute a reliable range.

19in (48cm)
1870s china
lady with
pierced ears.
*H & J Foulke,
Inc.*

Bawo and Dotter, "Pat. Dec. 7/80:"
  18-20in (46-51cm)   **$400-$450**

Dressel & Kister: Ca. 1890-1920. China shoulder head with varying hairdos and brush-stroked hair; delicately painted features; cloth body with china arms having beautifully molded fingers. Often used as ornamental dolls in only half form as for a boudoir lamp or candy box.
  13in (33cm)   **$1,500 up**
  Heads only   **$675-$750**

1890s Hairstyles: China shoulder head with black or blonde molded wavy hair; appropriate clothes; all in good condition.
  4½in (11cm)   **$55-$60**
  8-10in (20-25cm)   **$110-$135***
  13-15in (33-38cm)   **$165-$195***
  19-21in (48-53cm)   **$235-$285***
  24in.(61cm)   **$350**
Molded bonnet:
  8-10in (20-25cm)   **$165-$185**
Molded "Jewel" necklace:
  22in (56cm)   **$400-$425**
  8-1/2in (21cm)   **$150-$165**

Pet Name: Ca. 1905. Made by Hertwig & Co. for Butler Bros., New York. China shoulder head, molded yoke with name in gold; black or blonde painted hair (one-third were blonde). Used names such as **Agnes, Bertha, Daisy,**

Dorothy, Edith, Esther, Ethel, Florence, Helen, Mabel, Marion, and **Pauline.**
  12-14in (30-36cm)   **$200-$250**
  18-21in (46-53cm)   **$350-$400**
  24in (61cm)   **$450**
  Open mouth, 10in (25cm)   **$175-$200**

*Allow $50-$100 extra for lithographed body.

26in (66cm) Bawo & Dotter china head. *H & J Foulke, Inc.*

15in (38cm) Dressel & Kister china head man and lady. *Private Collection.*

Cloth, Printed

Cloth, Printed Doll: Names such as Dolly Dear, Merry Marie, Improved Foot Doll, Standish No Break Doll, and others:

7-9in (18-23cm)	**$60-$70**
16-18in (41-46cm)	**$110-$125**
22-24in (56-61cm)	**$135-$165**

Uncut sheet, bright colors:

13in (33cm) doll	**$110-$125**
20in (51cm) doll	**$135-$165**

Black Child, Art Fabric:

18in (46cm)	**$250**

Boys and Girls with printed outer clothes. Ca. 1903:

12-13in (31-33cm)	**$100-$125**
17in (43cm)	**$150-$175**

Aunt Jemima Family:

Four dolls	**$65-$75 each**
Ball, uncut	**$250-$275**

Brownies: Ca. 1892. Designed by Palmer Cox; marked on foot:

8in (20cm)	**$75-$85**
Uncut sheet of six	**$250**
Buster Brown and Tige	**$325**
Cream of Wheat Rastus	**$90-$110**

Darkey Doll, Cocheco, made up:

16in (41cm)	**$225-$250**

E.T. Gibson, Ca. 1912: Red bathing suit **$165-$185**

George & Martha Washington **$350/pair**

Hen and Chicks, uncut sheet **$65**

Hug-Me-Tight, Ca. 1916. Grace G. Drayton Mother Goose Characters:

11in (28cm)	**$225-$250**
Pitti Sing, uncut	**$65**
Punch & Judy	**$350/pair**
Red Riding Hood	**$150**
Santa, Peck, 1886	**$225**
Tabby Cat	**$70-$80**
Tabby's Kittens	**$45-$55**

Topsy, uncut: 8½in (22cm) two dolls on sheet **$195**

Pillow-type, printed and hand-embroidered, 1920s-1930s:

16in (41cm)	**$65-$85**

Oilcloth:

Orphan Annie: 17in (43cm)	**$185**
Sandy	**$75-$85**
Smitty	**$60-$70**
Skeezix	**$60-$70**

FACTS
Various American companies, such as Cocheco Mfg. Co., Lawrence & Co., Arnold Print Works, Art Fabric Mills and Selchow & Righter and Dean's Rag Book Co. in England. 1896-on.
Mark: Mark could be found on fabric part, which was discarded after cutting.

Santa by Peck, 1886.
Nancy A. Smith Collection.

Cloth, Russian

Russian Cloth Doll: All-cloth with stockinette head and hands, molded face with hand-painted features; authentic regional clothes; all in very good condition.

6½in (16cm) child	**$50-$55**
11in (28cm) child	**$110-$125**
15in (38cm)	**$200-$250**
Tea Cosy: 20in (51cm)	**$250-$275**

Columbian Doll

Columbian Doll: All-cloth with hair and features hand-painted on a flat face; treated limbs; appropriate clothes; all in very good condition, no repaint or touch up.

15in (38cm)	**$6,000**
19-23in (48-58cm)	**$7,000-$8,000**
Some wear:	
23in (58cm)	**$4,000-$4,200**
Worn: 20in (51cm)	**$2,200**

11in (28cm) Russian cloth child, all original. *H & J Foulke, Inc.*

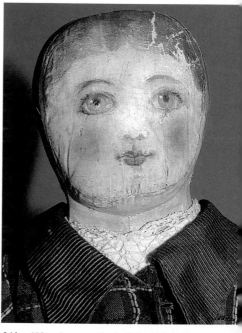

21in (53cm) unmarked Columbian-type doll. *Private Collection.*

<hr>

FACTS
Unknown craftsmen. Ca. 1930.
Mark: "Made in Soviet Union" sometimes with identification of doll, such as "Ukrainian Woman," "Village Boy," "Smolensk District Woman."

<hr>

FACTS
Emma and Marietta Adams.
1891-1910 or later.
Mark: Stamped on back of body.
Before 1900: "COLUMBIAN DOLL
EMMA E. ADAMS
OSWEGO CENTRE N.Y."
After 1906: "THE COLUMBIAN
DOLL MANUFACTURED BY
MARIETTA ADAMS RUTTAN
OSWEGO, N.Y."

Danel, Later Jumeau

Marked Paris Bébé: Ca. 1889-1892. Perfect bisque socket head with Jumeau look, good wig, paperweight eyes, closed mouth, pierced ears; composition jointed body; appropriately dressed; all in good condition. This doll was a copy of a Jumeau.

Mark: On Head   TÊTE DÉPOSÉ
PARIS BEBE

On Body

PARIS BÉBÉ
Breveté

16-18in (41-46cm)	$3,800-$4,200
22-24in (56-66cm)	$4,500-$4,800
32in (81cm)	$6,000-$6,200

Marked Paris Bébé: Ca. 1892-on. Character face developed by Jumeau for use with this trademark after he won a lawsuit against Danel. (For photograph, see *11th Blue Book,* page 144).

18-19in (46-48cm)	$5,000-$5,500
23-25in (58-64cm)	$6,000-$6,500

Marked B.F.: Ca. 1891. Bébé Française was used by Jumeau after 1892. Perfect bisque head, appropriate wig, paperweight eyes, closed mouth, pierced ears; jointed composition body; appropriate clothes; all in good condition.

Mark: B 9 F

16-19in (41-48cm)	$4,600-$5,000
23-25in (58-64cm)	$5,500-$6,000

FACTS
Danel & Cie., Paris & Montreuil-sous-Bois, France. 1889-1895.
Trademarks: Paris Bébé, Bébé Française. Both used by Jumeau after winning an 1892 lawsuit.

22in (56cm)
Bébé
Française.
H & J
Foulke, Inc.

DEP

DEP Closed Mouth: Ca. 1890. Perfect bisque head, swivel neck, lovely wig, set paperweight eyes, upper and lower painted eyelashes, closed mouth, pierced ears; jointed French composition and wood body (may be stamped Jumeau); pretty clothes; all in good condition.

Mark: **DEP**
(size number)

12in (31cm)	$1,950-$2,150
15in (38cm)	$2,500-$2,650
18-20in (46-51cm)	$3,100-$3,400
25-27in (63-68cm)	$4,500-$5,000
Open mouth, 22in (56cm)	
	$1,000-$1,200

Jumeau DEP: Ca. 1899-on. Heads possibly by Simon & Halbig. Perfect bisque socket head (sometimes with Tête Jumeau stamp), human hair wig, deeply molded eye socket, sleep eyes, painted lower eyelashes, upper hair eyelashes (sometimes gone), pierced ears; jointed French composition and wood body (sometimes with Jumeau label or stamp); lovely clothes; all in good condition.

Mark: **DEP**
8

9½in (20cm)	$1,000-$1,100
11-1/2in (29cm)	$850*
13-15in (33-38cm)	$900-$950*
18-20in (46-51cm)	$1,050-$1,200*
23-25in (58-64cm)	$1,400-$1,700*
29-30in (74-76cm)	$2,200-$2,500*
35in (89cm)	$3,000-$3,200

*Allow extra for Jumeau flowered shift.

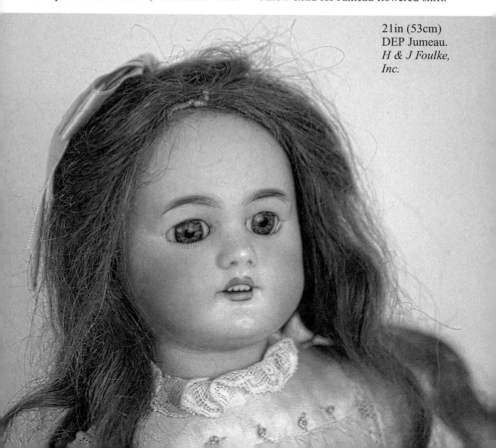

21in (53cm) DEP Jumeau. *H & J Foulke, Inc.*

Door of Hope

Dressel

Door of Hope: Carved wooden head with painted and/or carved hair; cloth body, some with stubby arms, some with carved hands; original handmade clothes, exact costuming for different classes of Chinese people; all in excellent condition. 25 dolls in the series.
Adult:

11-13in (28-33cm)	**$700-$1,000**
Child: 7-8in (18-20cm)	**$750-$850**
Amah and **Baby**	**$900-$1,000**

Manchu Lady:

Carved headdress	**$1,500**

Bride:

Old style	**$1,200**
New style	**$1,000**

Women or **Girls** with special carving in the hair: **$900-$1,100**

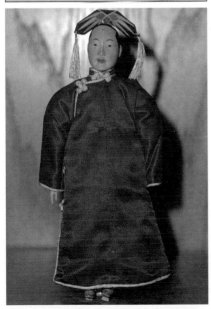

Door of Hope *Manchu Lady* with carved headdress. *Private Collection.*

Marked Holz-Masse: Ca. 1875-on. Papier-mâché or composition shoulder head; cloth/composition body. See page 163.

Child Doll: Ca. 1893-on. Perfect bisque head, good wig, glass eyes, open mouth; suitable clothes; all in good condition.
Mark:

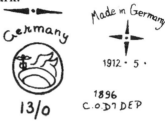

Composition body:

13in (33cm)	**$325**
15-16in (38-41cm)	**$375-$400**
19-21in (48-53cm)	**$450-$475**
24in (61cm)	**$525-$550**
32in (81cm)	**$1,000**
38in (96cm)	**$2,000**

#93, 1896 Kid body:

15-16in (38-41cm)	**$275-$325**
19-22in (48-56cm)	**$450-$500**

Character-type face, similar to **K★R** 117n. (For photograph, see *12th Blue Book,* page 151.):

14in (36cm)	**$1,100-$1,200**
26in (66cm)	**$1,600-$1,800**
41in (66cm)	**$3,100**

Portrait Series: 1896. Perfect bisque heads with portrait faces, glass eyes, some with molded mustaches and goatees; composition body; original clothes; all in good condition. Some marked "S" or "D" with a number.

Uncle Sam:
    12-14in (31-36cm) **$1,200-$1,500**
Admiral Dewey and **Officers:**
    15in (38cm)   **$1,600-$1,800**
Old Rip:
    11in (28cm)   **$1,200-$1,300**
Farmer: 13in (33cm)   **$1,500**
Buffalo Bill: 10in (23cm)   **$750**

Marked Jutta Child: Ca. 1906-1921. Perfect bisque socket head, good wig, sleep eyes, open mouth, pierced ears; ball-jointed composition body; dressed; all in good condition. Head made by Simon & Halbig.

Mold 1348 or 1349
Mark: 1349
    Jutta
    S&H
    11

14-16in (36-41cm)   **$700-$725***
19-21in (43-53cm)   **$750-$800***

24-26in (61-66cm)   **$900-$1,100***
30-32in (76-81cm)   **$1,500-$1,600**
38-39in (96-99cm)   **$3,000-$3,500**

Character Child: Ca. 1909-on. Perfect bisque socket head, mohair wig, painted eyes, closed mouth; ball-jointed composition body; suitable clothes; all in good condition. Glazed inside of head. (For photograph, see *10th Blue Book,* page 179.)
Mark: C.O.D.
    A/2

10-12in (25-31cm) **$1,500-$1,800****
16-18in (41-46cm)   **$3,000**
Limbach 8679 pouty, glass eyes (For photograph, see *14th Blue Book*, page 84.):
    14in (36cm)   **$1,800-$2,000****
Composition head:
    19in (48cm)   **$2,600-$3,000****
    13in (33cm) wear on nose and lips
         $1,300

*Allow $150 extra for flapper body with high knee joint.
**Not enough price samples to compute a reliable range.

18½in (47cm) COD 93 shoulder head. *Jensen's Antique Dolls.*

13in (33cm) *Uncle Sam* portrait, all original. *Private Collection.*

14in (36cm) 1914 *Jutta* character baby. *H & J Foulke, Inc.*

14in (36cm) COD 1469 lady. *Private Collection.*

Marked C.O.D. Character Baby: Ca. 1910 on. Perfect bisque character face with marked wig or molded hair, painted or glass eyes; jointed baby body; dressed; all in good condition.

12-13in (31-33cm)	**$350**
16-18in (41-46cm)	**$450-$475**
22-24in (56-61cm)	**$675-$725**

Marked Jutta Character Baby: Ca. 1910-1922. Perfect bisque socket head, good wig, sleep eyes, open mouth; bent-limb composition baby body; dressed; all in good condition.

Simon & Halbig:

16-18in (41-46cm)	**$650-$750**
23-24in (58-61cm)	**$1,300-$1,400**

Toddler, fully-jointed body:

23-25in (58-63cm)	**$1,900-$2,100**

Other Makers: (Armand Marseille, E. Heubach):

16-18in (41-46cm)	**$425-$475**
23-24in (58-61cm)	**$650-$750**

Toddler, fully-jointed body:

16-18in (41-46cm)	**$850-$900**

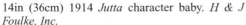

Marks: Heubach 6½ Koppelsdorf Jutta · Baby Dressel Germany 1922 10½   ⬭ Jutta 1914 8

Lady Doll: Ca. 1920s. Bisque socket head with young lady face, good wig, sleep eyes, closed mouth; jointed composition body in adult form with molded bust, slim waist and long arms and legs, feet modeled to wear high-heeled shoes; all in good condition.

Mark: 1469 C O. Dressel Germany 2.

#1469:

14in (36cm) naked	**$2,500-$3,000**
14in (36cm) original clothes	**$3,500-$4,300**

E.D. Bébé

Eden Bébé

Marked E. D. Bébé: Perfect bisque head, good wig, beautiful blown glass eyes, pierced ears; wood and composition jointed body; nicely dressed; good condition.
Closed mouth:
  15-18in (38-46cm)
    $2,800-$3,200
  22-24in (56-61cm)
    $3,600-$4,000
  28in (71cm)
    $4,200-$4,400
Open mouth:
  18-20in (35-51cm)
    $1,800-$2,000
  25-27in (64-69cm)
    $2,500-$2,700
  15in (38cm) all original, boxed, at auction   **$2,100**

Note: Dolls with Jumeau look but signed "E. D." are Jumeau factory dolls produced when Emile Douillet was director of the Jumeau firm, 1892-1899. They do not have the word "Déposé" under the "E. D." They should be priced as Jumeau dolls. (For photograph, see *10th Blue Book,* page 181.)

FACTS
Etienne Denamur of Paris, France. 1889-on.
Mark:

E 8 D
DEPOSÉ

Marked Eden Bébé: Ca. 1890. Perfect bisque head, beautiful wig, large set paperweight eyes, closed or open/closed mouth, pierced ears; fully-jointed or five-piece composition jointed body; lovely clothes; all in nice condition.
Closed mouth:
  14-16in (36-41cm)   **$2,200-$2,400**
  21-23in (53-58cm)   **$2,800-$3,000**
  Five-piece body: 12in (31cm) **$1,200-$1,500**
  Open mouth: 19-20in (48-51cm) **$1,900-$2,000**

FACTS
Fleischmann & Bloedel,
doll factory, Paris, France. 1890,
then into S.F.B.J. in 1899.
Trademark: Eden Bébé (1890),
Bébé Triomphe (1898).
Mark: "EDEN BEBE, PARIS"

11in (28cm) *Eden Bébé. H & J Foulke, Inc.*

French Fashion-Type
(Poupée)

French Fashion Lady (Poupée): Perfect unmarked bisque shoulder head, swivel or stationary neck, original or old wig, lovely blown glass eyes, closed mouth, earrings; kid body (*poupée peau*) or cloth body with kid arms — some with wired fingers; appropriate old clothes; all in good condition. Fine quality bisque.

12-13in (31-33cm)	**$2,000-$2,200***
15-16in (38-41cm)	**$2,500-$3,000***
18-19in (46-48cm)	**$3,500-$3,900***
21in (53cm)	**$4,100-$4,500***
33in (84cm)	**$6,750**

Dainty oval face:

12-14in (31-36cm)	**$2,300-$2,500**

Painted eyes, stiff neck:

16-17in (41-43cm)	**$1,800-$2,200**

Fully-jointed wood body (*poupée bois*):

16-18in (41-46cm)	**$6,200-$6,800**

Blown kid body: 17in (43cm) with hairline, at auction **$6,820**

F.B. Poupée: E. Barrois 1862-1877. Perfect bisque shoulder head (may have a swivel neck), appropriate wig, glass eyes (may be painted with long painted eyelashes), closed mouth; adult kid body, some with jointed wood arms or wood and bisque arms; appropriate clothing; all in good condition.

Mark: E . | DÉPOSÉ B

14-16in (36-41cm)	**$2,800-$3,200**
19-20in (48-51cm)	**$4,000-$4,200**
Wood body: 18in (46cm)	**$6,500**

Molded short curly hair, painted eyes:

19in (48cm) at auction	**$2,600**

*Allow extra for fancy original clothing and/or bisque lower arms.

> ### FACTS
> Various French firms. Ca. 1860-1930.
> (See also **Bru, Jumeau, Gaultier, Gesland** and **China Heads, French**.)

Benoit Martin, wood body, naked:

18in (46cm) at auction	**$17,500**

A. Dehors, 1860: 17in (43cm) shoulder head **$18,000-$19,000**

Dehors & Clement, blown kid body:

13in (33cm) at auction	**$9,750**

Marked Huret Poupée: Ca. 1850. China or bisque shoulder head, good wig, painted eyes, closed mouth; kid body; beautifully dressed; all in good condition.

16-17in (41-43cm)	**$15,000-$20,000**
Wood body	**$32,000**
Gutta-percha body	**$20,000****

Smiling man, wood body:

18in (46cm) at auction	**$16,000**

Character Lady:

19in (48cm) at auction	**$9,400**

Lavalée-Perrone, kid body:

17in (43cm)	**$7,500**

15in (38cm) *poupée peau* with swivel neck. *H & J Foulke, Inc.*

Radiquet and Cordonnier, molded breasts, bisque arms, one bent at elbow, bisque lower legs, original signed stand:
   17in (43cm)	**$13,000-$15,000**

Rohmer Poupée: Ca. 1857-1880. China or bisque swivel or shoulder head, lovely wig, set glass eyes, closed mouth, some ears pierced; jointed kid body, bisque or china arms, kid or china legs; fine costuming; entire doll in good condition.
   16-18in (41-46cm)	**$4,200-$4,750**
Zinc body: 17in (43cm) at auction
                              $7,750

Mark:

Parasol Doll, original silk outfit:
   18in (46cm)	**$2,200**
Rochard Head, with Stanhope necklace, 1868:
   6¾in (17cm) at auction	**$24,300**
Simonne,
   Kid body: 16in (41cm)
                $3,200-$3,500
   Wood body: 18in (46cm)
                $6,000-$6,500
Period Clothes, Fashion Lady clothing:
   Dress	**$500-$1,000 up**
   Boots	**$300-$350**
   Elaborate wig	**$300-$400**
   Nice wig	**$150-$250**

**Not enough price samples to compute a reliable average.

18in (46cm) *poupée bois* with swivel neck. *H & J Foulke, Inc.*

Frozen Charlotte
(Bathing Doll)

Frozen Charlotte: All-china doll, black or blonde molded hair, painted features; hands extended, legs separated but not jointed; no clothes; perfect condition. Good quality.

2-3in (5-8cm)	**$50-$65***
4-5in (10-13cm)	**$140-$165***
6-7in (15-18cm)	**$200-$225***
9-10in (23-25cm)	**$275-$325***
14-15in (36-38cm)	**$550-$600**
17in (43cm)	**$700-$750**

Pink tint, early hairdo:

2½-3½in (6-9cm)	**$225-$250**
3½in (9cm) *café-au-lait* hair	**$395**
5in (13cm)	**$375-$425**
10in (25cm)	**$750-$1,000**

Pink tint with bonnet:

3½in (9cm)	**$400-$450**
5in (13cm)	**$525-$575**

Black china: 5in (13cm)   **$165-$195**
Black boy, molded turban and pants:
3in (8cm)   **$275-$300**
Black boy, molded shift:
5in (13cm)   **$300-$350**
Blonde hair, molded bow:
5½in (14cm)   **$200-$225**
Wig, lovely painted boots:
5in (13cm)   **$200-$225**

All-Bisque:
Child: 5in (13cm)   **$150-$175**
Parian-type (1860s style):
5in (13cm)   **$225-$250**
Alice style with pink boots:
5in (13cm)   **$325-$375**
Fancy hairdo and boots:
4½in (11cm)   **$275-$300**
Molded clothes: 3¼in (9cm)   **$225**
Early boy, blonde hair:
9in (23cm)   **$450-$500**

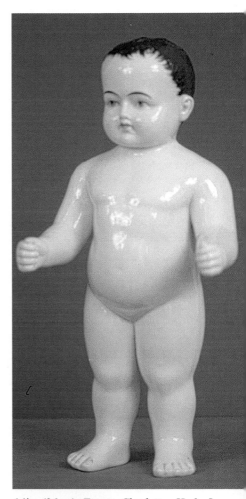

14in (36cm) *Frozen Charlotte. H & J Foulke, Inc.*

*Allow extra for pink tint, fine decoration and modeling, unusual hairdo.

FACTS
Various German firms. Ca. 1850s-early 1900s.
Mark: None, except for "Germany" or numbers or both.

Fulper

Fulper Child Doll: Perfect bisque head, good wig, set or sleep eyes, open mouth; kid jointed or composition ball-jointed body; suitably dressed; all in good condition. Good quality bisque.

Kid body:
  18-21in (46-53cm)   **$375-$425***
Composition body:
  16-18in (41-46cm)   **$400-$450***
  22-24in (56-61cm)   **$500-$550***
Character Baby:
  16-18in (41-46cm)   **$500-$550***
  22-24in (56-61cm)   **$700-$750***
Toddler: 15-17in (38-43cm)   **$800-$900***
Molded hair: 16in (41cm)   **$3,500-$4,000****

*Allow more for an especially pretty or cute doll.
**Not enough samples to compute a reliable range.

FACTS
Heads by Fulper Pottery Co., of Flemington, NJ, for other companies, often Amberg or Horsman. 1918-1921.
Mark:
"Fulper-Made in U.S.A."

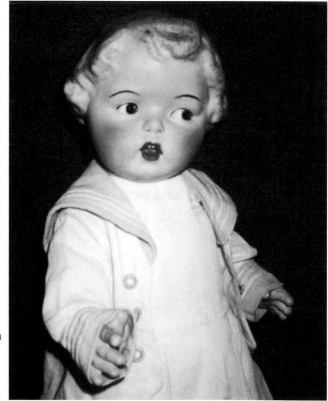

16in (41cm) rare Fulper toddler with molded hair.
Courtesy of Dorothy Hunt, Sweetbriar.

Gaultier

Marked F.G. Fashion Lady (Poupée Peau): Ca. 1860-1930. Perfect bisque swivel head on bisque shoulder plate, original or good French wig, lovely glass stationary eyes, closed mouth, ears pierced; original kid body, kid arms with wired fingers or bisque lower arms and hands; appropriately dressed; all in good condition.

Mark: "F.G." on side of shoulder.

10-11in (26-28cm)	**$1,850**
12-13in (30-33cm)	**$2,100-$2,250***
16-17in (41-43cm)	**$2,600-$2,850***

20in (51cm)	**$3,200-$3,400***
23-24in (58-61cm)	**$3,600-$3,900***
29-30in (71-76cm)	**$5,000-$6,000***
35in (89cm)	**$7,000-$7,400**
37in (94cm)	**$7,900**

Wood body, *(Poupée Bois):*

16-18in (41-46cm)	**$4,800-$5,200**

Late doll in ethnic costume:

8-9in (20-23cm)	**$750-$850**

Painted eyes:

16-17in (41-43cm)	**$1,800-$2,000**

*Allow extra for original clothes.

Left: 23in (58cm) early pale bisque shoulder head F. G. *poupée peau*, all original. *H & J Foulke, Inc.*

Below: 20in (51cm) F.G. 5 *poupée peau. H & J Foulke, Inc.*

FACTS
François Gauthier (name changed to Gaultier in 1875); St. Maurice, Charenton, Seine, Paris, France. (This company made only porcelain parts, not bodies.) 1860 to 1899 (then joined S.F.B.J.)

13½in (34cm) F.G. *bébé* with scroll mark. *H & J Foulke, Inc.*

Early model:
  13-15in (33-38cm)   **$3,600-$4,000**
  20-22in (51-56cm)   **$5,000-$6,000**
"Baggy pants," kid over wood arms:
  15in (38cm)   **$3,800**

Approximate size chart:	
Size 3/0 =	10½in (27cm)
2/0 =	11½in (29cm)
1 =	13½in (34cm)
2 =	15in (38cm)
3 =	17in (43cm)
5 =	20in (51cm)
6 =	22in (56cm)

Marked F.G. Bébé: Ca. 1879-1887. Perfect bisque swivel head, large bulgy paperweight eyes, closed mouth, pierced ears; dressed; all in good condition. So-called "Block letter" mark.
Mark:

F . 7.G

Composition body:
  13-15in (33-38cm)   **$4,300-$4,600**
  18-20in (46-51cm)   **$5,200-$5,700**
  22-23in (56-58cm)   **$5,800-$6,100**

  27-28in (69-71cm)   **$6,800-$7,200**
  33-35in (84-89cm)   **$7,500–$8,000**
Kid body:
  13in (33cm)   **$4,200–$5,200**
  16in (41cm)   **$5,500–$5,750**
  20-22in (51-56cm)   **$6,000–$7,000**

Marked F.G. Bébé: Ca. 1887-1900. Bisque head, beautiful large set eyes; well dressed; all in good condition. So-called "Scroll" mark.
Mark:

F.G

Closed mouth, very good quality bisque:
  5-6in (13-15cm)   **$750–$800**
  15-17in (38-43cm)   **$2,800–$3,100***
  22-24in (56-61cm)   **$3,600–$3,900***
  27-28in(69-71cm)   **$4,300–$4,600***
Open mouth:
  14-17in (38-43cm)   **$1,750–$1,950**
  20-22in(51-56cm)   **$2,100–$2,400**
  31in (79cm)   **$3,300–$3,600**

*For grainy or high color bisque, deduct $500 to $1,000.

Gesland

Fashion Lady (Poupée): Perfect bisque swivel head, good wig, paperweight eyes, closed mouth, pierced ears; stockinette body on metal frame with bisque hands and legs; dressed; all in good condition.

Early face:
16-20in (41-51cm) $5,500–$6,200*

F.G. face:
14in (36cm)	$3,600–$3,800*
16-20in (41-51cm)	$4,000–$4,500*
24in (61cm)	$5,500–$5,700*
28in (71cm)	$6,000–$6,500
Body only, for 14in (36cm)	$1,100

Bébé: Perfect bisque swivel head, composition shoulder plate, good wig, paperweight eyes, closed mouth, pierced ears; stockinette body on metal frame with composition lower arms and legs; dressed; all in good condition.

Beautiful early face:
14-16in (36-41cm)	$4,900–$5,100
22 – 24in (56-61cm)	$5,900–$6,400
29-30in (71-76cm)	$7,300-$7,500

"Scroll" mark face:
14-16in (36-41cm)	$2,800–$3,100
22-24in (56-61cm)	$4,000–$4,500

*Allow extra for original clothes.

FACTS
Heads: François Gaultier, Paris, France.
Bodies: E. Gesland, Paris, France. 1860-1928.
Mark: Head:

F G

Body: Sometimes stamped "E. Gesland."

16½ (42cm) *Bébé Gesland* with block mark. *H & J Foulke, Inc.*

Gladdie

Marked Gladdie: Biscaloid or ceramic head, molded and painted hair, glass eyes, open/closed smiling mouth with molded teeth; cloth torso, composition arms and legs; dressed; all in good condition.

 16-19in (41-48cm)   **$900-$1,000***
 22in (56cm)   **$1,250***

#1410 Bisque Head, Alt, Beck & Gottschalck, open mouth with teeth:

 15in (28cm)   **$2,500-$3,000**

*Allow extra for original clothes and exceptional condition.

FACTS
Designer: Helen W. Jensen
Distributor: George Borgfeldt & Co., New York, NY, 1929.
Mark:

Gladdie
Copyright By
Helen W. Jensen

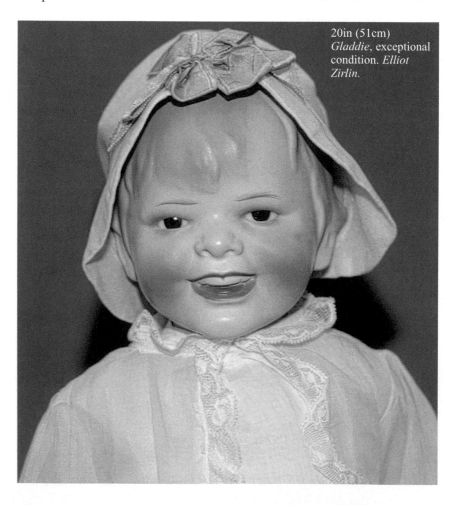

20in (51cm) *Gladdie*, exceptional condition. *Elliot Zirlin.*

Goebel

Goebel Child Doll: 1895 on. Perfect bisque socket head, good wig, sleep eyes, open mouth; composition jointed body; dressed; all in good condition. Some mold #120 or B.

    16-18in (41-46cm)   **$375-$425**
    23-25in (58-64cm)   **$475-$525**

Goebel Character Baby: Ca. 1910. Perfect bisque socket head, good wig, sleep eyes, open mouth; composition jointed baby body; dressed; all in good condition.

    13-15in (33-38cm)   **$350-$400**
    19-21in (48-53cm)   **$500-$550**

19in (48cm) B 5-10 character baby. *H & J Foulke, Inc.*

Goebel Character Doll: Ca. 1910. Perfect bisque head with molded hair in various styles, some with ornamentation, some with hats; character face with painted features; papier-mâché five-piece body; all in good condition.

    6½in (7cm)   **$275-$300**

FACTS

F & W Goebel porcelain factory, near Coburg, Thüringia, Germany. 1879 on

Marks:

"B" plus number "Germany" sometimes A, C, G, H, K, S, SA & T

Googly-Eyed Dolls

All-Bisque Googly: Jointed at shoulders and hips, molded shoes and socks; mohair wig, glass eyes, impish mouth; undressed; in perfect condition.
Glass Eyes:
#217, 501, 330 and others:

4½-5in (11-13cm)	**$750-$800**
5½-6in (14-15cm)	**$900-$1,000**

#189, 192 swivel necks:

4½-5in (11-13cm)	**$900-$1,100**
5½-6in (14-15cm)	**$1,150-$1,250**
7in (18cm)	**$1,350-$1,450**

#112 **Kestner,** jointed elbows and knees, swivel neck:

5in (13cm)	**$3,250**
7in (18cm)	**$4,500****
Baby: 4½in (12cm)	**$550-$600**
S.W.C. #405: 6½in (17cm)	**$1,350****

K & R 131:

7in (18cm)	**$3,500-$3,800****

Painted eyes, molded hair or wigged:
#217, 179 and others:

4½in (12cm)	**$450-$500**
6in (15cm)	**$600-$650**
7in (18cm)	**$750-$775**
S.W.C. #408: 5in (13cm)	**$350-$400***

Painted eyes, composition body: Perfect bisque swivel head; five-piece composition toddler or baby body; cute clothes; all in good condition.
A.M., E. Heubach, Goebel, R.A.:

6-7in (15-18cm)	**$550-$600***
9-10in (23-25cm)	**$900-$950***
12in (31cm)	**$1,100-$1,200***

#252 A.M. **Kewpie**-type baby:

9in (23cm)	**$1,200-$1,400****

*Allow extra for unusual models.
**Not enough price samples to compute a reliable range.

FACTS
J.D. Kestner; Armand Marseille; Hertel, Schwab & Co.; Heubach; H. Steiner; Goebel and other German and French firms. Ca. 1911-on.

5in (13cm) 217
all-bisque googly.
H & J Foulke, Inc.

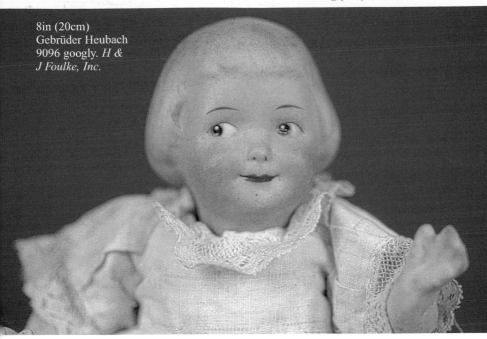

8in (20cm)
Gebrüder Heubach
9096 googly. *H &
J Foulke, Inc.*

Gebrüder Heubach:
  6-7in (15-18cm)   **$575-$625***
  7in (18cm) Winker   **$850-$900**
  9in (23cm) top knot   **$1,500-$1,600**
#246 G.K. Winker with molded hat:
  20in (51cm) at auction   **$2,100**

Glass eyes, composition body: Perfect bisque head; original composition body; cute clothes; all in nice condition. A.M. #323 and other similar models by H. Steiner, E. Heubach, Goebel and Recknagel:
  6-7in (15-18cm)   **$900-$1,100**
  10-11in (25-28cm) **$1,650-$1,850**
  13in (33cm)   **$2,500-$2,800**
  Baby body: 10-11in (25-28cm)
                       $1,400-$1,500
Armand Marseille:
  #253 (watermelon mouth):
  6-7in (15-18cm)   **$1,150-$1,350**
  9-10in (23-25cm) **$2,000-$2,250**
  9in (23cm) all original, at auction
                           $3,050
  #200:
  8in (20cm)   **$1,200-$1,500**
  11-12in (28-31cm) **$2,100-$2,300**
  #240: 10in (25cm) toddler
                     $3,000-$3,200

#241: 10in (25cm) at auction **$3,675**
Bähr & Pröschild 686: 10½in (26cm) at auction   **$3,900**
Demalcol (Dennis, Malley & Co., London, England):
  9-10in (23-25cm)   **$750-$850**
Max Handwerck:
  Molded hat:
  10-13in (25-33cm) **$2,100-$2,300**
  Double-faced   **$2,200-$2,400**
Hertel, Schwab & Co.:
  #163, baby:
  15in (38cm)   **$6,000-$6,500**
  Toddler, red molded hair:
    16in (41cm)   **$7,000-$7,500**
    12in (31cm)   **$4,000-$4,500**
  #165, baby:
  12-13in (31-33cm) **$4,200-$4,400**
  16in (41cm)   **$5,500**
  Toddler:
    11-12in (28-31cm)   **$4,500**
    16in (41cm)   **$6,500**
  #172, baby:
  15in (38cm)   **$6,800-$7,200****
  Toddler: 18in (46cm)   **$12,000****

*Allow extra for unusual models.
**Not enough price samples to compute a reliable range.

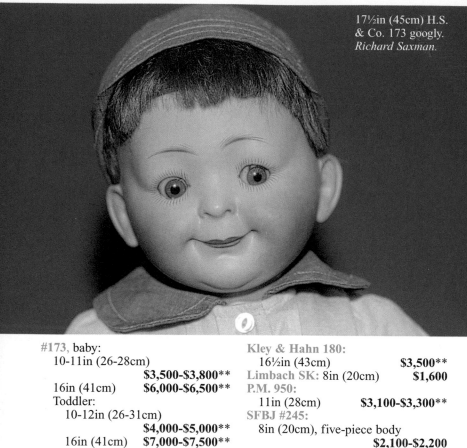

17½in (45cm) H.S. & Co. 173 googly. *Richard Saxman.*

#173, baby:
  10-11in (26-28cm)
                        $3,500-$3,800**
  16in (41cm)   **$6,000-$6,500****
  Toddler:
    10-12in (26-31cm)
                        $4,000-$5,000**
  16in (41cm)   **$7,000-$7,500****
Ernst Heubach:
  #310, 13in (33cm) at auction **$4,300**
  #322, 9in (23cm), at auction **$2,100**
Gebrüder Heubach:
  Einco: 11in (28cm) five-piece body
                        $3,500-$3,800
  Elizabeth:
    7-9in (18-23cm)   **$1,850**
  #8678, 9573:
    6-7in (15-18cm)   **$900-$1,100**
    9in (23cm)   **$1,500-$1,700**
  #10542: 8in (20cm)   **$850**
Oscar Hitt:
  13in (33cm) at auction **$26,000**
K & R 131:
  15-16in (38-41cm)   **$13,000**
JDK 221:
  12in (30cm)   **$6,900-$7,300**
  14in (35cm)   **$8,300-$8,600**
  16½in (43cm) largest size
                        $13,000-$14,500

Kley & Hahn 180:
  16½in (43cm)   **$3,500****
Limbach SK: 8in (20cm) **$1,600**
P.M. 950:
  11in (28cm)   **$3,100-$3,300****
SFBJ #245:
  8in (20cm), five-piece body
                        $2,100-$2,200
  15in (38cm)   **$4,200-$4,600****
Schieler:
  15in (38cm) at auction **$3,045**

Disc Eyes:
DRGM 954642 black or white:
  11-12in (28-31cm) **$1,250-$1,500****

Composition face: 1911-1914.
Hug Me Kids, Little Bright Eyes and other trade names. Round all-composition or composition mask face, wig, round glass eyes looking to the side, watermelon mouth; felt body; original clothes; all in very good condition.
  10in (25cm)   **$700-$800**
  12in (31cm)   **$950**
  16in (41cm)   **$1,250**

**Not enough price samples to compute a reliable range.

Greiner

Marked Greiner: Papier-mâché shoulder head with blonde or black molded hair, painted features; homemade cloth body, leather arms; nice old clothes; entire doll in good condition, some wear acceptable.

'58 label:

15-17in (38-43cm)	**$900-$1,000**
20-23in (51-58cm)	**$1,250-$1,500**
28-30in (71-76cm)	**$1,750-$2,000**
38in (97cm)	**$2,800**

21in (53cm) excellent, all original,
at auction   **$2,625**

Much worn:

20-23in (51-58cm)	**$650-$750**
28-30in (71-76cm)	**$850-$950**

Glass eyes: 20-23in (51-58cm)
                                $2,200-$2,500**

**Not enough price samples to compute reliable range.

'72 label:

19-22in (48-56cm)	**$500-$550**
29-31in (71-79cm)	**$800-$900**
35in (89cm)	**$1,100-$1,200**

FACTS

Ludwig Greiner of Philadelphia, PA,
U.S.A. 1858-1883,
but probably as early as 1840s.
Mark: Paper label on back shoulder:

GREINER'S
IMPROVED
PATENTHEADS
Pat.March 30th'58
or
GREINER'S
PATENT DOLL HEADS
No7
Pat. Mar.30'58.Ext.'72

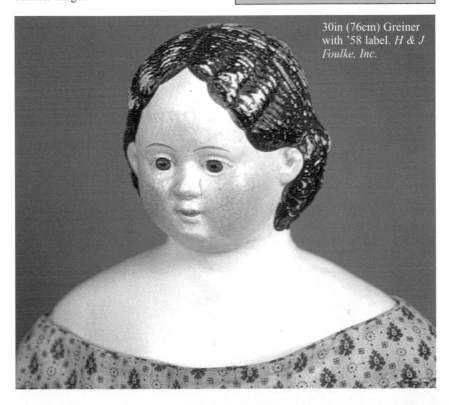

30in (76cm) Greiner with '58 label. *H & J Foulke, Inc.*

Heinrich Handwerck

Marked Handwerck Child Doll: Ca. 1885-on. Perfect bisque socket head, original or good wig, sleep or set eyes, open mouth, pierced ears; composition ball-jointed body with Handwerck stamp; dressed; entire doll in good condition.

#69, 79, 89, 99, 109, 119 or no mold #:
10-12in (25-31cm), all original

	$550–$650
14-16in (36-41cm)	**$650-$700**
19-21in (43-53cm)	**$700-$800**
23-25in (58-64cm)	**$800-$900**
28-30in (71-76cm)	**$1,100-$1,200**
32-33in (79-84cm)	**$1,500**
35-36in (89-91cm)	**$2,000-$2,200**
42in (107cm)	**$3,800-$4,200**

#109: 31in (79cm) all original with wig extensions, at auction **$1,700**
#79: 34in (86cm) all original with long curly wig, at auction **$4,100**

HH/S&H: 33in (84cm) all original, fancy silk dress and hat **$3,300**
Bébé Cosmopolite: 19in (48cm) all original, boxed **$1,000**
Ladies' Home Journal "Daisy," blonde mohair wig, blue eyes:
18in (46cm) only **$1,250-$1,450**
#139 and other shoulder heads, kid body:

16-18in (41-46cm)	**$350-$400**
22-24in (56-61cm)	**$450-$500**

#79, 89 closed mouth:

18-20in (46-51cm)	**$2,300-$2,500****
24in (61cm)	**$2,800-$3,200****

#189, open mouth:

18-20in (46-51cm)	**$900-$950**

#160 character child:

22in (56cm) at auction	**$7,250**

**Not enough price samples to compute a reliable range.

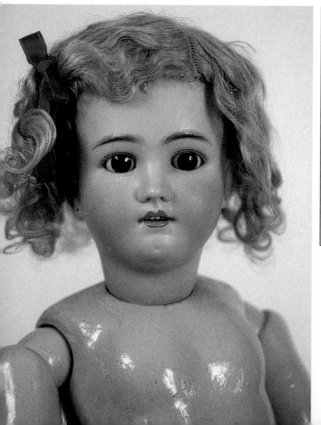

FACTS
Heinrich Handwerck,
doll factory,
Waltershausen,
Thüringia, Germany.
Heads by
Simon & Halbig.
1885-on.
Trademarks:
Bébé Cosmopolite,
Bébé de Réclame,
Bébé Superior.
Mark:

Germany
HANDWERCK
109-N
Germany

27in (69cm) Heinrich Handwerck/Simon & Halbig (HH/S&H) child, original wig. *H & J Foulke, Inc.*

Max Handwerck

Marked Max Handwerck Child Doll:
Perfect bisque socket head, original or
good wig, set or sleep eyes, open
mouth, pierced ears; original ball-jointed body; well dressed; all in good
condition.
#283, 297:

16-18in (41-46cm)	**$375-$400**
22-24in (56-61cm)	**$525-$575**
31-32in (79-81cm)	**$900-$1,000**
#421: 15-18in (38-46cm)	**$550-$750**

Bébé Elite Character Baby:

19-21in (48-53cm)	**$550-$650**

FACTS
Max Handwerck, doll factory,
Waltershausen, Thüringia, Germany.
Some heads by Goebel. 1900-on.
Trademarks: Bébé Elite, Triumph-
Bébé.
Mark:

MAX HANDWERCK. Germany
Au Handwerck Baba Elite 8 an/101 6 germany
Max HANDWERCK Germany

Hertel, Schwab & Co.

Marked Character Baby: Perfect
bisque head; bent-limb baby body;
dressed; all in good condition.
#130, 142, 150, 151, 152:

10-12in (25-31cm)	**$375-$425**
15-17in (38-43cm)	**$525-$600**
19-21in (48-53cm	**$700-$750**
24-25in (61-64cm)	**$900-$1,000**

Toddler:

16in (41cm)	**$750**
24in (61cm)	**$1,500**
#150 all-bisque: 6in (15cm)	**$400-$450**

#142 all-bisque, painted eyes:

11in (28cm)	**$850-$900**

#159, two faces:

10in (25cm) at auction	**$850**

#125 (so-called **Patsy Baby**):

12-13in (30-33cm)	**$950-$1,000**

#126 (so-called **Skippy**):

9in (23cm) baby	**$850**
16in (41cm) toddler	**$1,500**

Child Doll: Ca. 1910. Perfect bisque
head, mohair or human hair wig, sleep
eyes, open mouth with upper teeth;
good quality jointed composition body
(some marked "K & W"); dressed; all
in good condition.
Mold #136:

7in (18cm) five-piece body	**$250-$300**
18-20in (46-51cm)	**$475-$525**
24-25in (61-64cm)	**$650-$700**

FACTS
Hertel Schwab & Co., porcelain factory,
Hertel, Stutzhaus,
near Ohrdruf, Thüringia, Germany.
1910-on.
Mark:

Made in Germany 151/2   152 4   Made in Germany 136/10   152 LW&C. 3

18in (46cm) Max Handwerck 421 child.
H & J Foulke, Inc.

Marked Character Child: Perfect bisque head, painted or sleep eyes, closed mouth; jointed composition body; dressed; all in good condition.
#134, 141:
    16-18in (41-46cm) **$8,000-$10,000**
#149:
    16-18in (41-46cm) **$8,000-$9,000**
#154 (closed mouth):
    14-16in (36-41cm) **$2,300-$2,500**
    19in (48cm) **$3,100**
#154, 166 (open mouth):
    16-18in (41-46cm) **$1,300-$1,500**
#169 (closed mouth):
    19-21in (48-53cm) toddler
                $3,500-$4,000
#127 (so-called **Patsy**):
    17in (43cm) **$2,100-$2,500**

Right: 18in (46cm) 150 character baby. *H & J Foulke, Inc.*

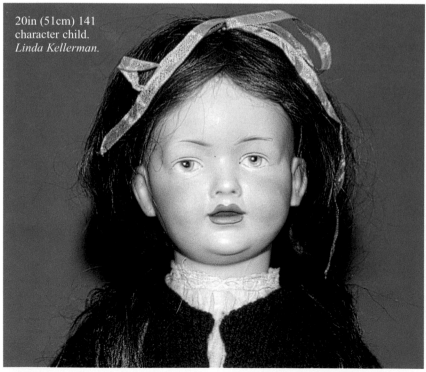

20in (51cm) 141 character child. *Linda Kellerman.*

Hertwig & Co.

Half-Bisque Dolls: 1911-on. Head and body to waist of one-piece bisque, molded hair, painted features; bisque hands, lower legs with white stockings and painted shoes, some with heels and bows; other parts of body are cloth; appropriate clothes; all in good condition.

4½in (11cm) children   **$225-$275**
6½in (17cm) adults   **$325-$375**
Family of seven dolls, boxed, at auction   **$3,300**

4½in (11cm) half-bisque boy and girl. *H & J Foulke, Inc.*

See the "All-Bisque" section for Hertwig children with molded clothes, pink bisque characters and nodders.

See the "Bisque, German" section for shoulder heads with molded bonnets.

See the "China" section for china heads with gold-painted names.

FACTS
Hertwig & Co., porcelain factory, Katzhutte, Thüringia, Germany. 1864-on.
Mark: Germany

Ernst Heubach

Heubach Child Doll: Ca. 1888-on. Perfect bisque head; dressed; all in good condition.

#275 or horseshoe, kid or cloth body:
19-21in (48-53cm)	**$275-$325**
24in (61cm)	**$425-$450**

#250, 251, composition body:
8-9in (20-23cm) five-piece body	**$210-$235**
16-18in (41-46cm)	**$350-$400**
23-24in (58-61cm)	**$500-$550**

Painted bisque, **#250, 407:**
7-8in (18-20cm)	**$110-$135**

#312 SUR (for Seyfarth & Reinhard):
14in (36cm)	**$350-$375***
28in (71cm)	**$750-$850***
45-46in (113-115cm)	**$3,500**

Character Children: 1910-on. Perfect bisque shoulder head with molded hair in various styles, some with hair bows, painted eyes, open/closed mouth; cloth body with composition lower arms.

#261, 262, 271 and others:
12in (31cm)	**$400-$450****

*Allow $150 to $250 extra for a flapper body.
**Not enough price samples to compute a reliable range.

FACTS
Ernst Heubach, porcelain factory, Köppelsdorf, Thüringia, Germany. 1887-on.
Mark:

D.E.P. 1902

Heubach · Kopplesdorf.
300·14/0
Germany

2/0

22in (56cm) 1900 child with horseshoe trademark. *H & J Foulke, Inc.*

13in (33cm)
300 character
baby with
reflecting glass
eyes. *H & J
Foulke, Inc.*

Character Baby: 1910-on. Perfect bisque head, good wig, sleep eyes, open mouth (sometimes also wobbly tongue and pierced nostrils): composition bent-limb baby; dressed; all in good condition.

#300, 320, 342 and others:

5½-6in (14-15cm)	**$250-$275**
8-10in (20-25cm)	**$250-$275**
14-17in (36-43cm)	**$400-$450**
19-21in (48-53cm)	**$500-$575**
24-25in (61-64cm)	**$750**

**Not enough price samples to compute a reliable range.

Toddler: 9-10in (23-25cm) five-piece body   **$375-$425**

Fully-jointed body:

15-17in (38-43cm)	**$550-$650**
23-25in (58-64cm)	**$1,000-$1,150**

Painted Bisque Toddler: 11in (28cm) factory original   **$500-$550**

Infant: Ca. 1925. Perfect bisque head; cloth body.

#349, 339, 350:

10½in (26cm)	**$450-$475**
13-16in (33-41cm)	**$575-$675**

#338, 340:

14-16in (36-41cm)	**$725-$825****

Gebrüder Heubach

Heubach Character Child: Ca. 1910. Perfect bisque head; jointed composition or kid body; dressed; all in good condition. (For more photographs of Heubach dolls see *Focusing on Dolls*, pages 30-68 and previous *Blue Books*.)

#5636, 7663, laughing child, glass eyes:
12-13in (31-33cm)	**$1,600-$1,900**
15-18in (38-46cm)	**$2,500-$2,800**

#5689 smiling child:
26in (66cm)	**$4,000-$4,500**

#5730 Santa:
19-21in (48-53cm)	**$1,800-$2,200**

#5777 Dolly Dimple:
19-22in (48-56cm)	**$3,000-$3,200**
Shoulder head,	
17-19in (43-48cm)	**$900-$1,100**

#6969, 6970, 7246, 7347, 7407, 8017, pouty child (must have glass eyes):
7in (18 cm)	**$900**
12-13in (31-33cm)	**$2,250-$2,750**
16-19in (41-48cm)	**$3,800-$4,200**
24in (61cm)	**$5,500-$6,000**
28in (71cm)	**$8,500****

#6969, painted eyes:
16in (41cm)	**$1,800-$2,000**

#6692 and other shoulder head pouties:
14-16in (36-41cm)	**$750-$850**
20in (51cm)	**$1,100-$1,200**

#7054 and other smiling shoulder heads:
12-14in (30-36cm)	**$600-$700**
19in (48cm)	**$900-$1,000**

#7407 painted eye, wigged:
16in (41cm)	**$2,350**

#7604, 7820 and other smiling socket heads:
14-16in (36-41cm)	**$800-$1,000**
20in (51cm)	**$1,650**

#7602, 6894, 7622 and other socket head pouties:
16-18in (41-46cm)	**$1,000-$1,250**

#7658, smiling face, molded short curly hair, bangs:
15in (38cm) at auction	**$6,400**

#7661 squinting eyes, crooked mouth:
19in (48cm)	**$6,750****

#7665 Smiling: 16in (41cm) **$1,800**

#7679, 8774 Whistler:
10in (25cm)	**$800-$900**
14in (36cm)	**$1,100-$1,300**

#7684 Screamer:
10in (25cm)	**$1,500**
16-19in (41-48cm)	**$2,500-$3,000****

#7711:
9in (23cm)	**$900-$1,000**
12-14in (31-36cm)	**$1,400**

#7743 big ears:
17in (43cm)	**$5,500-$6,000****

#7764 singing girl:
16in (41cm)	**$10,000****

#7788, 7850 Coquette:
11in (28cm)	**$950**
14in (36cm)	**$1,200**
20in (51cm)	**$1,650**
Shoulder head,	
12in (31cm)	**$700-$775**

13in (33cm) 5636 laughing character child. *H & J Foulke, Inc.*

FACTS
Gebrüder Heubach, porcelain factory, Licht and Sonneberg, Thüringia, Germany. 1820-on; doll heads, 1910-on. **Mark:**

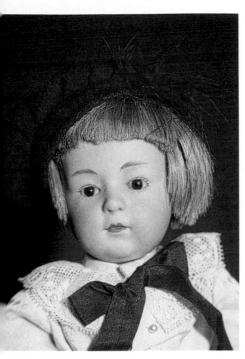

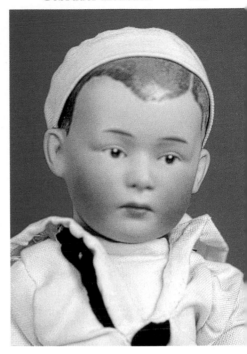

11in (28cm) 6970 pouty character child. *Rhoda Shoemaker Collection.*

16in (41cm) 7602 pouty character boy. *H & J Foulke, Inc.*

#7852 shoulder head, molded coiled braids: 16in (41cm)   **$2,200****
#7853 shoulder head, downcast eyes: 14in (36cm)   **$1,650-$1,850**
#7911, 8191 grinning:
    11in (28cm)   **$850-$900**
    15in (38cm)   **$1,200-$1,250**
#7920: 18in (46cm)   **$2,700****
#7925, 7926 lady:
    11in (28cm)   **$1,300-$1,500**
    18-19in (46-48cm) **$2,800-$3,100**
#8050 smiling girl with hair bow:
    18in (46cm)   **$12,500****
#8192:
    9-11in (23-28cm)   **$450**
    14-16in (36-41cm)   **$750**
    18-22in (46-56cm)   **$1,000**
#8381 Princess Julianna:
    16in (41cm)   **$10,000-$12,000**
#8548 Grumpy:
    25in (64cm)   **$13,500****

**Not enough price samples to compute a reliable range.

17in (43cm) 7850 *Coquette* character girl. *H & J Foulke, Inc.*

#8550, molded tongue sticking out:
13in (33cm) intaglio eyes
$950-$1,050
17in (43cm) glass eyes   **$1,500**
#8556, googly-type face   **$11,500****
#8420, pouty with glass eyes:
9½in (24cm) twin toddlers **$1,800pr**
13in (33cm)   **$1,950**
16in (41cm)   **$2,500**
#9102 Cat:
6in (15cm)   **$1,000-$1,150****
#9141 Winker:
9in (23cm) glass eye   **$1,500**
7in (18cm) painted eye   **$850-$950**
#9145: 23in (58cm) at auction **$20,500**
#10532:
8½in (21cm) chubby five-piece
toddler, all original   **$900**
20-22in (51-53cm)   **$1,200-$1,300**
#10586, 10633:
12in (30cm)   **$425**
18-20in (46-51cm)   **$750-$850**
#11173 Tiss Me:
8in (20cm)   **$1,850-$2,000****
Baby Bo Kaye, Bonnie Babe:
7-8in (18-20cm)   **$900-$950**
#1907 Jumeau:
16in (41cm)   **$1,800-$2,000**
20-22in (51-56cm)   **$2,400-$2,500**

All-Bisque:
Position Babies and Action Figures:
5in (13cm)   **$450-$550**
Girl with bobbed hair:
9in (23cm)   **$900-$1,000**
Girl with headband (coquette):
6in (15cm) swivel neck   **$895**
9in (23cm)   **$1,000-$1,100**
Girl with three bows:
6in (15cm)   **$1,350**
9in (23cm)   **$1,650**
9in (23cm) swivel neck   **$2,400**
Boy: 8in (20cm)   **$1,200**
Boy or girl: 4½in (11cm)   **$300-$400**
Chin Chin: 4½in (11cm)   **$325-$365**

Heubach Babies: Ca. 1910. Perfect
bisque head; composition bent-limb
body; dressed; all in nice condition.
#6894, 7602, 6898, 7759 and other
pouty babies; **#7604** laughing:
4½in (12cm)   **$225**
6in (15cm)   **$250**

7926 shoulder head lady. *H & J Foulke, Inc.*

10-12in (25-31cm)   **$400-$500**
14in (36cm)   **$600-$700**
20in (51cm)   **$1,000**
#7877, 7977 Baby Stuart:
Painted eyes:
9in (23cm)   **$800-$850**
13-15in (33-38cm)   **$1,300-$1,500**
Glass eyes: 13in (33cm)   **$2,250**
#8649, blue quilted bonnet:
12in (31cm)   **$1,400**
#7622, dimples and full lips:
14in (36cm) at auction   **$1,400**
#8420, glass eyes:
14in (36cm)   **$1,250-$1,300**
#7959, molded pink cap:
14in (36cm) at auction   **$4,200**
#8413, open/closed mouth with tongue:
12in (31cm) at auction   **$900**

**Not enough price samples to compute a
reliable range.

Indian Dolls
Bisque Heads

Jullien

American Indian Doll: Perfect bisque head, tinted complexion, wrinkles between eyebrows, wavy eyebrows, set brown glass eyes, black mohair wig; original clothes, head feathers, moccasins or molded shoes; all in good condition.
Marked "A.M." (Armand Marseille) or unmarked.

7-8in (18-20cm)	**$175-$225**
12in (30cm)	**$375-$425**
15in (38cm)	**$500-$550**
18in (46cm)	**$750-$850**

Bähr & Pröschild 244, closed mouth:

14-15in (36-38cm)	**$1,800-$2,200**

Gebrüder Heubach 8457, 9467, shoulder head on cloth body:

14in (36cm)	**$2,500**

Simon & Halbig 1303:

21in (53cm)	**$17,000****

**Not enough price samples to compute a reliable range.

Marked Jullien Bébé: Perfect bisque head, lovely wig, paperweight eyes, closed mouth, pierced ears; jointed wood and composition body; pretty old clothes; all in good condition.

17-19in (43-48cm)	**$3,200-$3,500**
24-26in (61-66cm)	**$4,000-$4,300**

Open mouth:

19-21in (48-53cm)	**$1,600-$1,800**
29-30in (74-76cm)	**$2,400-$2,600**

FACTS
Jullien, Jeune of Paris, France.
1875-1904 when joined with S.F.B.J.
Mark: "JULLIEN" with size number

JuLLieN
1

FACTS
Various German factories.
Ca 1895-on.

10in (25cm) unmarked German bisque head Indian, all original.
H & J Foulke, Inc.

Jumeau

Poupée Peau Fashion Lady: Late 1860s-on. Perfect bisque swivel head on shoulder plate, old wig, paperweight eyes, closed mouth, pierced ears; all-kid body; appropriate old clothes; all in good condition.

Mark on body: JUMEAU
ME DAILLE D'OR
PARIS

Standard face:
11½-13in (29-33cm) **$2,600-$3,000***
17-18in (43-46cm) **$3,600-$3,800***
20in (51cm) **$4,200-$4,600***
19in (48cm) all original, with three extra outfits, at auction **$8,500**

Poupée Bois, wood body with bisque limbs: 18in (46cm) **$6,500-$7,500**
Later face with large eyes:
10½-11in (27-28cm) **$2,000-$2,500***
14-15in (36-38cm) **$2,800-$3,000***
So-called "Portrait Face:"
19-21in (48-53cm) **$7,000-$7,250***
Wood body (*poupée bois*):
19-21in (48-53cm) **$11,000***

*Allow extra for original clothes.

26in (66cm) Jumeau *poupée* with portrait face. *Private Collection.*

FACTS
Maison Jumeau,
Paris, France.
1842-on.
Trademark:
Bébé Jumeau (1886)
Bébé Prodige (1886)
Bébé Français (1896)

25in (64cm) Jumeau *triste* or long face.

Period Clothes for Bébés:

Jumeau shift	**$400-$600**
Jumeau shoes	**$350-$450**
Jumeau dress and hat	**$1,000up**

Long-Face Triste Bébé: 1879-1886. Designed by Carrier-Belleuse. Marked with size (9 to 16) number only on head, blue stamp on body. Perfect bisque socket head with beautiful wig, paperweight eyes, closed mouth, applied pierced ears; jointed composition body with straight wrists (separate ball joints on early models); lovely clothes; all in good condition.

20-21in (51-53cm)	**$16,000-$20,000**
28-30in (71-76cm)	**$22,500-$25,000**

Size	
9 = 21in (53cm)	
11 = 24in (61cm)	
13, 14 = 29-30in (74-76cm)	

Portrait Jumeau: 1877-1883. Usually marked with size number only on head, blue stamp on body; skin or other good wig, spiral threaded enamel paperweight eyes, closed mouth, pierced ears; jointed composition body with straight wrists and separate ball joints; nicely dressed; all in good condition.

Premiere:

9in (23cm)	**$7,000-$8,000**
12 in (30cm)	**$6,500-$7,500**
14-15in (36-38cm)	**$7,500-$8,000**
18-19in (46-48cm)	**$8,000-$9,000**
23in (58cm)	**$11,000-$12,000**

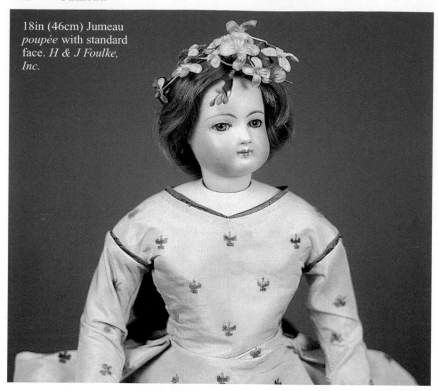

18in (46cm) Jumeau *poupée* with standard face. *H & J Foulke, Inc.*

16in (41cm) Jumeau *poupée* with later face. *H & J Foulke, Inc.*

Almond-Eyed or Deluxe:

Sizes:
    4/0 = 12in (30cm)
    3/0 = 13½in (34cm)
    2/0 = 14½in (37cm)
     0 = 16in (41cm)
     1 = 17in (43cm)
     2 = 18½in (47cm)
     3 = 20in (51cm)
     4 = 23in (58cm)
     5 = 25in (64cm)

12-14½in (30-37cm)
                   $13,000-$15,000*
16-18½in (41-47cm)
                   $18,000-$22,000*
20in (51cm)   **$25,000-$30,000***
23in (58cm)   **$33,000-$38,000***
25in (64cm)   **$55,000***

Second Series, excellent quality, larger dolls have applied ears:
    13in (29cm)   **$7,000-$7,200**
    15in (38cm) Size 6   **$8,000-$8,500**
    18-20in (46-51cm) Size 8   **$10,000**
    22in (56cm) Size 10   **$12,500**
    25in (64cm) Size 12
                      $16,000-$18,000

*Allow extra for unusually large eyes.

13½in (34cm) Second Series Jumeau. *H & J Foulke, Inc.*

20in (51cm) early almond-eyed portrait Jumeau. *Linda Kellerman.*

E.J. Bébé: 1881-1886. Perfect bisque socket head with good wig, paperweight eyes, closed mouth, pierced ears; jointed composition body with straight wrists, early models with separate ball joints; lovely clothes; all in good condition.

Early Mark:

8
E.J.

17-18in (43-46cm) size 6	**$10,500**
19-21in (48-53cm) size 8	**$12,500**
23in (58cm) size 9	**$17,500**
E.J.A.: 25in (64cm)	**$30,000-$32,000**

Mid to Late Period Mark:

DÉPOSÉ
E.8J.

11in (28cm)	**$5,750**
14-16in (36-41cm)	**$6,850-$7,250**
19-21in (48-53cm)	**$7,850-$8,250**
25-26in (64-66cm)	**$9,500-$10,500**
30in (76cm)	**$13,000**

Déposé 9 or 9x:

20-21in (51-53cm)	**$6,500-$7,500**
9x, bisque lower arms:	
21in (53cm) at auction	**$17,050**

Incised "Jumeau Déposé" Bébé: 1886-1889. Head incised as below, blue stamp on body. Perfect bisque socket head with good wig, paperweight eyes, closed mouth, pierced ears; jointed composition body with straight wrists; lovely clothes; all in good condition.
Mark: Incised on head:

DÉPOSÉ
JUMEAU
8

9in (23cm) Size 1, all original, in store box, at auction	**$15,250**
14-15in (36-38cm)	**$5,000-$5,500**
18-20in (46-51cm)	**$6,000-$6,500**
23in (58cm)	**$6,800**
25in (64cm)	**$7,500**

Approximate sizes of E.J.s and Têtes:
1 = 10in (25cm)
2 = 11in (28cm)
3 = 12in (31cm)
4 = 13in (33cm)
5 = 14-15in (36-38cm)
6 = 16in (41cm)
7 = 17in (43cm)
8 = 19in (48cm)
9 = 20in (51cm)
10 = 21-22in (53-56cm)
11 = 24-25in (61-64cm)
12 = 26-27in (66-69cm)
13 = 29-30in (74-76cm)

15in (38cm) *Bébé Jumeau* with "E.J." mark. *H & J Foulke, Inc.*

22in (56cm) *Tête Jumeau. H & J Foulke, Inc.*

Tête Jumeau Bébé: 1885-1899, then through S.F.B.J. Red stamp on head as indicated below, blue stamp or "Bébé Jumeau" oval sticker on body. Perfect bisque head, original or good French wig, beautiful stationary eyes, closed mouth, pierced ears; jointed composition body with jointed or straight wrists; original or lovely clothes; all in good condition.

Mark:
```
            DÉPOSÉ
      TETE JUMEAU
       Bᵀᴱ SGDG
           6
```

9-10in (23-25cm) #1	$5,000-$5,500
12-13in (31-33cm)	$3,500-$4,000
15-16in (38-41cm)	$4,200-$4,600
18-20in (46-51cm)	$4,800-$5,200
21-23in (53-58cm)	$5,200-$5,500
25-27in (64-69cm)	$6,000-$6,500
30in (76cm)	$6800-$7,200
34-36in (86-91cm)	$8,000-$8,500
41in (104cm)	$12,500*
20in (51cm) all original couturier costume	$7,750
Lady body, 20in (51cm)	$6,000*

Open mouth:

14-16in (36-41cm)	$2,650-$2,950
20-22in (51-56cm)	$3,200-$3,500
24-25in (61-64cm)	$3,600-$3,800
27-29in (69-74cm)	$3,800-$4,000
32-34in (81-86cm)	$4,500

Bébé Phonographe: 1894-1899.

24-25in (61-64cm)	$6,500-$7,500

Marked E.D. Bébé: Mark used during the Douillet management, 1892-1899. Perfect bisque head, closed mouth.

17-19in (43-48cm)   **$4,750-$5,000**

Mark:

E.8.D

Marked B.L. Bébé: 1892 on. For the Louvre department store. Perfect bisque socket head, closed mouth.

Mark: **B.9L.**

13in (33cm)	$3,500-$4,000
18-21in (46-53cm)	$4,800-$5,200

Marked R.R. Bébé: 1892 on. Perfect bisque head, closed mouth.

Mark: **R 10 R**

21-23in (53-58cm)	$4,900-$5,300
26in (66cm) open mouth	$3,950

#230 Character Child: Ca. 1910. Perfect bisque socket head, good wig, open mouth, set or sleep eyes; jointed composition body; dressed; all in good condition:

13in (33cm)	$1,400
18in (46cm)	$1,750

*Allow extra for original clothes.

#1907 Jumeau Child: Ca. 1907-on. Sometimes red-stamped "Tête Jumeau." Perfect bisque head, open mouth:

16in (40cm)	$2,500-$2,600
19-22in (48-56cm)	$2,900-$3,200
25-27in (64-69cm)	$3,600-$3,800
33in (84cm)	$4,500

Papier-mâché face:

22-24in (56-61cm)	$800-$1,000**

DEP Tête Jumeau: See page 78 for details.

SFBJ Tête Jumeau: See page 172 for details.

Jumeau Characters: 1892-1899. Perfect bisque head with glass eyes, character expression:

#203, 208 and others	$50,000 up
#221 Great Ladies: 10-11in (25-28cm) all original	$600-$650

#203, 211 Double faced laughing and crying 18in (46cm) at auction **$14,500**

Princess Elizabeth Jumeau: 1938 through S.F.B.J. Perfect bisque socket head highly colored, glass flirty eyes.
Mark:

UNIS
FRANCE 149
306

Body Incised:

JUMEAU
PARIS
Princess

18-19in (46-48cm)	$1,600-$1,800
32-33in (81-84cm)	$2,700-$3,200**

**Not enough price samples to compute a reliable range.

18in (46cm) 1907 Jumeau, all original, in costume of Savoie. *H & J Foulke, Inc.*

Kamkins

Marked Kamkins: Molded mask face with painted features, wig; cloth body and limbs; original clothing; all in excellent condition.

18-20in (46-51cm)	**$2,500-$3,000**
Good	**$1,200-$1,600**
Fair	**$850-$950**
Dirty, face wear, naked	**$500-$600**
With swivel joints or molded derriére	
	$2,500-$3,500

FACTS
Louise R. Kampes Studios, Atlantic City, NJ, U.S.A. 1919-1928 and perhaps longer.
Mark:
Red paper heart on left side of chest:

Also sometimes stamped with black on foot or back of head:

KAMKINS
A DOLLY MADE TO LOVE
PATENTED BY L.R. KAMPES
ATLANTIC CITY,   N.J.

Left and above: 19in (48cm) *Kamkins* with rare wrist label. *H & J Foulke, Inc.*

Very rare *Kamkins* baby with curved arms and legs. No prices available. *Dorothy Hunt , Sweetbriar.*

Kämmer & Reinhardt

Child Doll: 1886-1895. Perfect bisque head; ball-jointed composition body; appropriate clothes; all in good condition.

#192:

Closed mouth:

5in (13cm)	**$550**
6-7in (15-18cm)	**$600-$700***
11in (28cm)	**$1,350-$1,450**
16-18in (41-46cm)	**$2,800-$3,000**
22-24in (56-61cm)	**$3,200-$3,400**

Open mouth:

7-8in (18-20cm)	**$550-$600***
12in (31cm)	**$700-$800**
14-16in (36-41cm)	**$900-$1,000**
20-22in (51-56cm)	**$1,200-$1,300**
26-28in (66-71cm)	**$1,700-$1,900**
9in (23cm) doll in original dressmaker set	**$2,100**

*Allow $100 to $200 extra for a fully-jointed body.

FACTS
Kämmer & Reinhardt of Waltershausen, Thüringia, Germany. Bisque heads often by Simon & Halbig. 1886-on.
Trademarks: Majestic Doll, Mein Liebling (My Darling), Der Schelm (The Flirt), Die Kokette (The Coquette), My Playmate.
Mark:
Size number is height in centimeters.

K ✡ R
SIMON & HALBIG
116/A
50

11in (28cm) 192 child with closed mouth. *H & J Foulke, Inc.*

26in (66cm) K & R child. *H & J Foulke, Inc.*

Child Doll: 1895-1930s. Perfect bisque head, open mouth; K & R ball-jointed composition body; appropriate clothes; all in good condition.

#191, 290, 402, 403 or size number only+:

Five-piece body:

4½-5in (12-13cm)	**$450-$495**
7-8in (18-20cm)	**$425-$475**
10in (25cm)	**$650-$675**

Fully-jointed body:

8-10in (20-25cm)	**$650-$750**
12-14in (31-36cm)	**$650-$750***
16-17in (41-43cm)	**$750-$800***
19-21in (48-43cm)	**$850-$950***
23-25in (58-64cm)	**$1,050-$1,150***
28in (71cm)	**$1,300-$1,400***
30-31in (76-79cm)	**$1,600-$1,800***
33in (84cm)	**$2,200-$2,300***
36in (91cm)	**$2,500-$2,800***
39-42in (99-107cm)	**$3,600-$4,200***

Closed mouth: 6in (15cm)

$550-$600

Child Doll: Shoulder head, kid body; all in good condition.

17-18in (41-46cm)	**$425-$475**
22in (56cm)	**$550-$600**

+Numbers 15 to 100 low on neck are centimeter sizes, not mold numbers.
*Allow $100 to $200 additional for flirty eyes; allow $200 extra for flapper body; allow $100 for walking body.

Character Babies or Toddlers: 1909-on. Perfect bisque head; K & R composition body; nicely dressed; all in good condition. (See *Simon & Halbig Dolls, The Artful Aspect* for photographs of mold numbers not pictured here.)

#100 Baby, painted eyes:

11-12in (28-31cm)	$525-$575
14-15in (36-38cm)	$700-$750
18-20in (46-51cm)	$900-$1,100
Glass eyes, 16in (41cm)	$2,000**

#118A, baby body:

11in (28cm)	$1,200-$1,500

#119, baby body:

24in (61cm), at auction	$16,000

#121, 122, baby body:

10-11in (25-28cm)	$600-$650
15-16in (38-41cm)	$900-$1,000
23-24in (58-61cm)	$1,500

#121, 122, toddler body:

10in (25cm) five-piece body	$1,000+
13-14in (33-36cm)	$1,200-$1,300

20-23in (51-58cm)	$1,700-$1,900
26-27in (66-69cm)	$2,200-$2,400

#126, 22, baby body:

10-12in (25-31cm)	$450-$525*
14-16in (36-41cm)	$550-$600*
18-20in (46-51cm)	$700-$800*
22-24in (56-61cm)	$850-$950*

#126, all-bisque baby:

6 in (15cm)	$750-$800
8½in (21cm)	$1,000-$1,100**

#126, all-bisque toddler:

7in (18cm)	$1,400-$1,500**

#126, 22, five-piece toddler body:

6-7in (15-18cm)	$900+
9-10in (23-25cm)	$950-$1,000+
15-17in (38-43cm)	$700-$800*
23in (58cm)	$1,050-$1,150*

+With "starfish" hands.

*Allow $50 to $100 additional for flirty eyes.

**Not enough price samples to compute a reliable range.

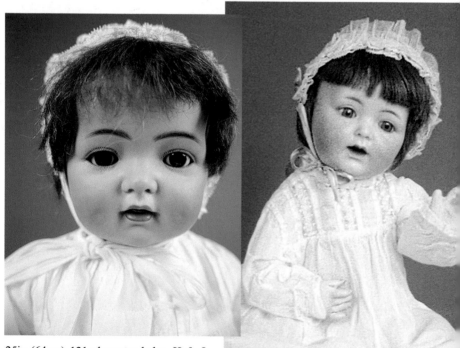

25in (64cm) 121 character baby. *H & J Foulke, Inc.*

15in (38cm) 116a character baby with open mouth. *H & J Foulke, Inc.*

#126, toddler fully-jointed:

   12-13in (31-33cm)   **$750-$850**

   15-17in (38-41cm)**$1,000-$1,200***

   23-25in (58-64cm)**$1,500-$1,700***

   28-30in (71-76cm)**$2,000-$2,200***

#128, baby body:

   10in (25cm)   **$650-$675**

   15-16in (38-41cm)   **$900-$1,000**

   20in (51cm)   **$1,500-$1,600***

   24in (61cm)   **$2000-$2,200****

#128, toddler body:

   16-18in (41-46cm)   **$1,650****

Composition Heads:

   #926, five-piece toddler body:

      18in (46cm)   **$500-$600***

   "Puz" baby, cloth body:

      16-17in (41-43cm)   **$400-$450***

      25in (64cm)   **$650-$750***

Character Children: 1909-on. Perfect bisque socket head; K & R composition ball-jointed body; nicely dressed; all in good condition. (See *Simon & Halbig, The Artful Aspect* for photographs of mold numbers not pictured here.)

#101 (Peter or Marie):

   12in (31cm)   **$2,800-$3,200**

   14-15in (36-38cm)   **$3,800-$4,200**

   17in (43cm)   **$4,500-$4,650**

   19-20in (48-51cm)   **$5,500-$6,000**

Glass eyes:

   15in (38cm)   **$11,500**

   20in (51cm)   **$14,000-$15,000**

#102:

   12in (31cm)   **$20,000 up****

   22in (55cm)   **$75,000 up****

#103, 104:

   22in (56cm)   **$100,000 up****

#105: 22in (56cm)   **$170,000****

#106: 22in (56cm)   **$145,000****

#107 (Carl):

   12in (30cm)   **$16,000-$19,000**

   22in (56cm)   **$50,000-$55,000**

#108: at auction   **$277,095**

*Allow $50 to $100 additional for flirty eyes.

**Not enough price samples to compute a reliable range.

8in (20cm) 101 *Peter* character child. *H & J Foulke, Inc.*

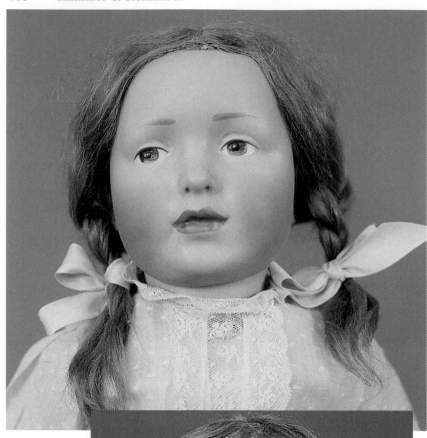

Above: 109 *Elise* character child. *Private Collection.*

Right: 21in (53cm) 114 *Gretchen* character child with glass eyes. *Connie & Jay Lowe.*

#109 (Elise):
7in (18cm)	$2,500-$2800
9-10in (23-25cm)	$3,000-$3,500
14in (36cm)	$7,500-$8,500
21in (53cm)	$20,000

Glass eyes:
20in (51cm)	$25,000-$26,000

#112, 112x:
16-18in (41-46cm)	$16,000-$17,000

Glass eyes:
10-11in (25-28cm)	$8,000**
17in (43cm) at auction	$18,000

#114 (Hans or Gretchen):
8-9in (20-23cm) jointed body	$1,800-$2,200
12in (31cm)	$3,200
15-16in (38-41cm)	$4,500
19-20in (48-51cm)	$5,500-$6,000
21-22in (53-56cm)	$6,200-$6,600

Glass eyes:
15in (38cm)	$9,250
24in (61cm)	$18,000

#115: 15-16in (38-41cm) toddler
$6,000-$6,500**

#115A:
10-12in (25-31cm)	$2,800-$3,100
Baby: 14-16in (36-41cm)	$3,500-$3,850

Toddler:
15-16in (38-41cm)	$4,500-$5,000
19-20cm (48-51cm)	$5,800-$6,200
23in (58cm)	$6,600-$7,000

#116:
16in (41cm) toddler
$4,500-$5,000**

20in (51cm) baby	$4,000**

#116A, open/closed mouth:
Baby:
10-11in (25-28cm)	$2,100-$2,300
14-16in (36-41cm)	$3,000-$3,500

Toddler:
16-18in (41-46cm)	$3,800-$4,300
27in (69cm)	$5,500-$5,800

#116A, open mouth:
Baby: 14-16in (36-41cm)
$1,800-$2,200
Toddler: 25in (64cm) $3,600-$3,800

#117, 117A, closed mouth (may have an H. Handwerck body):
8in (20cm)	$2,400-$2,500
12in (30cm)	$3,500-$3,800
14-16in (36-41cm)	$4,300-$4,800
18-20in (46-51cm)	$5,300-$5,800
22-23in (56-58cm)	$6,300-$6,800
30-32in (76-81cm)	$7,500-$8,500

#117n, flirty eyes:
14-16in (36-41cm)	$1,400-$1,500
20-22in (51-56cm)	$1,900-$2,100
28-30in (71-76cm)	$2,500-$2,800

#117n, sleep eyes:
14-16in (36-41cm)	$1,100-$1,200
22-24in (56-61cm)	$1,500-$1,600
30-32in (76-81cm)	$1,900-$2,100

#117x, flapper: 14in (36cm) $3,900**
#117, open mouth:
27in (69cm) $4,700-$5,200**

**Not enough price samples to compute a reliable range.

29in (74cm) 117 character child. *Mary Barnes Kelley Collection.*

16in (41cm) 171 infant.
Lesley Hurford Collection.

#123, 124 (Max & Moritz):
17in (43cm) each   **$23,000****
#127:
Baby: 10in (25cm)   **$800-$850**
14-15in (36-38cm)   **$1,300-$1,400**
20-22in (51-56cm)   **$1,800-$2,000**
Toddler:
15-16in (38-41cm) **$1,600-$1,750**
25-27in (64-69cm)   **$2,500**
#135, child:
14-16in (36-41cm) **$1,500-$1,900****
#201: 13in (33cm)   **$1,500****
#214: 15in (38cm)   **$2,100-$2,500****
Infant: 1924-on. Perfect bisque head;
cloth body, composition hands; nicely
dressed; all in good condition.

#171, 172:
14-15in (36-38cm)   **$3,500****
#173, toddler (composition body):
14in (36cm)   **$1,650****
#175:
11in (28cm) h.c.   **$1,100-$1,200****

Cloth Characters: 1927. Stockinette
faces with needle-sculpted and hand-
painted features; straw-filled torso;
wire-armature arms and legs, wood
feet; all original; excellent condition.
12in (31cm)   **$350-$400.**

**Not enough price samples to compute a
reliable range.

Kestner

Child doll, early socket head: Ca. 1880. Perfect bisque head, plaster dome; Kestner composition ball-jointed body, some with straight wrists and elbows; well dressed; all in good condition. Many marked with size numbers only.

#169, 128, long face and round face with no mold number, closed mouth:

7in (18cm)	**$1,000**
10in (25cm)	**$1,500-$1,650**
12in (31cm)	**$1,900-$2,100**
14-16in (36-41cm)	**$2,200-$2,500**
19-21in (48-53cm)	**$2,700-$3,000**
24-25in (61-64cm)	**$3,200-$3,500**
29in (74cm)	**$4,000**
33in (84cm)	**$4,500**

Face with square cheeks or white space between lips, no mold number, closed mouth:

11-12in (38-30cm)	**$2,000-$2,200**
14-16in (36-41cm0	**$2,200-$2,500**
19-21in (48-53cm)	**$2,600-$2,800**
24-25in (61-64cm)	**$3,000-$3,200**

Very pouty face, closed mouth:

10-12in (25-31cm)	**$2,800-$3,000**
14-16in (36-41cm)	**$3,200-$3,500**
19-21in (48-53cm)	**$3,800-$4,000**
24in (61cm)	**$4,200-$4,500**
#X: 15in (38cm) only	**$3,500-$4,000**
#XI: 16in (41cm) only	**$4,200-$4,800**
#XII: 17in (43cm)	**$4,500**

#103, closed mouth:

28-32in (71-78cm)	**$3,500-$4,500**

A.T.-type, closed mouth:

15in (38cm)	**$9,000**
18in (46cm)	**$12,500**

Bru-type, molded teeth, jointed ankles:

15in (38cm)	**$3,750**
20in (51cm)	**$5,000-$6,000**

Open mouth, square cut teeth:

12-14in (31-36cm)	**$1,200**
16-18in (41-46cm)	**$1,400-$1,600**
24-25in (61-64cm)	**$1,900-$2,000**
40in (103cm)	**$4,300-$4,600**

Wax-over papier-mâché head:
11in (38cm) all original, at auction **$1,000**

FACTS
J.D. Kestner, Jr., doll factory, Waltershausen, Thüringia, Germany. Kestner & Co., porcelain factory, Ohrdruf. 1816-on.

13in (33cm) pouty Kestner 7. *Kay & Wayne Jensen Collection.*

Child doll, early shoulder head: Ca. 1880s. Perfect bisque head, plaster dome, good wig, set or sleep eyes; sometimes head is slightly turned; kid body with bisque lower arms; marked with size letters or numbers. (No mold numbers.)

Closed mouth:
12in (31cm)	**$650-$675***
14-16in (36-41cm)	**$750-$850***
20-22in (51-56cm)	**$900-$950***
26in (66cm)	**$1,100-$1,300***

A.T.-type, closed mouth:
21in (53cm)	**$8,000**

Open/closed mouth:
16-18in (41-46cm)	**$650-$750**

Open mouth (turned shoulder head):
16-18in (41-46cm)	**$500-$600**
22-24in (56-61cm)	**$700-$750**

Open mouth, square cut teeth:
14-16in (36-41cm)	**$1,000-$1,200**

Child doll, bisque shoulder head, open mouth: Ca. 1892. Plaster dome, good wig, sleep eyes, open mouth; kid body, some with rivet joints; dressed, all in good condition. (See *Kestner, King of Dollmakers* for photographs of mold numbers not pictured here.)

Head Mark:

154 8 dep
D made in Germany

Body Mark:

*Allow $100 to $200 extra for a very pouty face or swivel neck.

19in (48cm) pouty Kestner 13. *H & J Foulke, Inc.*

20in (51cm) turned shoulder head G, open mouth. *H & J Foulke, Inc.*

#145, 154, 147, 148, 166, 195:
  12-13in (31-33cm) $300-$350*
  16-18in (41-46cm) $400-$500*
  20-22in (51-56cm) $550-$600*
  26-28in (66-71cm) $800-$900*

*Allow additional for a rivet jointed body and/or jointed composition arms.

Child doll, open mouth: Bisque socket head on Kestner ball-jointed body; dressed; all in good condition. (See *Kestner, King of Dollmakers* for photographs of mold numbers not pictured here.)

Head Mark: *made in Germany. 8. 162.*

Body Mark:

Germany		Excelsior
5-1/2	or	DRP N. 70686
		Germany

Mold numbers 142, 144, 146, 164, 167, 171, 214:
  9in (23cm) all original $850
  10-12in (25-31cm) $550-$650*
  14-16in (36-41cm) $750-$850*
  18-21in (46-43cm) $850-$950*
  24-26in (61-66cm)
                      $1,000-$1,100*
  30in (76cm) $1,200-$1,500
  33in (84cm) $1,650-$1,850
  36in (91cm) $2,200-$2,500
  42in (107cm) $3,750-$4,250
  21in (43cm) with original trunk and trousseau, at auction $2,700

*Allow 30% additional for all original clothes, wig and shoes.

30in (76cm) 214 child, all original. *H & J Foulke, Inc.*

22in (56cm) 167 child. *H & J Foulke, Inc.*

13½in (35cm) 143 character child. *H & J Foulke, Inc.*

#128, 129, 149, 152, 160, 161, 173, 174:

10-12in (25-31cm)	**$700-$800***
14-16in (36-41cm)	**$900-$1,000***
18-21in (46-53cm)	**$1,100-$1,250***
24-26in (61-66cm)	**$1,300-$1,400***

#133, five-piece body:

6in (15cm)	**$350**

#155, fully-jointed body:

7-8in (18-20cm)	**$800-$900**
10in (25cm) five-piece body	**$750-$800**

#171 Daisy, blonde mohair wig, blue sleep eyes:

18in (46cm) only	**$1,250-$1,450**
All original shift, shoes, socks, wig	**$1,750**

#168, 196, 215:

18-21in (46-53cm)	**$700-$750**
26-28in (66-71cm)	**$800-$900**
32in (81cm)	**$1,000-$1,100**

Character Child: 1909-on. Perfect bisque head character face, plaster pate, wig, painted or glass eyes, closed, open or open/closed mouth; Kestner jointed composition body; dressed; all in good condition. (See *Kestner, King of Dollmakers* for photographs of mold numbers not pictured here.)

#143 (Pre 1897):

7in (18cm)	**$800**
9-10in (23-25cm)	**$800-$850**
12-14in (31-36cm)	**$900-$1,000**
18-20in (46-51cm)	**$1,300-$1,700**
24-27in (58-69cm)	**$2,000-$2,500**

#178-190:

Painted eyes:

12in (31cm)	**$2,200-$2,500**
15in (38cm)	**$3,600-$4,000**
18in (46cm)	**$5,000-$5,500**

Glass eyes:

12in (31cm)	**$3,200-$3,500**
15in (38cm)	**$4,800-$5,200**
18in (46cm)	**$6,000-$6,500**

*Allow 30% additional for all original clothes, wig and shoes.

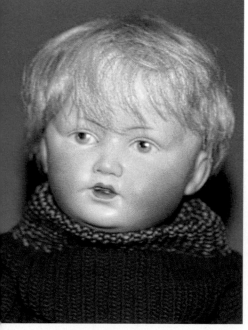

15in (38cm) 179 character child. *Nancy A. Smith.*

Boxed set, doll with three character heads:

Painted eyes:
12in (31cm)	**$10,000-$11,000**
15in (38cm)	**$13,000-$14,000**
Glass eyes: 15in (38cm)	**$20,000**

#206:
12in (31cm)	**$10,000****
19in (48cm)	**$25,000****

#208:

Painted eyes:
12in (31cm)	**$10,000****
23-24in (58-61cm)	**$25,000****

#212: 12in (31cm) at auction **$8,750**

#220, toddler:
11in (28cm)	**$3,700-$4,000**
14-16in (36-41cm)	**$5,000-$6,000**
24in (61cm)	**$7,500-$8,000**
27in (69cm) size Q20	**$8,500**

#239, toddler:
15-17in (38-43cm)	**$4,000****

#241:
17-18in (43-46cm)	**$6,200-$6,400**
21-22in (53-56cm)	**$7,000-$7,500**
27-29in (68-75cm)	**$8,500-$9,500**

#249:
13-14in (33-36cm)	**$1,100-$1,200**
20-22in (51-56cm)	**$1,800**
26in (66cm)	**$2,250**

17½in (45cm) 239 toddler. *Mary Barnes Kelley Collection.*

**Not enough price samples to compute a reliable range.

Below: 27in (68cm) 249 character child. *H & J Foulke, Inc.*

#260:
Toddler, five-piece body:

8-10in (20-25cm)	**$900-$1,100**
19-20in (48-51cm)	**$1,200**

Jointed body:

12-14in (31-36cm)	**$750-$800**
18-20in (46-51cm)	**$900-$1,000**
29in (75cm)	**$1,300-$1,400**
35in (88cm)	**$2,000****
42in (107cm)	**$4,000****

Teenage body: 19in (48cm)   **$1,600**

Max & Moritz: 12in (31cm) pair, at auction   **$17,000**

Character Baby: 1910-on. Perfect bisque head, molded and/or painted hair or good wig, sleep eyes, open or open/closed mouth; Kestner bent-limb body; well dressed; nice condition. (See *Kestner, King of Dollmakers* for photographs of mold numbers not pictured here.)
Mark:

made in
F. Germany. 10
211
J.D.K.

#211, 226, 257:

11-13in (28-33cm)	**$700-$725***
16-18in (41-46cm)	**$800-$900***

20-22in (51-56cm)	**$1,000-$1,200**
25in (64cm)	**$1,650-$2,000**

#211, Toddler:

13in (33cm)	**$1,500***
16in (41cm)	**$2,000***

#257, Toddler:

8in (20cm)	**$1,000-$1,100**

JDK, solid dome:

12-14in (31-36cm)	**$600-$700**
18in (46cm)	**$800**
23-25in (58-64cm)	**$1,200-$1,500**

Painted eyes:

14in (36cm)	**$525-$575**

#262, 263: See page 64.
#210, 234, 235, 238, shoulder heads:

11in (28cm)	**$900-$1,000**
14-16in (36-41cm)	**$1,200-$1,300**

Hilda, #237, 245 and solid dome baby **1070:**

11-13in (28-33cm)	**$2,200-$2,500**
16-17in (41-43cm)	**$2,800-$3,200**
20-22in (51-56cm)	**$3,800-$4,000**
24in (61cm)	**$5,000**

Toddler:

17-19in (43-48cm)	**$4,800-$5,000**
25in (64cm)	**$6,000-$6,500**

*Allow $50 to $100 extra for an original skin wig.
**Not enough price samples to compute a reliable range.

22in (56cm) 245
Hilda toddler.
*Mary Barnes
Kelley collection.*

#247:
 14-16in (36-41cm) **$1,800-$2,100**
 Toddler:
  13in (33cm)   **$2,200-$2,300**
  18-20in (46-51cm) **$2,200-$3,200**
#267, molded hair:
 22-24in (56-61cm) **$3,700-$4,200**
JDK, solid dome, fat-cheeked (so-called **Baby Jean**):
 12-13in (31-33cm) **$1,100-$1,200**
 17-18in (43-46cm) **$1,450-$1,550**
 15in (38cm) toddler **$1,500-$1,600**

All-Bisque Baby:
Painted eyes, stiff neck:
 5-6in (13-15cm)   **$225-$275**
Swivel neck, painted eyes:
 7½in (19cm)   **$450-$500**
 9in (23cm)   **$650-$750**
 12in (31cm)   **$850-$950**
Glass eyes, swivel neck:
 8in (20cm)   **$900-$1,000**
#177, Toddler: 8in (20cm) **$1,000**
#178, Toddler: 8in (20cm) **$1,250**

All-Bisque Child: Perfect all-bisque child, jointed at shoulders and hips; glass eyes; very good quality.
#130, 150, 160, 184 and **208:**
 4-5in (10-13cm) **$250-$350***
 6in (15cm)   **$375-$400***
 7in (18cm)   **$450-$500***
 8in (20cm)   **$600-$650***
 9in (23cm)   **$800-$900***
 10in (25cm)   **$1,000-$1,200**
 12in (31cm)   **$1,400-$1,600**
#208, swivel neck, yellow boots:
 6in (15cm)   **$750-$850**
 8in (20cm)   **$1,250-$1,500**
#310, yellow stockings:
 8in (20cm)   **$1,265**
#620/130, swivel neck:
 Glass eyes:
  4in (10cm)   **$300**
  5-6in (13-15cm) **$400-$500**
 Painted eyes:
  4in (10cm)   **$150**
  5-6in (13-15cm) **$225-$275**

*Allow 30-40% extra for swivel neck and $50-$150 extra for yellow boots.

11in (28cm) character baby on a kid body. *H & J Foulke, Inc.*

4½in (11cm) 150 all-bisque child. *H & J Foulke, Inc.*

Early All-Bisque Dolls: See page 26.

Gibson Girl: Ca. 1910. Perfect bisque shoulder head with appropriate wig, closed mouth, up-lifted chin; kid body with bisque lower arms (cloth body with bisque lower limbs on small dolls); beautifully dressed; all in good condition; sometimes marked "Gibson Girl" on body.

#172:

10in (25cm)	$950-$1,050
15in (38cm)	$1,800-$2,000*
19-21in (48-53cm)	$3,000*
Head only to make a 20in (51cm) doll	$825

Lady Doll: Perfect bisque socket head, plaster dome, wig with lady hairdo; Kestner jointed composition body with molded breasts, nipped-in waist, slender arms and legs; appropriate lady clothes; all in good condition.

Mark: made in
D Germany. 8.
162.

#162:

16-18in (41-46cm)	$1,600-$2,000
Naked: 16-18in (41-46cm)	$1,200

All original clothes:

16-18in (41-46cm)	$2,300-$2,500

O.I.C. Baby: Perfect bisque solid dome head, wide open mouth with molded tongue; cloth body; dressed; all in good condition. Mold #255.

10in (25cm) h.c.	$1,200**

Siegfried: Perfect bisque head; cloth body with composition hands; dressed; all in good condition. Mold #272.

MARK: Siegfried
made in Germany
9

10in (25cm)	$1,500**
14in (36cm)	$2,000**

Marked Century Doll Co. Infant: Ca. 1925. Perfect bisque head; cloth body. Some with smiling face are mold #277. Head circumference:

17-18in (43-46cm)	$850-$950
Double-face	$2,500**

Mama Doll, bisque shoulder head
#281: 21in (53cm) $650-$750**

*Allow extra for original clothes.
**Not enough price samples to compute a reliable range.

20in (51cm) 172 *Gibson Girl. H & J Foulke, Inc.*

Kewpie

All-Bisque: 1913-on. Made by J.D. Kestner and other German firms. Often have manufacturing imperfections. Sometimes signed on foot "O'Neill." Standing, legs together, arms jointed, blue wings, painted features, eyes to side.

2-2½in (5-6cm)	$110-$125
4in (10cm)	$150*
5in (13cm)	$185*
6in (15cm)	$235*
7in (18cm)	$300-$350*
8in (20cm)	$450-$500*
9in (23cm)	$600-$700*
10in (25cm)	$800*
12in (31cm)	$1,300-$1,500*
Jointed hips:	
4in (10cm)	$500-$550
6in (15cm)	$850

8in (20cm)	$1,250
Shoulder head: 3in (8cm)	$425
Perfume bottle:	
4½in (11cm)	$550-$600
Black Hottentot:	
5in (13cm)	$600-$800
Molded Dress and Hat:	
4½in (11cm)	$1,800
Buttonhole: 2in (5cm)	$165-$175
Pincushion: 2-3in (5-8cm)	$250-$300
Painted shoes and socks:	
4-5in (10-13cm)	$600-$700
11in (28cm)	$1,500-$1,800
With glass eyes and wig:	
6in (15cm) at auction	$2,400
With wig: 6in (15cm)	$425

*Allow extra for original clothes.

FACTS
Designer: Rose O'Neill.
Mark: Red and gold paper heart or shield on chest and round label on back.

7½in (19cm) *Kewpie* with original ribbon dress. *H & J Foulke, Inc.*

Action Kewpies (sometimes stamped "©"):

Thinker:

4in (10cm)	$275-$325
7in (18cm)	$500-$550

Kewpie with cat: 3½in (9cm) **$650**

Kewpie holding pen:

3in (8cm)	$450-$475

Kneeling, with outstretched arms:

3¾in (9cm)	$1,100

Reclining or sitting:

3-4in (8-10cm)	$550

Crawling: 4in (10cm) **$900**

Tumbling: 3in (8cm) **$625**

Farmer, Fireman (molded hats):

4in (10cm)	$600-$750

Kewpie: 2in (5cm) with rabbit, rose, turkey, pumpkin, shamrock and others **$500-$550**

Doodle Dog:

1½in (4cm)	$1,000
3in (9cm)	$2,500
4½in (11cm)	$3,200

Huggers: 3½in (9cm) **$200-$225**

Guitar player: 3½in (9cm) **$400-$500**

With **Doodle Dog:**

4in (10cm)	$2,600

Traveler: 3½in (9cm) **$325-$350**

Baby Sister, molded blue hair bow: 3½in (9cm), large chip on bow, at auction **$892**

Kewpie with molded gray top hat and red umbrella: 4½in (11cm) **$2,000**

Kewpie in eggshell:

2½in (6cm)	$3,000

Kewpie Hero, soldier with nurse:

5½in (14cm)	$8,400

Kewpie with drum:

3½in (9cm)	$1,575

Governor or **Mayor:**

4in (10cm)	$450-$500

Kewpie and **Doodle Dog** on bench:

3½in (9cm)	$4,500

Kewpie sitting on inkwell:

3½in (9cm)	$750

Traveler with **Doodle Dog:**

3½in (9cm)	$1,350-$1,650

2in (5cm) *Kewpie* reading book. *H & J Foulke, Inc.*

4½in (11cm) *Kewpie Traveler. H & J Foulke, Inc.*

Soldiers:
3½ (9cm) lying Confederate   **$675**
5-6in (13-15cm) standing
$1,200-$1,700
3½in (9cm) sitting   **$1,500**
Kewpie on sled: 2½in (6cm)   **$1,000**
Two **Kewpies** reading book:
3½in (9cm), standing   **$850-$950**
5½in (13cm)   **$2,200**
Kewpie at tea table:
4½in (11cm)   **$3,200**
Kewpie with basket: 4in (10cm)**$1,000**
Kewpie Mountain with 17 figures:
$17,000 up
Kewpie, holding teddy bear:
4in (10cm)   **$850-$950**
Kewpie in bisque swing:
2½in (6cm)   **$4,000**
Glazed **Kewpie** shaker with animal:
2in (5cm) each   **$500-$600**
Kewpie Bellhop in green:
4in (10cm)   **$1,700**
Place Card: 2in (5cm)   **$425-$525**
Kewpie with broom and dustpan:
5in (10cm)   **$850**
Kewpie with hunting babies:
3½in (9cm)   **$4,000**
Kewpie riding hobby horse:
4½in (11cm)   **$5,500**
Kewpie riding animal:
4½in (11cm)   **$5,000-$5,300**

Bisque head on chubby jointed composition toddler body, glass eyes:
Made by J.D. Kestner.
Mark:

"Ges. gesch.
O'Neill J.D.K."

10in (25cm) five-piece body **$5,000**
12-14in (31-36cm)   **$6,500**

Bisque head on cloth body: Mold #1377 made by Alt, Beck & Gottschalck.
12in (31cm) glass eyes
$2,600-$2,800**
Painted eyes   **$1,600-$2,000****

Celluloid: Made by Karl Standfuss, Saxony, Germany.
2½in (6cm)   **$40-$50**
5in (13cm)   **$90-$110**

8in (20cm)   **$200-$225**
12in (31cm)   **$350**
22in (56cm)   **$550-$600**
Black: 2½in (6cm)   **$125**
5in (13cm)   **$200**
Kewpie/Billiken double face:
2½in (6cm)   **$150**

All-Composition: Made by Cameo Doll Co., Rex Doll Co. and Mutual Doll Co. All-composition, jointed at shoulders, some at hips; good condition.
8in (20cm)   **$200-$250**
11-12in (28-31cm)   **$325-$375**
All original, boxed   **$550-$600**
Black: 12-13in (31-33cm) **$400-$450**
Talcum container:
7in (18cm)   **$225-$250**
Composition head, cloth body:
12in (31cm)   **$250-$275**

**Not enough price samples to compute a reliable range.

12in (31cm) *Kewpie* with composition head and hands, cloth body. *H & J Foulke, Inc.*

All-Cloth: Made by Richard G. Krueger, Inc., or King Innovations, Inc., New York. Patent number 1785800. Mask face with plump cloth body.

10-12in (25-31cm)	**$275-$300**
18-22in (46-56cm)	**$600-$650**

Hard Plastic: Ca. 1950s.
Standing **Kewpie,** one-piece with jointed arms: 8in (20cm)   **$150-$165**
Boxed   **$225-$250**
Fully-jointed with sleep eyes; all original clothes: 13in (33cm)   **$500**

Vinyl: Ca. 1960s, Cameo Dolls. All original and excellent condition.

12-13in (31-33cm), boxed	**$90-$100**
16in (41cm), boxed	**$125**
27in (68cm)	**$150-$200**
Black: 12in (31cm) boxed	**$125**

Kewpie Baby with hinged body:
16in (41cm)   **$250**
Kewpie Gal:

8in (20cm), boxed	**$65-$75**
14in (36cm), boxed	**$125**

Ragsy, molded clothes:
8in (20cm)   **$30-$40**
Jesco Dolls, 1980s, boxed:

8in (20cm) black	**$40-$5**
12in (31cm)	**$60**
18in (46cm)	**$85**
24in (61cm)	**$130-$160**

Cloth Krueger *Kewpie. H & J Foulke, Inc.*

10in (25cm) *Kewpie* bride and groom, all original. *Private Collection.*

13in (33cm) hard plastic *Kewpie. H & J Foulke, Inc.*

Kley & Hahn

Character Baby: Perfect bisque head; bent-limb baby body; nicely dressed; all in good condition.

#138, 158, 160, 167, 176, 458, 525, 531, 680 and others:

11-13in (28-33cm)	**$475-$500**
18-20in (46-51cm)	**$700-$750**
24in (61cm)	**$1,000**
28in (71cm)	**$1,500**
Toddler:	
14-16in (36-41cm)	**$1,300-$1,450**
18-20in (46-51cm)	**$1,700-$1,900**

Two-face baby: 15in (38cm)　**$1,550**

FACTS
Kley & Hahn, doll factory, Ohrdruf, Thüringia, Germany. Heads by Hertel, Schwab & Co. (100 series), Bähr & Pröschild (500 series) and J.D. Kestner (200 series, 680 and Walküre). 1902-on.
Trademarks: Walküre, Meine Einzige, Special, Dollar Princess.
Mark:

Σ K&H ⟨　κ π
Germany　Walküre

18in (46cm) 680 toddler with flirty eyes. *H & J Foulke, Inc.*

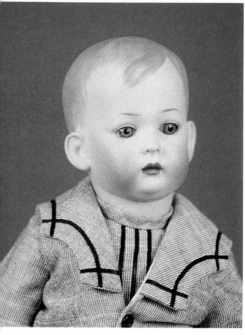

20in (51cm) 166 toddler with closed mouth. *H & J Foulke, Inc.*

Character Child: Perfect bisque head, closed mouth; jointed composition child or toddler body; fully dressed; all in good condition.

#520, 526:

15-16in (38-41cm)	**$3,500-$3,800**
19-21in (48-53cm)	**$4,500-$5,000**

#536, 546, 549:

15-16in (38-41cm)	**$4,000-$4,500**
19-21in (48-53cm)	**$5,000-$5,500**

#547: 18½in (47cm) at auction **$6,825**

#548, 568, Toddler:

21-23in (53-58cm)	**$1,900-$2,100**

#154, 166, closed mouth, toddler or jointed body:

16-17in (41-43cm)	**$2,500-$2,650**
19-20in (48-51cm)	**$3,200**

#154, 166, open mouth:

17-18in (43-46cm) jointed body	**$1,400-$1,500**
25in (64cm)	**$1,850-$1,950**
20in (51cm) baby	**$1,300-$1,400**

#169, closed mouth:

13-14in (33-36cm) toddler	**$2,200-$2,400**
17-19in (43-48cm) toddler	**$3,200-$3,500**

#169, open mouth:

23in (58cm) baby	**$1,500-$1,650**

Child Doll: Perfect bisque head; jointed composition child body; fully dressed; all in good condition.

#250, 282 or **Walküre:**

7½in (19cm)	**$325-$375**
12-13in (31-33cm)	**$425-$450**
16-18in (41-46cm)	**$500-$550***
22-24in (56-61cm)	**$600-$700***
28-30in (71-76cm)	**$900-$1,000**
35-36in (89-91cm)	**$1,500-$1,600**
Head only: 5in (13cm)	**$235**

Special, Dollar Princess:

23-25in (58-64cm)	**$525-$575**

*Allow $100 to $150 additional for flapper body.

**Not enough price samples to compute a reliable range.

12in (31cm) 546 character child. *H & J Foulke, Inc.*

Kling

Bisque shoulder head: Ca. 1880. Molded hair or mohair wig, painted eyes, closed mouth; cloth body with bisque lower limbs; dressed; in all good condition. Mold numbers in 100 and 200 Series.

12-14in (31-36cm)	$300-$375*
18-20in (46-51cm)	$500-$550*
23-25in (58-64cm)	$600-$700*

Glass eyes and molded hair:

15-16in (38-41cm)	$500-$600*
22in (56cm)	$900-$950*

Boy styles, such as 131:

16-18in (41-46cm)	$900-$1,000

Girl styles, such as #186, 176:

15-17in (38-43cm)	$900-$1,000

Lady styles with decorated bodice, such as:

#135, 170:

21-23in (53-58cm)	**$1,500 up**

#116, lady with molded blue bonnet:

16in (41cm) at auction	**$1,600**

#106, lady with molded stand-up collar, glass eyes:

17in (43cm) at auction	**$2,100**

China shoulder head: Ca. 1880. Black- or blonde-haired china head with bangs, sometimes with a pink tint; cloth body with china limbs; dressed; all in good condition.

#188, 189, 200, 203 and others:

13-15in (33-38cm)	$275-$325
18-20in (46-51cm)	$400-$450
24-25in (61-64cm)	$525-$575

*Allow extra for unusual or elaborate hairdo.

FACTS
Kling & Co., porcelain factory, Ohrdruf, Thüringia, Germany. 1870-on.
Mark:

23in (58cm) 189 china shoulder head. *H & J Foulke, Inc.*

Bisque head: Ca. 1890. Perfect bisque head, glass eyes; appropriate body; dressed; all in good condition.

#123, closed mouth shoulder head:
6½in (17cm)	**$250-$275**
10-12in (25-31cm):	
Original costume	**$500-$700**
Re-dressed	**$250-$300**
15in (38cm)	**$500-$600**

#166 or **167,** closed mouth shoulder head: 16-18in (41-46cm) **$750-$850**

#182, 190, socket head, closed mouth, composition body:
14in (36cm)	**$1,600-$1,800**

#373, 377, 245, shoulder head, open mouth:
13-15in (33-38cm)	**$375-$425**
19-22in (48-56cm)	**$475-$525**

#370, 372, 182, socket head, open mouth:
14-16in (36-41cm)	**$450-$500**
22-24in (56-61cm)	**$600-$700**
27in (69cm)	**$900-$1,000**

All Bisque: Glass eyes, wig; shirred pink or blue hose, **#61, #71:**
5-6in (11-15cm)	**$290-$325**

black boots **#36, #69:**
5-6in (11-15cm)	**$350-$400**

15in (38cm) Kling 245 child. *H & J Foulke, Inc.*

König & Wernicke

K & W Character: Perfect bisque head; composition baby or five-piece toddler body; appropriate clothes; all in good condition.

#98, 99, 100, 1070:
8½in (21cm)	**$350-$375**
10-11in (25-28cm)	**$450-$475**
14-16in (36-41cm)	**$550-$650***
19-21in (48-53cm)	**$700-$750***
24-25in (61-64cm)	**$1,000-$1,100**

Toddler, fully-jointed body:
13-15in (33-38cm)	**$800-$1,000**
19-20in (48-51cm)	**$1,450-$1,650**

All-Composition Toddler:
22in (56cm)	**$700**

Child #4711, Mein Stolz (My Pride):
37in (94cm)	**$1,800-$2,000**

*Allow extra for flirty eyes.

18in (46cm) König & Wernicke 99 character toddler. *H & J Foulke, Inc.*

FACTS
König & Wernicke, doll factory, Waltershausen, Thüringia, Germany. Heads by Hertel Schwab & Co. and Bähr & Pröschild. 1912-on.
Trademarks: Mein Stolz, My Playmate
Mark:

K & W
1070

Käthe Kruse

Cloth Käthe Kruse: Molded muslin head, hand-painted; jointed at shoulders and hips:
Doll I (1910-1929), 16in (41cm):
Early model, wide hips:

Mint, all original	**$4,800-$5,500**
Very good	**$3,200-$3,800**
Fair	**$1,800-$2,200**
Jointed knees, very good	
	$6,500 up**
"Frog" hands, good	**$5,000**

Doll I (1929-on), 17in (43cm):
Later model, slim hips:

Molded hair, mint	**$3,300-$3,800**
Very good	**$2,200-$2,600**

Doll 1H (1930-on), (wigged):

Mint, all original	**$3,200-$3,600**
Very good	**$2,000-$2,500**
U.S. Zone, all original excellent:	
18in (46cm)	**$2,500-$3,000**

Doll II "Schlenkerchen" Smiling Baby (1922-1936), 13in (33cm):

Excellent	**$10,000**
Very worn	**$4,500**

**Not enough price samples to compute a reliable range.

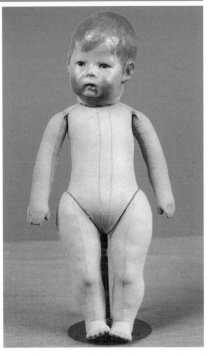

16in (41cm) *Doll I* with wide hips. *H & J Foulke, Inc.*

17in (43cm) *Doll I* U.S. Zone Germany, all original. *H & J Foulke, Inc.*

Doll V and VI Babies "Traumerchen" (1925-on) (five-pound weighted "Sand Baby") and **Du Mein** (unweighted):
Cloth head: 19½-23½in (50-60cm)
$5,000-$6,000
Magnesit head: 21in (53cm) **$1,600**

Doll VII (1926-1952), 14in (36cm), with **Doll I** head (1930-on):
All original   **$2,000-$2,500**
With **Du Mein** head (1926-1929):
14in (36cm):
Showing wear **$1,800-$2,200**
Mint   **$2,900**

Doll VIII "German Child" (1929-on), 20½in (52cm) wigged, turning head:
Mint, all original   **$2,000-$2,500**
Good condition, suitably dressed
$1,200-$1,500

Doll IX "Little German Child" (1929-on), wigged, turning head, 14in (36cm):
Mint, all original   **$1,350-$1,650**
U.S. Zone: cloth head **$1,100-$1,300**
Doll X (1930-1952), turning **Doll I** head:
14in (36cm) all original
$2,000-$2,500

U. S. Zone, cloth head **$1,100-$1,300**
Dolls XII and XIII "Hampelchen" (1931-on), with dangling legs:
14in (36cm)   **$1,400-$1,600**
18in (46cm)   **$2,000-$2,500**

14in (36cm) hard plastic baby, all original. *H & J Foulke, Inc.*

20½in (52cm) *Doll VIII. H & J Foulke, Inc.*

Hard Plastic (Synthetic) Head: Ca. 1948-on. Hard plastic head with human hair wig, painted eyes; pink muslin body; original clothes; all in excellent condition.
US. Zone:
  14in (36cm)   **$600-$700**
  21in (53cm)   **$950**
Ca. 1952-1975:
  14in (36cm)   **$375-$425**
  19-21in (48-53cm)
                       $500-$575
1975-on:
  14in (36cm)   **$300-$350**
  19-21in (48-53cm)
                       $400-$450
  20in (51cm) Du Mein
                       $600-$700
  18in (46cm) Slim
    Grandchild   **$900**

Hanna Kruse Dolls:
Däumlinchen, 25H (1957-on):
  10in (25cm) with foam
    rubber stuffing
                       $225-$250
Rumpumpel Baby or **Toddler, 32 H,** (1959-on):
  13in (33cm)   **$325-$350**
Doggi, (1964-1967), (vinyl head):
  10in (25cm)   **$225-$250**
Hard Plastic Baby:
  14in (36cm) all   **$100-$125**

All-Hard Plastic (Celluloid) Käthe Kruse: Wig or molded hair, sleep or painted eyes; jointed neck, shoulders and hips; original clothes; all in excellent condition. Turtle mark. 1955-1961.
  16in (41cm)   **$450-$500**
  Re-dressed   **$225-$275**
Vinyl head:
  16in (41cm)   **$300-$350**

Mannikin, Ca. 1950: 46-52in (116-132cm) **$2,200-$2,500**

Kruse-Type

Bing Art Dolls: Nurnberg, Germany. 1921-1932. Cloth head, molded face, hand-painted features; cloth body with jointed shoulders and hips (some with pinned joints), mitten hands; all original clothing; very good condition. "Bing" stamped or impressed on sole of shoe.
Cloth head, painted hair:
  10-12in (25-30cm)   **$425-$475**
  14in (36cm)   **$850-$950**
Cloth head, wigged: 10in (25cm) **$300-$350**
Composition head, wigged:
  7in (18cm)   **$100-$120**

Heine & Schneider Art Doll: Bad-Kösen, Germany. 1920-1922. All cloth or head of pressed cardboard covered with cloth, molded hair; cloth body with jointed shoulders and hips (some with cloth-covered composition arms and hands); appropriate or original clothes; all in good condition. Mark stamped on foot.
  17-19in (43-48cm)   **$1,500**

Unmarked Child Dolls: Ca. 1920s.
  15-17in (38-43cm)   **$375 up***

*Depending upon quality.

Below: 14in (36cm) Bing child, all original. *H & J Foulke, Inc.*

Gebrüder Kuhnlenz

G.K. doll with closed mouth: Ca. 1885-on. Perfect bisque socket head (some with closed Belton-type crown), inset glass eyes, closed mouth, round cheeks; jointed composition body; dressed; all in good condition.

#28, 31, 32:

8-10in (20-25cm)	**$850-$1,100**
15-16in (38-41cm)	**$1,600-$1,700**
21-23in (53-58cm)	**$2,400-$2,600**

#34, Bru-type, French body:

15in (38cm)	**$3,500-$4,000****
18in (46cm)	**$5,200-$5,600****

#38 shoulder head, kid body:

14-16in (36-41cm)	**$675-$750**
22-23in (56-58cm)	**$1,000-$1,100**

**Not enough price samples to compute a reliable range.

20in (51cm) 38-28 shoulder head child. *Private Collection.*

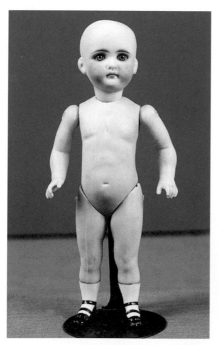
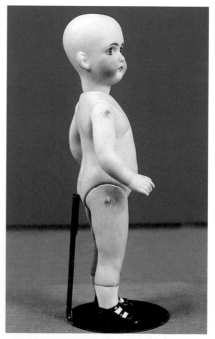

8½in (21cm) 31-32 all-bisque child. *H & J Foulke, Inc.*

G.K. Child Doll: Ca. 1890-on. Perfect bisque socket head, sleep or paperweight-type eyes, open mouth, molded teeth; jointed composition body, sometimes French; dressed; all in good condition.

#41, 44, 56 (character-type face):

9-10in (23-25cm)	**$700**
16-19in (41-48cm)	**$900-$1,000**
24-26in (61-66cm)	**$1,300-$1,500**

#165:

18in (46cm)	**$375-$425**
22-24in (56-61cm)	**$500-$525**
30-32in (76-81cm)	**$850-$950**

#61, 47 shoulder head:

19-22in (48-56cm)	**$650-$750**

G.K. Tiny Dolls: Perfect bisque socket head, wig, stationary glass eyes, open mouth with molded teeth; five-piece composition body with molded shoes and socks; all in good condition. Usually mold #44.

7-8in (18-20cm):

Crude body	**$185-$210**
Better body	**$250-$300**

All-Bisque: Swivel neck, usually mold **#31, #41,** or **#44:**

Bootines:

7-8in (18-20cm)	**$1,200-$1,500**
9½in (24cm)	**$2,200-$2,500**

Mary Janes:

5in (13cm)	**$550-$650**
7in (18cm)	**$1,250**
8½in (22cm)	**$1,650**

Black: See page 57.

FACTS

Gebrüder Kuhnlenz, porcelain factory, Kronach, Bavaria. 1884-on.

Mark:

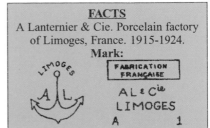

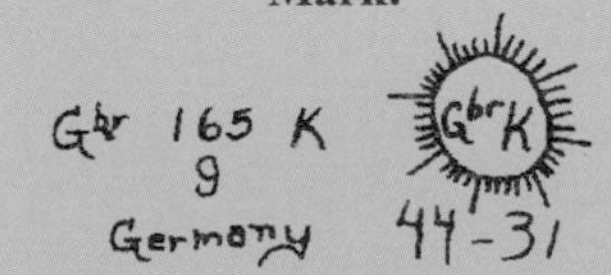
Gbr 165 K
9
Germany
GbrK
44-31

and/or numbers, such as:

41-28 56-18 44-15

The first two digits are mold numbers; second two are size number.

Lanternier

Marked Lanternier Child: Ca. 1915. Perfect bisque head, good or original wig, large stationary eyes, open mouth, pierced ears; papier-mâché jointed body; pretty clothes; all in good condition.

Cherie, Favorite or **La Georgienne**:

16-18in (41-46cm)	**$655-$750**
22-24in (56-61cm)	**$850-$900**
28in (71cm)	**$1,250-$1,350**

Lorraine Lady: Ca. 1915. Composition lady body:

16-18in (41-46cm)	**$850-$1,000***

Characters, "Toto" and others: Ca. 1915. Smiling character face:

17-19in (43-48cm)	**$900-$1,100**

*Depending upon costume and quality.

18in (46cm) unmarked character of the type made by Lanternier. *Mary Barnes Kelley Collection.*

FACTS

A Lanternier & Cie. Porcelain factory of Limoges, France. 1915-1924.

Mark:

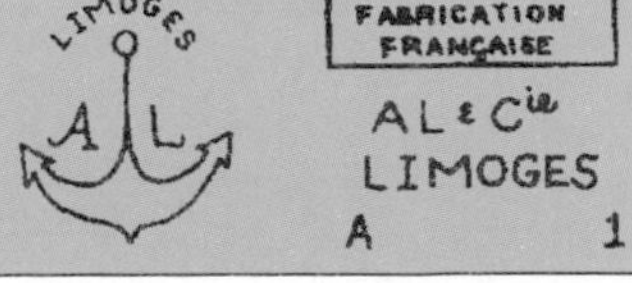
LIMOGES
A L
FABRICATION FRANÇAISE
AL & Cie
LIMOGES
A 1

Lenci

Lenci: All-felt (sometimes cloth torso); pressed felt head, painted features, eyes usually side-glancing; jointed shoulders and hips; original clothes, often of felt or organdy; in excellent condition.

Miniatures and Mascottes:
8-9in (20-23cm) Regionals
$350-$400
Children or unusual costumes
$450-$600
Cupido: 7in (18cm) boxed, at auction $4,200
Roly Poly: 8in (20cm) at auction
$250
Purse $300
Jackie Coogan with cigarette
$1,800

Children #300, 109, 149, 159, 111:
13in (33cm) $850-$1,000
17in (43cm) $1,200-$2,000
19-22in (48 56cm) $1,600-$2,200
#300 children, 17in (43cm):
Tyrolean Boy $2,600
Boy with Pipe (European) $3,900
Hiker $6,600

Fascist Boy or Girl $3,500-$4,200
Soldiers $10,000
Huntsman $3,500
Drummer Boy $2,600
Sports Series $3,500-$4,500
#1500, scowling face:
17-19in (43-48cm) $2,000-$2,500
#500: 21in (53cm) $1,650-$1,850
Baby: 18-21in (46-53cm)
$2,000-$2,500
Googly, watermelon mouth:
22in (56cm) $1,600-$2,000

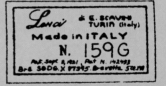

FACTS
Enrico & Elandi Scavini, Turin, Italy.
1920-on
Mark: "LENCI" on cloth and various paper tags; sometimes stamped on bottom of foot.

21in (53cm) 1500 series child, all original. *H & J Foulke, Inc.*

17in (43cm) 300 series child, all original. *H & J Foulke, Inc.*

9in (23cm) *Mascotte*, all original, in regional costume. *H & J Foulke, Inc.*

1930s Children:
"Lucia" face: 14in (36cm)
Child clothes	$800-$1,200
Regional outfits	$700-$900

"Laura" face: 16in (41cm) **$1,000 up**
"Mariuccia" face:
17in (43cm)   **$1,100 up**
"Benedetta" face:
19in (48cm)   **$1,300 up**
"Henriette" face:
25in (63cm)   **$1,700 up**

Becassine:
11in (28cm)   **$950**
20in (51cm) glass eyes   **$3,000**

Ladies and long-limbed novelty dolls:
24-28in (61-71cm)   **$1,500-$2,500**
40in (102cm), faded color
                       $1,000-$1,250
Pierrot (Dudovich):
20in (51cm)   **$3,500**
Opium Smoker:
20in (51cm)   **$3,200**
Valentino:
25in (63cm)   **$5,750**
30in (76cm) at auction   **$8,500**
Marilyn Miller, Follies Star:
28in (71cm)   **$3,100**
Lotte #800A: 45in (113cm)**$6,000**
Glass Eyes, 20in (51cm): Valentine,
Widow Allegra and others
                       $3,000-$4,000
"Surprised Eye" (round painted eyes),
fancy clothes:
20in (51cm)   **$2,200-$2,600**
Kufi #261, black child:
31in (78cm)   **$12,500**
Hand Puppet   **$400-$500**
Winkers:
12in (31cm)   **$750-$950**
Black Bellhop, at auction **$3,100**
1935 Round face:
11in (28cm)   **$450-$500**
20in (51cm)   **$800-$1,000**
1950 Characters   **$300 up**
Wood head: 6in (15cm)   **$60-$90**
Mask face, disc eyes:
23in (58cm)   **$600-$700**
Flocked hard plastic:
11in (28cm)   **$200-$250**
Celluloid-type, 6in (15cm) **$60-$75**
Catalogs   **$900-$1,200**

Modern Series: 1979 on:
13in (28cm)	**$110-$135**
22-21in (51-53cm)	**$225-$275**
22in (56cm) surprised eyes	
	$300-$330
26in (66cm) lady	**$275-$375**
27-28in (69-71cm) long gown	
	$325-$425

13in (33cm) 450 series child, all original.
H & J Foulke, Inc.

Lenci-Type

Felt or Cloth Doll: Mohair wig, painted features; stuffed cloth body; original clothes or costume; excellent condition.
Child dolls: 16-18in (41-46cm) depending upon quality, up to **$750**
Regional costume, very good quality:
7½-8½in (19-22cm) **$40-$50**
12in (31cm) **$90-$110**

Alma, Turin, Italy:
11in (28cm) **$200-$250**
16in (41cm) **$400-$500**

Dean's Rag Book Company, England:
14-16in (36-41cm) **$500-$600**
Composition face:
18in (46cm) **$600-$700**
Dancing Dolls:
12in (31cm) **$225-$250**
Ronnaug Petterssen, Norway:
8in (20cm) **$100-$125**
15in (38cm) **$650-$750**
18½ (47cm) at auction **$1,950**

Farnell's Alpha Toys, London, England:
Child: 14in (36cm) **$300-$350**
Black character:
14in (36cm) **$275-$300**
King George VI, 1937:
16in (41cm) **$400-$450**

Allwin Nightdress Case:
20in (51cm) **$400**

Eugenie Poir, Gre-Poir French doll makers, Paris and New York:
16-18in (41-46cm)
Cloth face **$300-$350**
Felt face **$450-$550**

Raynal, Venus, Marina, Clelia, Paris, France: 17-18in (43-46cm) mint
$500-$600
Poupées Nicette: 14in (36cm) Regional costumes **$250-$300**

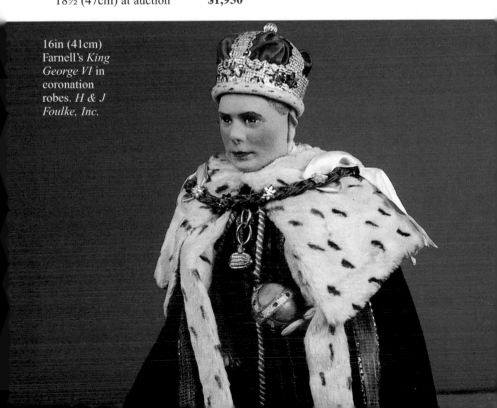

16in (41cm) Farnell's *King George VI* in coronation robes. *H & J Foulke, Inc.*

Liberty of London

British Coronation Dolls: 1939. All-cloth with painted and needle-sculpted faces; original clothes; excellent condition. The **Royal Family** and **Coronation Participants:**

    9-9½in (23-24cm) **$175-$200**
    Princess Margaret:
      6in (15cm) **$400-$425**
    Princess Elizabeth:
      7in (17cm) **$400-$425**
English Historical and Ceremonial Characters: 9-10in (23-25cm)
                         $135-$165
Beefeater (Tower Guard) **$85**

FACTS
Liberty & Co. of London, England. 1906-on.
Mark: Cloth label or paper tag "Liberty of London."

Unidentified Liberty character in historical costume. *H & J Foulke, Inc.*

Armand Marseille (A.M.)

Child Doll: 1890-on. Perfect bisque head, nice wig, sleep eyes, open mouth; composition ball-jointed body; pretty clothes; all in good condition.

#390 (larger sizes marked only "A. [size] M."), **Florodora, 1894:**

9-10in (23-25cm)	**$235-$265***
12-14in (31-36cm)	**$225-$275***
16-18in (41-46cm)	**$325-$375***
20in (51cm)	**$400-$425***
23-24in (58-61cm)	**$450-$500***
28-29in (71-74cm)	**$650-$700**
30-32in (76-81cm)	**$750-$850**
35-36in (89-91cm)	**$1,000-$1,250**
38in (96cm)	**$1,500-$1,800**
40-42in (102-107cm)	**$2,500-$2,800**

Head only with sleep eyes:

6in (15cm)	**$85**

Five-piece composition body, (excellent quality body):

6-7in (15-18cm)	**$200-$225**
9-10in (23-25cm)	**$260-$285**
Closed mouth:	
5-5½in (12-14cm)	**$250-$275**

Cardboard and stick leg body:

9-10in (23-25cm)	**$125**
12-14in (31-36cm)	**$135-$165**
16-18in (41-46cm)	**$210-260**

*Add $100 to $200 for factory original clothes.

FACTS
Armand Marseille of Köppelsdorf, Thüringia, Germany (porcelain and doll factory). 1885-on.
Marks:

24in (61cm) 390 child, all original.
H & J Foulke, Inc.

#1894 (composition body; early pale bisque):

14-16in (36-41cm)	**$475-$525**
21-23in (53-58cm)	**$725-$775**
26in (66cm)	**$850**

#370, 3200, 1894, Florodora, Anchor 2015, Rosebud, Lily, Alma, Mabel, Darling, Beauty, Princess: shoulder heads on kid or cloth bodies

11-12in (28-31cm)	**$125-$150**
14-16in (36-41cm)	**$175-$225**
22-24in (56-61cm)	**$375-$425**
25-26in (64-66cm)	**$450-$500**

#2000: 14in (36cm)   **$900****

Queen Louise, Rosebud (composition body):

12in (31cm)	**$340-$365**
23-25in (58-64cm)	**$550-$600**
28-29in (71-74cm)	**$700-$750**

Baby Betty:

14-16in (36-41cm) composition body	**$550-$600**
19-21in (48-53cm) kid body	**$525-$575**

#1894, 1892, 1896, 1897 shoulder heads (excellent quality):

19-22in (48-56cm)	**$475-$525**

Character Children: 1910-on. Perfect bisque head, molded hair or wig, glass or painted eyes, open or closed mouth; composition body; dressed; all in good condition. (For photographs of dolls not shown here, see previous *Blue Books*.)

#230 Fany (molded hair):

15-16in (38-41cm)	**$6,000-$7,000**
18in (46cm) at auction	**$9,750**

#231 Fany (wigged):

14-15in (36-38cm)	**$5,500-$6,500**

#250: 11-13in (28-33cm)   **$750**

#251/248 (open/closed mouth):

12in (31cm)	**$1,650**
16-18in (41-46cm)	**$2,600-$3,000**

#340: 13in (33cm)   **$2,600****

#345, (wig, intaglio eyes):

12in (31cm) at auction	**$2,800**

#372 Kiddiejoy, shoulder head, "mama" body: 19in (48cm)   **$650****

#400 (child body):

13in (33cm)	**$1,600-$1,800****
17in (43cm)	**$2,600-$2,800****

#500, 600:

13-15in (33-38cm)	**$700-$800**

#550 (glass eyes):

12in (31cm)	**$2,200-$2,500**
18-20in (46-51cm)	**$3,400-$3,600***

#560: 11-13in (28-33cm)   **$750-$850**

#590, (open/closed mouth):

15-16in (38-41cm)	**$1,300-$1,400**

#620, shoulder head:

16in (41cm)	**$1,250****

#640, shoulder head (same face as 550 socket): 20in (51cm)   **$1,500-$1,650****

#700:

11in (28cm) painted eyes	**$2,100****
14in (36cm) glass eyes	**$4,000-$4,500****

A.M. (intaglio eyes):

16-17in (41-43cm)	**$6,000 up**
23in (58cm)	**$15,000 up**

**Not enough price samples to compute a reliable range.

19in (48cm) 1894 child. *H & J Foulke, Inc.*

17in (43cm) *Baby Betty.*
H & J Foulke, Inc.

15in (38cm) 550 character girl.
Jensen's Antique Dolls.

Character Babies and Toddlers:
1910-on. Perfect bisque head, good
wig, sleep eyes, open mouth, some with
teeth; composition bent-limb body;
suitably dressed; all in nice condition.
Marks:

Armand Marseille
Germany
990
A 9/0 M

Germany
326

A 11 M

Mold #990, 985, 971, 996, 1330, 326,
(solid dome), 980, 991, 327, 329, 259
and others:

10-11in (25-28cm)	$275-$300
13-15in (33-38cm)	$325-$375
18-10in (46-51cm)	$400-$500
22in (56cm)	$625-$650
24-25in (61-64cm)	$750

#233:

13-15in (33-38cm)	$500-$550
20in (51cm)	$700-$800

#250: 11-13in (28-33cm) $400-$500
#251/248 (open/closed mouth):
11-12in (28-31cm) $800-$900

#251/248 (open mouth):
12-14in (31-36cm) $550-$650
#410 (two rows of teeth):
15-16in (38-41cm) **$1,200-$1,500****
#518:
16-18in (41-46cm) $500-$600
25in (64cm) $900-$1,000
#560A:
10-12in (25-31cm) $450-$500
15-17in (38-43cm) $600-$650
#580, 590 (open/closed mouth):
9in (23cm) $650-$750
15-16in (38-41cm)   **$1,200-$1,500**
#590 (open mouth):
12in (31cm) $600
16-18in (41-46cm) $850-$950
#920, shoulder head, "mama" body:
21in (53cm)   **$650****
Melitta:
19in (48cm) toddler   **$1,100-$1,250**
#995, painted bisque toddler:
18in (46cm) $500-$600

**Not enough price samples to compute a
reliable range.

15in (38cm) 329
character baby.
H & J Foulke, Inc.

Left: 14in (36cm) 975 character baby. *H & J Foulke, Inc.*

Below: 9in (23cm) 250 character baby. *H & J Foulke, Inc.*

Infant: 1924-on. Solid-dome bisque head with molded and/or painted hair, sleep eyes; composition body or hard-stuffed jointed cloth body or soft-stuffed cloth body; dressed; all in good condition.

Mark: A. M.
        Germany.
        351. 14ĸ

#351, 341, Kiddiejoy and **Our Pet:**
Head circumference:

8-9in (20-23cm)	$225-$250*
10in (25cm)	$275-$300*
12-13in (31-33cm)	$350-$425*
15in (38cm)	$600*
Composition body:	
8-10in (21-25cm) long	$250-$275

24in (61cm) wigged toddler	
	$1,000-$1,100
Hand Puppet	$300
#352: 17-20in (43-51cm) long	
	$575-$625
#347, head circumference:	
12-13in (31-33cm)	$475-$525
Baby Phyllis, head circumference:	
9in (23cm) black	$500
12-13in (31-33cm)	$425-$475
Baby Gloria, RBL, New York:	
12in (31cm)	$450-$500
15-16in (38-41cm)	$700-$800
Kiddiejoy, open mouth with tongue:	
13½in (34cm) h.c.	$650

*Allow $25 to $75 extra for composition body.

Marked "Just Me" Character: Ca. 1925. Perfect bisque socket head, curly wig, glass eyes to side, closed mouth; composition body; dressed; all in good condition. Some of these dolls, particularly the painted bisque ones, were used by the Vogue Doll Company in the 1930s and will be found with original Vogue labeled clothes.

Mark: Just ME
Registered
Germany
A 310/5/0 M

7½-8in (19-20cm)	**$1,400-$1,500**
9in (23cm)	**$1,750-$2,000**
11in (28cm)	**$2,500**
13in (33cm)	**$3,000**

Painted bisque:
7-8in (18-20cm) all original
$900-$1,000
10in (25cm) all original
$1,200-$1,400
9in (23cm) all original and boxed, at auction **$3,000**

Lady: 1910-1930. Bisque head with mature face, mohair wig, sleep eyes, open or closed mouth; composition lady body with molded bust, long slender arms and legs; appropriate clothes; all in good condition.

#401 and **400** (slim body), 14in (36cm):
Open mouth	**$1,250-$1,450**
Closed mouth	**$2,250-$2,500**
Painted bisque	**$900-$1,000**

#300, (M.H.):
9in (23cm)	**$1,400-$1,500****
All original	**$1,650***

#400, flapper body:
16-19in (41-48cm)	**$2,500-$3,000**

**Not enough price samples to compute a reliable range.

24in (61cm) long 351 character baby on composition body. *Jensen's Antique Dolls.*

9in (23cm) *Just Me. H & J Foulke, Inc.*

Metal Dolls

Missionary Ragbabies

German Metal Head Child: Ca. 1888 on. Marked Minerva, Juno and Diana or unmarked. Metal shoulder head on cloth or kid body; dressed; very good condition, not repainted.

Molded hair, painted eyes:
12-14in (31-36cm)	**$125-$150**
20-22in (51-56cm)	**$175-$195**

Molded hair, glass eyes:
12-14in (31-36cm)	**$160-$185**
20-22in (51-56cm)	**$235-$265**

American All-Metal Child: Ca. 1917 on. Giebeler-Falk, Atlas Doll & Toy Co. and others. Wig, sleep eyes; fully-jointed body; dressed; all in good condition.

16-20in (41-51cm)	**$325-$425**

All-Metal Baby:
11-13in (28-33cm)	**$100-$125**

Beecher Baby: Handmade stuffed stockinette doll with looped wool hair, painted eyes and mouth, needle sculpted face; appropriately dressed; all in good condition.

21-23in (53-59cm)	**$3,500-$4,000**
Excellent	**$5,000**
Fair	**$1,800-$2,000**

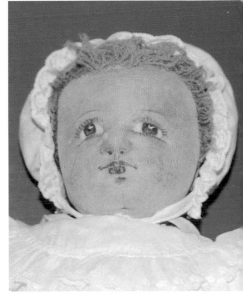

23in (58cm) *Missionary Ragbaby. Nancy A. Smith.*

14in (36cm) German metal head doll. *H & J Foulke, Inc.*

FACTS
Julia Beecher, Elmira, NY, U.S.A. 1893-1910.
All-cloth. 16-23in (41-58cm)
Designer: Julia Jones Beecher
Mark: None

Multi-Faced Dolls

Marked C.B. Doll: Carl Bergner, Sonneberg, Germany. Perfect bisque head with two or three different faces, usually sleeping, laughing and crying, papier-mâché hood hides the unwanted face(s); a ring through the top of the hood attached to a dowel turns the faces; cloth torso, composition limbs or jointed composition body; dressed; all in good condition.

Two or three faces:
12-13in (31-33cm)	**$1,800**
16in (41cm)	**$2,250**

#202 dep, two-faced black and white:
13in (33cm)	**$1,800-$2,200**

Red Riding Hood, Grandmother and Wolf: 13in (33cm)   **$6,000****

German Character Babies: Ca. 1910. Perfect bisque head with two faces, usually crying, sleeping or smiling; swivel neck; composition or cloth body; dressed; all in good condition. Some have papier-mâché hoods to cover unwanted faces, while some use cloth bonnets.

HvB (von Berg) two-faced baby:
17in (43cm)	**$1,200-$1,400**

Gebrüder Heubach three-faced baby:
13in (33cm)	**$1,800-$2,000**

Gebrüder Heubach two-faced baby, crying and smiling with glass eyes:
16in (41cm) at auction	**$3,800**

Kley & Hahn two-faced baby:
13in (33cm)	**$2,000-$2,200**

Max Schelhorn two-faced baby:
9in (23cm)	**$650-$750**

American Composition Dolls:
Trudy, 3-in-1 Doll Corp., New York, sleeping, crying, smiling, all original:
14in (36cm)	**$275-$295**

Johnny Tu-Face. Effanbee, New York, crying and smiling: 16in (41cm)
$400-$450

FACTS
Various German, French and American companies.
1888 and perhaps earlier.

 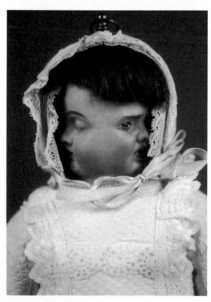

14in (36cm) three-faced C.B.(Carl Bergner). *H & J Foulke, Inc.*

Munich Art Dolls

Nelke

Munich Art Dolls: Molded composition character heads with hand-painted features; fully-jointed composition bodies; appropriate regional or "country style" clothes; all in good condition.

13-14in (33-36cm)	**$4,000-$5,000**
18-19in (46-48cm)	**$7,500-$8,500**

Nelke or Nelke-type Dolls: One-piece stockinette dolls, some with attached limbs, hand-painted faces with large eyes and rosy cheeks, painted hair; clothing was an integral part of the body, but some had an added ribbon, collar, hat or other item; excellent condition.

8-10in (20-25cm)	**$85-$95**
14-16in (36-41cm)	**$150-$175**

12in (31cm) *Munich Art Doll. Courtesy of Dorothy Hunt, Sweetbriar.*

Nelke-type stockinette doll, all original. *H & J Foulke, Inc.*

FACTS
Marion Kaulitz. 1908-1912.
All-composition, fully-jointed bodies.
Designer: Paul Vogelsanger and others.
Mark:
Sometimes signed on doll's neck.

FACTS
The Nelke Corporation,
Philadelphia, PA
1917-1930
Mark: woven label

Ohlhaver

Revalo Character Baby or **Toddler:**
Perfect bisque socket head, good wig,
sleep eyes, hair eyelashes, painted
lower eyelashes, open mouth; baby
bent-limb body; dressed; all in good
condition.
#22:

15-17in (38-41cm)	**$500-$550**
22in (56cm)	**$750-$800**

Toddler:

17-19in (41-48cm)	**$900-$1,100**

Revalo Child Doll: Bisque socket head,
good wig, sleep eyes, hair eyelashes,
painted lower eyelashes, open mouth;
ball-jointed composition body; dressed;
all in good condition. Mold **#150** or
#10727.

14-15in (36-38cm)	**$450-$500**
18-20in (46-51cm)	**$650-$700**
24-25in (61-64cm)	**$850-$900**
28in (71cm)	**$1,250**
Shoulder head: 22in (56cm)	**$650-$675**

Revalo Character Doll: Bisque head
with molded hair, painted eyes,
open/closed mouth; composition body;
dressed; all in good condition.
Coquette: 12-13in (31-33cm) **$850**
Coquette with hair bows:
13-14in (33-36cm) **$1,000-$1,100**

Above: 18in (46cm) *Revalo* child. *H & J
Foulke, Inc.*

Left: 14in (36cm) *Revalo* character baby.
H & J Foulke, Inc.

Oriental Dolls

Japanese Traditional Dolls:
Ichimatsu (play doll): 1868-on. Papier-mâché swivel head on shoulder plate, hips, lower legs and feet (early ones have jointed wrists and ankles); cloth midsection, cloth (floating) upper arms and legs; hair wig, dark glass eyes, pierced ears and nostrils; original clothes; all in very good condition.

Meiji Era (1868-1912):

3-5in (8-13cm)	**$200-$250**
12-14in (31-36cm)	**$350-$450***
18-20in (46-51cm)	**$600-$700***
24-26in (61-66cm)	**$1,200-$1,400***

Early three-bend body (Mitsuore):

14-16in (36-41cm)	**$1,500 up**

Ca. 1920s:

13-15in (33-38cm)	**$175-$225**
17-18in (43-46cm)	**$275-$325**
Ca. 1940s: 12-14in (31-36cm)	**$85-$95**

Traditional Lady (Kyoto or Fashion Doll):

Ca. 1900: 12in (31cm)	**$500 up**

1920s:

10-12in (25-31cm)	**$150-$175**
16in (41cm)	**$235-$265**

1940s:

12-14in (31-36cm)	**$85-$95**
6½in (16cm) Geisha with six wigs, boxed	**$95**

Traditional Warrior:

1880s: 16-18in (41-46cm)	**$800 up**
1920s: 11-12in (28-31cm)	**$250 up**

Royal Personages:

Ca. 1890: 10in (25cm)	**$800 up**

1920s-1930s:

4-6in (10-15cm)	**$100-$125**
12in (31cm)	**$350 up**

Baby with bent limbs:

Ca. 1910: 11in (28cm)	**$250 up**

Ca. 1930s, souvenir dolls:

8-10in (20-25cm)	**$65-$85**

Carved Ivory, Ca. 1890:

2-3in (5-8cm) fully jointed, exquisite carving	**$350**
Lesser quality	**$225**

Chinese Papier-mâché: Ca 1930-1940. All original, so-called "Opera" dolls:

8in (20cm)	**$80-$85**
26in (66cm)	**$500**

*Allow extra for a sexed boy.

16in (41cm) *Ichimatsu*, all original. *H & J Foulke, Inc.*

15in (38cm) French *poupée* on wood body. *Private Collection.*

Oriental Bisque Dolls: Ca. 1900-on. Made by French and German firms. Bisque head tinted yellow; matching ball-jointed or baby body; original or appropriate clothes; all in excellent condition. (See previous *Blue Books* for photographs of dolls not pictured here.)

B.P. #220:

11in (33cm)	**$2,300****
16-17in (41-43cm)	**$3,200-$3,500****

Belton-type: 12in (31cm) 127   **$1,700**

BSW #500:

11in (28cm)	**$1,100-$1,300**
14-15in (36-38cm)	**$1,800-$2,200***

Bru Jne: 20in (51cm)   **$26,000****

Jumeau:

Closed mouth: 19-20in (48-51cm)
$48,000-$62,000**
Open mouth: 18in (46cm) **$4,500****
French *Poupée*, wood body:
15in (38cm)   **$7,500****

JDK 243:

13-14in (33-36cm)	**$4,300-$5,300**
16-18in (41-46cm)	**$5,800-$6,500**

A.M. 353:

9½ (24cm)	**$750-$800**
12in (31cm)	**$900-$1,000**
15-16in (38-41cm)	**$1,200-$1,400**
10in (25cm) cloth body	**$700**

A.M. Girl: 8-9in (20-23cm)   **$650**

S&H 1329:

14-15in (36-38cm)	**$1,800-$2,200***
18-19in (46-48cm)	**$2,700-$2,800***

S&H 1099, 1129, and **1199:**

15in (38cm)	**$2,700-$2,800***
19-20in (48-51cm)	**$3,200-$3,500***

S PB H:

9in (23cm)	**$650**
19in (48cm)	**$2,000***

#164: 16-17in (41-43cm)
$1,850-$2,000*

Unmarked:

4½in (12cm) painted eyes	**$175-$195**
4¾in (12cm) glass eyes	**$400-$500**
11-12in (28-31cm) glass eyes	**$850-$950**

All-Bisque Dolls:
JDK Baby: 7in (18cm)   **$2,200****
Heubach Chin Chin: 4in (10cm)
$325-$365

*Allow extra for elaborate original outfits.
**Not enough price samples to compute a reliable range.

S&H Child:
4½in (12cm)   **$625-$675**
5½in (14cm)   **$750-$775**
7in (18cm)   **$850-$950**
Man with molded hat and mustache:
3½in (9cm)   **$330**

Bisque Heads of Unknown Origin:
Lady with molded hair or hat, wood
jointed body: 13in (33cm)   **$750-$850**
Character man with molded mustache,
jointed body: 11in (28cm)   **$1,100****

German Papier-mâché: Ca. 1925.
August Möller: 14in (36cm) all original, boxed, at auction   **$650**
#419, Papier-mâché man, molded hat
and mustache, cloth body:
13in (33cm)   **$300-$350**

American Cloth: Oil painted stockinette in the Chase manner; original
clothes: 16in (41cm)   **$1,050**

**Not enough price samples to compute a
reliable range.

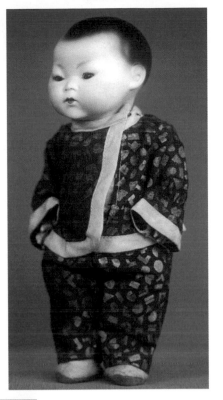

Above: 10in (25cm) Armand
Marseille 353 on cloth body,
all original. *H & J Foulke,
Inc.*

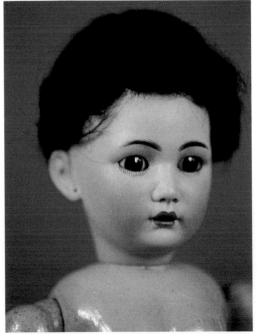

Left: 16in (41cm) Simon &
Halbig 1329 lady. *H & J
Foulke, Inc.*

Papier-Mâché
(So-Called French-Type)

French-type Papier-mâché: Shoulder head with painted black pate, brush marks around face, nailed-on human hair wig (often missing), set-in glass eyes, closed or open mouth with bamboo teeth, pierced nose; French pink kid body with stiff arms and legs; appropriate old clothes; all in good condition, showing some wear.

14-16in (36-41cm)	**$1,800-$2,200**
19-21in (48-51cm)	**$2,500-$2,600**
24-26in (61-66cm)	**$2,800-$3,000**
32in (81cm)	**$3,500-$3,800**

Painted eyes:

6-8in (15-20cm)	**$375-$475**
14-16in (36-41cm)	**$1,000-$1,200**

Wood-jointed body:

6in (15cm)	**$750-$800**

Shell decoration:

8in (20cm) pair	**$1,300-$1,600**
18in (46cm) pair	**$2,500**

Poupard, molded bonnet and clothes:

18in (46cm)	**$400-$500**

FACTS
Heads by German firms such as Johann Müller of Sonneberg and Andreas Voit of Hildburghausen, were sold to French and other doll makers. 1835-1850.
Mark: None.

16in (41cm) French papier-mâché lady, all original, in Pyrenees costume. *H & J Foulke, Inc.*

Papier-Mâché
(German)

Papier-mâché Shoulder Head: Johann Müller and others. Ca. 1840s to 1860s. Unretouched shoulder head, molded black hair, painted eyes; some wear and crazing; cloth or kid body; original or appropriate old clothing; entire doll in fair condition.

16-18in (41-46cm)	**$900-$1,000***
22-24in (56-61cm)	**$1,100-$1,300***
32in (81cm)	**$1,900-$2,200***

18½in (47cm) all original, exceptional model and condition **$5,000**

Long curls: 19in (48cm) **$2,300**

Brown hair with molded flowers and ornaments: 17in (43cm) **$3,190**

Glass eyes, short hair:

19in (48cm)	**$1,650-$1,850**
24in (61cm)	**$2,400**

21in (53cm) all original provincial costume **$2,600**

Glass eyes, long hair:

22in (56cm) **$1,700-$2,000**

Glass eyes, bun and exposed ears:

20-22in (51-56cm) **$4,000-$5,000**

Flirty eyes, long hair:

23in (58cm) **$2,700-$3,000**

Unmarked So-called Pre-Greiner: Unknown makers, some may be American. Ca. 1850. Papier-mâché shoulder head; molded and painted black hair, pupil-less black glass eyes; stuffed cloth body, mostly homemade, wood, leather or cloth extremities; dressed in good old or original clothes; all in good condition, showing some wear.

18-22in (46-56cm)	**$1,000-$1,350**
28-32in (71-81cm)	**$2,000-$2,300**

Fair condition, much wear:

20-24in (51-61cm)	**$700-$800**
Flirty eye: 30in (76cm)	**$3,000**

Molded Hair Papier-mâché: So-called Milliners' Model. Ca. 1820s-1860s. Unretouched shoulder head, various molded black hairdos, blue, black or brown eyes, painted features; original kid body, wooden arms and legs; original or very old handmade clothing; entire doll in fair condition.

*Allow extra for unusual model.

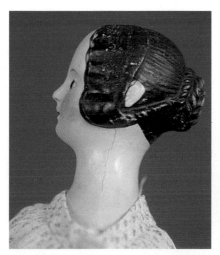

22in (56cm) 1840s lady with bun and glass eyes. *H & J Foulke, Inc.*

17½in (43cm) molded hair lady. *Private Collection.*

Long curls:
9in (23cm) **$550***
13in (33cm) **$675-$725***
23in (58cm) **$1,400-$1,500***

Covered wagon hairdo:
7in (18cm) **$275-$325***
11in (28cm) **$450-$500***
15in (38cm) **$675-$775***
Side curls with braided bun:
9-10in (23-25cm) **$750-$850***
13-15in (31-38cm) **$1,300-$1,500***
28in (71cm) at auction **$4,100**
Center part with molded bun:
7in (18cm) **$525***

11in (28cm) **$950-$1,000***
Wood-jointed body **$1,200-$1,350**
Side curls with high beehive (Apollo knot):
11in (28cm) **$950-$1,000***
18in (46cm) **$1,900-$2,100***
Coiled braids at ears, braided bun:
10-11in (25-28cm) **$1,000-$1,100***
20in (51cm) **$2,000-$2,200***
Braided coronet:
11in (28cm) **$1,250-$1,450***
Molded bonnet and red snood:
13in (33cm) **$1,250-$1,500***

*Allow extra for excellent condition.

Above: 25in (64cm) Sonneberg Täufling. *H & J Foulke, Inc.*

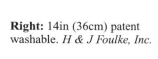

Right: 14in (36cm) patent washable. *H & J Foulke, Inc.*

Sonneberg Täufling So-called Motschmann Baby*: Heinrich Stier and other Sonneberg factories. Ca. 1850 on. Papier-mâché or wax-over-composition head with painted hair, dark pupil-less glass eyes; composition lower torso, composition and wood arms and legs, jointed at the ankles and wrists, cloth-covered midsection with voice box, cloth-covered upper arms and legs, called floating joints; dressed in shift and bonnet. (For body photograph, see *11th Blue Book*, page 336.)
Very good condition:

6in (15cm)	**$650-$750**
12-14in (31-36cm)	**$1,000-$1,200**
18-20in (46-51cm)	**$1,600-$2,000**
24in (61cm)	**$2,800-$3,000**

Fair condition, with wear:

12-14in (31-36cm)	**$600-$750**
18-20in (46-51cm)	**$950-$1,150**

*Some are found stamped "Ch. Motschmann," but he was the holder of the patent for the voice boxes, not the manufacturer of the dolls.

Patent Washable Dolls: F.M. Schilling and other Sonneberg factories. 1880-1915. Composition shoulder head with mohair or skin wig, glass eyes, closed or open mouth; cloth body with composition arms and lower legs, sometimes with molded boots; appropriately dressed; all in good condition.
Superior Quality:

12-14in (31-36cm)	**$500-$600**
16-18in (41-46cm)	**$700-$750**
22-24in (56-61cm)	**$850-$900**
30in (76cm)	**$1,200-$1,400**
21in (53cm) all original baby costume, at auction	**$1,300**

Standard Quality:

11-12in (28-31cm)	**$150-$175**
14-16in (36-41cm)	**$225-$250**
22-24in (56-61cm)	**$350-$375**
30-33in (76-84cm)	**$450-$500**
38in (97cm)	**$600-$700**
Lady: 13-16in (33-41cm)	**$750-$850**
Oriental: 12in (31cm)	**$250**

Sonneberg-type Papier-mâché: Müller & Strasburger, A. Wislizenus, Cuno & Otto Dressel and other Sonneberg

18½in (47cm) Sonneberg-type papier-mâché. *H & J Foulke, Inc.*

factories. Ca. 1880-1910. Shoulder head with molded and painted black or blonde hair, painted eyes, closed mouth; cloth body, sometimes with leather arms; old or appropriate clothes; all in good condition, showing some wear.
Mark: Usually unmarked. Some marked:

> M & S
> Superior
> 2015

13-15in (33-38cm)	**$300-$350**
18-19in (46-48cm)	**$450-$500**
23-25in (58-64cm)	**$600-$700**
Glass eyes: 18in (46cm)	**$550-$600**
Topsy Turvy: 7½in (19cm) all original	**$300**

Papier-mâché child: Ca. 1920-on. Papier-mâché head, good wig, painted features; hard stuffed body; original clothes, all in good condition.

10-12in (25-31cm)	**$90-$110**

Parian-Type
(Unpainted Bisque)

Unmarked Parian: Pale or untinted shoulder head, sometimes with molded blouse, beautifully molded hairdo (may have ribbons, beads, comb or other decoration), painted eyes, closed mouth; cloth body; lovely clothes; entire doll in fine condition.

Common, plain style:

8-10in (20-25cm)	**$135-$185**
16in (41cm)	**$300-$350**
24in (61cm)	**$475-$525**
Swivel neck: 17½in(45cm)	**$525-$575**

Molded white blouse, blue scarf:

22in (56cm)	**$550-$575**

Child, short blonde hair:

15-16in (38-41cm)	**$600-$650**

Pretty hairdo, may have simple ribbon, comb or snood:

14-15in (36-38cm)	**$550-$650**
18-20in (46-51cm)	**$800-$900**

Tan hair, applied Dresden flowers:

17in (43cm)	**$1,100-$1,200**

Man, molded collar and tie:

16-17in (41-43cm)	**$750**

Child, glass eyes, molded blonde curls:

14-16in (36-41cm)	**$1,150-$1,250**

"Augusta Victoria:"

17in (43cm)	**$1,200-$1,300**

Decorated shoulder plate:

17-19in (43-48cm)	**$1,300-$1,900**

Man with collar and glass eyes:

19in (48cm) at auction	**$1,760**

"Alice" hairdo:

14in (36cm)	**$450-$500**
21in (53cm)	**$850-$950**

"Countess Dagmar:"

19in (48cm)	**$850-$950**

"Irish Queen," Limbach 8552:

16in (41cm)	**$600-$700**

"Dolly Madison," glass eyes, swivel neck:

18in (46cm)	**$750-$800**

Decorated plate:

17in (43cm)	**$1,250-$1,350**

FACTS
Various German firms.
Ca. 1860s through 1870s.
Mark: Usually none,
sometimes numbers.

15in (38cm) parian boy.
H & J Foulke, Inc.

"**Empress Eugenie**," pink lustre hat or snood: 17in (43cm)   **$1,700-$1,800**

Pink lustre tiara, gold earrings:
   14-16in (36-41cm)   **$1,500**

Molded straw bonnet, fancy shoulder plate: 16in (41cm)   **$2,500**

Fancy brown hair, inserted metal tiara:
   19in (48cm)   **$1,500-$1,600**

Molded flowers and gold coronet, all original: 14½in (37cm)   **$1,650**

Light brown hair waving past shoulders, applied Dresden flowers:
   21in (53cm)   **$1,700**

Fancy black hair with ribbon, glass eyes: 22in (56cm)   **$2,000**

Molded yellow bonnet with flowers:
   10in (25cm)   **$1,650**

Molded necklace, fancy hair, glass eyes: 16in (41cm)   **$1,400**

All-parian, pink lustre boots, fine quality: 5½in (14cm)   **$250-$275**

Head only, decorated shoulder plate, painted eyes: 5in (13cm)   **$450**

Head only, molded blouse with black bow, pierced ears, blonde hair:
   3½in (8cm)   **$325**

16in (41cm) parian lady with applied ornamentation in her hair. *Private Collection.*

10½in (27cm) parian lady with molded hat. *Private Collection.*

16in (41cm) parian lady with fancy snood. *H & J Foulke, Inc.*

Philadelphia Baby

Philadelphia Baby: All-cloth with treated shoulder-type head, lower arms and legs; painted hair, well-molded facial features, ears; stocking body; very good condition.

18-22in (46-56cm)	**$4,200**
Mint condition	**$5,000-$5,500**
Fair, showing wear	**$2,500**
Very worn	**$1,600-$1,800**

Rare style face (See *6th Blue Book*, page 302, for exact doll.), at auction **$9350**

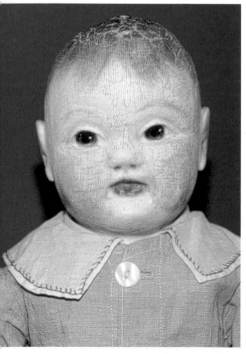

21in (53cm) *Philadelphia Baby. Nancy A. Smith.*

Rabery & Delphieu

Marked R.D. Bébé: Ca. 1880s. Perfect bisque head, lovely wig, paperweight eyes, closed mouth; jointed composition body; beautifully dressed; entire doll in good condition; very good quality bisque, very pretty.

12-14in (31-36cm)	**$2,500-$3,000**
18-19in (46-48cm)	**$3,600-$3,800**
24-25in (61-64cm)	**$4,000-$4,500**
28in (71cm)	**$5,000-$5,500**
Open mouth:	
19-22in (48-56cm)	**$1,900-$2,200**
26-28in (66-71cm)	**$2,800-$3,000**

28in (71cm) *Bébé Rabery. Betty Harms Collection.*

Raggedy Ann and Andy

Early Raggedy Ann or **Andy:** Volland. All-cloth with movable arms and legs; brown yarn hair, button eyes, painted features; legs of striped fabric for hose and black for shoes; original clothes; all in good condition.

Mark: "PATENTED SEPT. 7, 1915"
Early hand painted face Ann
$2,200-$2,500
Single eyelash $3,500
Printed face $1,300-$1,500

FACTS
Various makers.
1915 to present. All-cloth
Creator: Johnny B. Gruelle.

Wear, stains, not original clothes
$800-$900
Characters **$2,500**
Beloved Belindy **$2,500**
Molly'es Raggedy Ann or **Andy:** 1935-1938, manufactured by Molly'es Doll Outfitters. Red hair and printed features; original clothes; all in good condition.
Mark:
"Raggedy Ann and Raggedy Andy Dolls, Manufactured by Molly'es Doll Outfitters" (printed writing in black on front torso)
18-22in (46-56cm)
$1,400-$1,800 each
30in (76cm) at auction **$5,200**
Babies:
14in (36cm) pair **$4,000-$5,000**

16in (41cm)
early Volland
Raggedy Ann.
H & J Foulke,
Inc.

Georgene Raggedy Ann or Andy: 1938-1963, manufactured by Georgene Novelties, Inc. Red hair, black button eyes; original clothes; all in good condition, light wear and fading acceptable.

Mark: Various cloth labels sewn in side seam of body.

Black Outline Nose, Ca. 1938-1944:
19-20in (48-51cm)	**$1,200-$1,500**
32in (81cm)	**$2,500-$2,800**

Asleep/Awake, Black Outline Nose:
13in (33cm)	**$1,800**
Pair	**$1,800**

Asleep/Awake, plain nose:
12in (30cm)	**$650**

Face #2, long nose, Ca. 1944-1946:
19in (48cm)	**$1,000-$1,200**

Silsby Label, 1946:
15in (38cm)	**$500-$550**
20in (51cm) pair	**$1,500-$1,800**

Small nose, curved sides, bright color, excellent condition:
15in (38cm)	**$350-$400**
boxed	**$500-$600**
19-20in (48-51cm)	**$450-$550**
boxed	**$650-$700**

23in (58cm)	**$550-$650**
49in (124cm) at auction	**$1,800**

Small nose, worn faded, all original:
15in (38cm)	**$175-$200**
19in (48cm)	**$225**
23in (58cm)	**$275**

Beloved Belindy:
19in (48cm)	**$1,500-$2,000**
Boxed with label, at auction	**$3,800**

Handmade, 1930-1940:
15-19in (38-48cm)	**$185-$225**

Knickerbocker Toy Co. Raggedy Ann or Andy: 1963-1982. Bright color, excellent condition.

Early, 1964: 15in (38cm) boxed with clouds **$250**

Various print dresses:
15in (38cm)	**$135-$150**
19in (48cm)	**$165-$185**

Common print dress:
15in (38cm)	**$65-$85**
19in (48cm)	**$85-$95**
Boxed	**$125**
32-35in (81-86cm) pair	**$300-$400**

Beloved Belindy:
15in (38cm)	**$800-$900**

19in (48cm) Georgene Novelties *Raggedy Ann* with black outlined nose, all original. *H & J Foulke, Inc.*

Georgene Novelties *Raggedy Andy* with Silsby label, all original. *H & J Foulke, Inc.*

15in (38cm) Georgene Novelties, *Raggedy Andy,* all original. *H & J Foulke, Inc.*

19in (48cm) Georgene Novelties, *Raggedy Ann,* all original and boxed. *H & J Foulke, Inc.*

Camel with Wrinkled Knees:

15in (38cm)	**$300-$350**

Musical, 1966:

15in (38cm) boxed	**$225**

Teach N Play, 1971:

18in (46cm)	**$125-$135**

Embraceables, 1973:

7in (18cm) boxed	**$100-$125**

Talking, 1973:

18in (46cm) boxed	**$225**

Hand Puppets, 1973:

9½in (24cm) pair	**$27**

Applause, 1981-on:
Embroidered eyes:

12in (31cm)	**$10-$12**
17in (43cm)	**$15-$18**

Classic model, button eyes:

17-20in (43-51cm)	**$25**
25in (63cm)	**$35**
Black: 12in (30cm) pair	**$40-$45**
Asleep/Awake: pair	**$65-$75**

1992 75th Anniversary: 19in (48cm)

Ann or Andy, boxed	**$90-$110**

1993 Molly-E Baby Raggedy Ann:

13in (33cm)	**$90-$110**

1994 Raggedy Ann or Andy:

13in (33cm) boxed	**$90-$110**
Camel with Wrinkled Knees	**$110**

19in (48cm) Georgene Novelties, *Raggedy Ann,* all original and boxed. *H & J Foulke, Inc.*

1995 Raggedy Ann, U.S. Patent:

17in (43cm)	**$125-$150**

1997 Stamp Doll:

17in (43cm) boxed	**$55-$65**

1998 Stars & Stripes:

17in (43cm) boxed	**$85-$95**

Hasbro, Inc., 1983-on:

12in (31cm), boxed	**$12-$15**
18in (46cm), boxed	**$20-$22**
24in (61cm)	**$35**
Baby: pair, boxed	**$38-$42**

1989 Christmas Ann:

boxed	**$75-$85**

1996 Anniversary pair:

11in (28cm) boxed	**$55-$65**

Playskool, 1989-on:
1989 Valentine Ann:

12in (31cm)	**$32**

1989 Christmas Ann: boxed	**$40**
1989 Baby Ann or Andy: boxed	**$30-$40**

1991 Dress Me Raggedy Ann:

14in (35cm) boxed	**$30-$35**
Mint-in-box, at auction	**$122.50**

Alexander
1993 Mop Top Wendy & Billy: pair

$90-$100

Recknagel

R.A. Child: Ca. 1890s-World War I. Perfect marked bisque head, good wig, set or sleep eyes, open mouth; jointed composition or wooden body; some dolls with molded painted shoes and socks; all in good condition.

1907, 1909, 1914:
8-9in (20-23cm) five-piece body
$140-$165
16-18in (41-46cm) **$300-$350**
24in (61cm) **$450-$500**

R.A. Character Baby: 1909-World War I. Perfect bisque head, painted or glass eyes; cloth baby body or composition bent-limb baby body; nicely dressed; all in good condition.

#121, 126, 127, 1924 infants:
8-9in (20-23cm) long **$235-$285**
#23 character babies:
7-8in (18-20cm) **$300-$350**
#22, 28, and **44** bonnet babies:
8-9in (20-23cm) **$550-$600**
11in (28cm) **$800**

Character children:
6-8in (15-20cm) composition body
$275-$300
18in (46cm) smiling face, at auction
$1,700

#31 Max and **#32 Moritz,** molded hair, painted features: 8in (20cm) **$650-$700**

#45 and **46,** googlies:
7in (18cm) **$500-$550**
#43, 44, googlies with molded hats:
7in (18cm) **$600**

> **FACTS**
> Th. Recknagel, porcelain factory,
> Alexandrienthal, Thüringia, Germany.
> 1886-on.
> **Mark:**
> 1907
> R/A DEP
> I 9/0

9in (23cm) 28 character baby. *H & J Foulke, Inc.*

7in (18cm) 46 googly. *H & J Foulke, Inc.*

Rollinson Doll

Marked Rollinson Doll: All molded cloth with painted head and limbs; painted hair or human hair wig, painted features (sometimes teeth also); dressed; all in good condition.

Chase-type with painted hair:
  18-22in (46-51cm) **$800-$1,200**
Child with wig:
  16in (41cm) **$800-$1,200**
  26in (66cm) **$1,500-$2,000**

FACTS
Utley Doll Co., Holyoke, MA, U.S.A. 1916-on.
Designer: Gertrude F. Rollinson
Mark: Stamp in shape of a diamond with a doll in center, around border: "Rollinson Doll Holyoke, Mass."

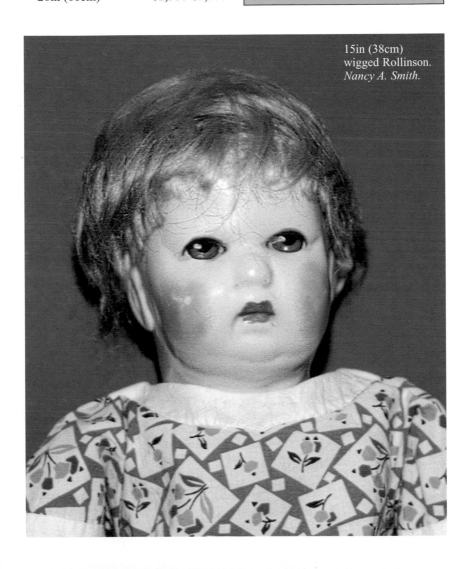

15in (38cm) wigged Rollinson. *Nancy A. Smith.*

S.F.B.J.

Child Doll: 1899-on. Perfect bisque head, good French wig, set or sleep eyes, open mouth, pierced ears; jointed composition body; nicely dressed; all in good condition.

Jumeau-type, paperweight eyes (no mold number), 1899-1910:

14-16in (36-41cm)	**$1,100-$1,250**
21-23in (53-58cm)	**$1,700-$1,900**
25-27in (64-69cm)	**$2,200-$2,500**

#301, (some stamped "Tête Jumeau" on labeled Jumeau body):

10in (25cm)	**$650-$675**
12-14in (31-36cm)	**$700-$800**
20-23in (51-58cm)	**$900-$1,000**
28-30in (71-76cm)	**$1,200-$1,500**
37in (94cm)	**$2,500-$2,800**
14in (36cm) boxed, all original with Jumeau shift and shoes	**$1,700**
22in (56cm) lady body	**$1,200**

Above: 12in (31cm) Jumeau mold SFBJ, all original costume from Arles in Provence. *H & J Foulke, Inc.*

FACTS
Société Française de Fabrication de Bébés & Jouets, Paris, France. 1899-on.
Mark:

DÉPOSÉ
S.F.B.J.

S.F.B.J
301
PARIS

Left: 27½in (70cm) 301 child. *H & J Foulke, Inc.*

#60, end of World War I on:
7½in (19cm) with Jumeau tag
$425-$450
12-14in (31-36cm) $600-$650
19-21in (48-53cm) $750-$800
28in (71cm) $900-$1,000

Bleuette #301:
10½-11in (27-29cm) $1,000-$1,200
With trunk, wardrobe, and catalog, at
auction $3,500
Walking, kissing and flirting:
22in (56cm) $1,300-$1,500
All original, fancy outfit, at auction
$1,900
Papier-mâché head #60, fully-jointed
body:
17in (43cm) $250-$300
22in (56cm) $350-$400
18in (46cm) child in original sailor
outfit, like new $1,400

Character Dolls: 1910-on. Perfect
bisque head, wig, molded, sometimes
flocked hair on mold numbers 237, 266,
227 and 235, sleep eyes; composition
body; nicely dressed; all in good condition.
Mark:
    S F B J
    230
    PARIS
       S F B J
       236
       PARIS

#226: 14-16in (36-41cm)
$1,700-$1,900
#227: 17in (43cm) $1,850-$1,900
#229: 16in (41cm) $2,000-$2,200**
#230, (sometimes Jumeau):
12-14in (30-36cm) $1,200-$1,400
19-22in (48-56cm) $1,900-$2,100
#233: 16in (41cm) $3,300-$3,500
#234: 15in (38cm) baby $2,500
#235:
16in (41cm) child $1,850-$1,900
5in (38cm) baby, all original Au Nain
Bleu outfit $2,200
#236, baby:
12-13in (31-33cm) $700-$800
15-17in (38-43cm) $900-$1,100
20-22in (51-56cm) $1,400-$1,500
25in (64cm) $1,700-$1,800
Toddler:
15-16in (38-41cm) $1,250-$1,350
24in (61cm) $1,950-$2,000

#237:
15-16in (38-41cm) $2,200-$2,500
All original boy, at auction $4,000
#238, child: 15-16in (38-41cm)
$2,200-$2,500
Lady: 18-19in (46-48cm) $3,000
#239:
13in (33cm) Poulbot, all original
$8,000**
Boxed pair, at auction $31,000
#242, nursing baby:
13-14in (33-35cm) $3,250**
#245 Googly: See page 94.
#246: 16½in (42cm) at auction $3,100
#247, toddler:
18-21in (46-53cm) $2,100-$2,600

**Not enough price samples to compute a
reliable range.

16in (41cm) 239 Poulbot character.
Dorothy Hunt, Sweetbriar.

#248:
10-12in (25-30cm) **$7,500-$8,500****
#250:
19-20in (48-51cm) **$3,250-$3,500****
#251, toddler:
14-15in (36-38cm)   **$1,300-$1,500**
24in (61cm)   **$2,200-$2,400**
#252, baby:
10in (25cm)   **$2,500-$3,000**
15in (38cm)   **$4,000-$4,200**
Toddler:
13in (33cm)   **$4,800**
20in (51cm)   **$6,500-$7,500**
27-28cm (69-71cm)
                     $9,000-$11,000
Boxed set: 12in (30cm) baby with three
character heads (233, 235, 237)
                     $7,500-$8,500**

**Not enough price samples to compute
a reliable range.

Right: 12in (31cm) 248 character.
Dorothy Hunt, Sweetbriar.

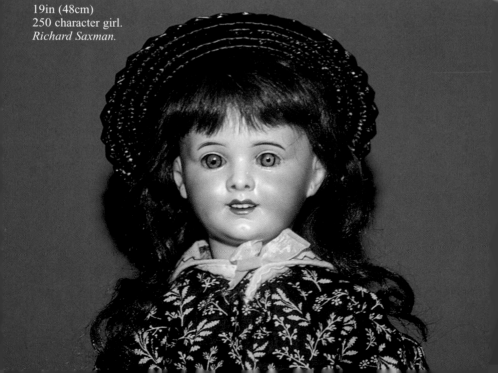

19in (48cm)
250 character girl.
Richard Saxman.

Bruno Schmidt

Marked B.S.W. Child Doll: Ca. 1898-on. Bisque head, good wig, sleep eyes, open mouth; jointed composition child body; dressed; all in good condition.

18-20in (46-51cm)	**$450-$500**
24-26in (61-66cm)	**$650-$750**

Marked B.S.W. Character Dolls: Bisque socket head, glass eyes; jointed composition body; dressed; all in good condition.

#2048, 2094, 2096, (so-called "Tommy Tucker"), molded hair, open mouth:

13-14in (33-36cm)	**$900-$1,100**
19-21in (48-53cm)	**$1,350-$1,450**
25-26in (64-66cm)	**$1,700-$1,900**

#2048, (closed mouth) toddler:

20-21in (51-53cm)	**$3,250-$3,500**

#2042, (molded hair, painted eyes):

16in (41cm) toddler, at auction	**$2,600**

FACTS
Bruno Schmidt, doll factory, Waltershausen, Thüringia, Germany. Heads by Bähr & Pröschild, Ohrdruf, Thüringia, Germany. 1898-on.
Mark:

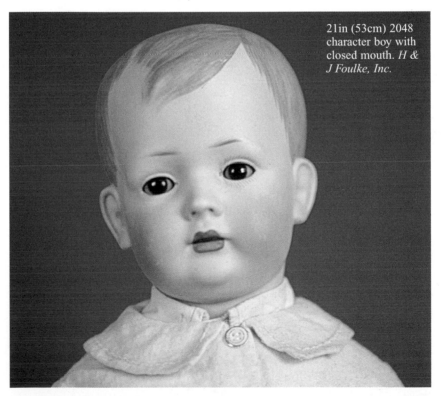

21in (53cm) 2048 character boy with closed mouth. *H & J Foulke, Inc.*

#2048 (closed mouth) toddler:
20-21in (51-53cm)   **$3,250-$3,500**
#2072:
23in (58cm) toddler
$4,500-$5,000**
17in (43cm)   **$3,000-$3,500****
#2033, (so-called "Wendy") **(537):**
12-13in (30-33cm)   **$14,000**
15-17in (38-43cm) **$18,000-$22,000**
20in (51cm)   **$30,000**
#2023 (539):
24in (61cm) at auction   **$3,000**
#2025 (529), closed mouth, wigged:
22in (56cm)   **$6,500-$7,000**
#2097, #692, character baby, open
mouth:
13-14in (33-36cm)   **$450-$500**
18in (46cm)   **$650-$750**
24in (61cm)   **$1,000**
#2097, toddler:
17in (43cm)   **$950-$1,050**
#425, all-bisque baby:
5½-6in (13-15cm)   **$300-$350**
#426, all-bisque toddler:
9½in (24cm)   **$1,200****

**Not enough price samples to compute
a reliable range.

Franz Schmidt

Marked S & C Child Doll: Ca. 1890-
on. Perfect bisque socket head, good
wig, sleep eyes, open mouth; jointed
composition child body; dressed; all in
good condition. Some are Mold #293
or 269.

6in (15cm)   **$250-$300**
16-18in (41-46cm)   **$400-$450**
22-24in (56-61cm)   **$550-$650**
29-30in (74-76cm)   **$900-$1,100**
Flapper: 20in (51cm), flirty eyes
$750

11in (28cm) 537 character girl. *Private Collection.*

16in (41cm) 1294 character baby. *H & J Foulke, Inc.*

42in (107cm)   **$3,000-$3,200**
Shoulder head, kid body:
   26in (66cm)   **$550-$600**
Mark:

    S & C
SIMON & HALBIG
    28

Marked F.S. & Co. Character Baby:
Ca. 1910. Perfect bisque character head,
good wig, sleep eyes, open mouth, may
have open nostrils; jointed bent-limb
composition body; suitably dressed; all
in good condition.

#1271, 1272, 1295, 1296, 1297, 1310:
Baby:
   12-14in (31-36cm)   **$500-$550**
   20-21in (51-53cm)   **$750-$800**
   26-27in (66-69cm)   **$1,400-$1,500**
Toddler:
   7in (18cm), five-piece body   **$850**
   13-15in (33-38cm)   **$850-$950**
   19-21in (48-53cm)   **$1,300-$1,500**
   26-27in (66-69cm)   **$1,750-$1,950**

#1266, bald head, painted eyes, closed
mouth:
   16-17in (41-43cm) **$3,500-$3,900****
#1267, open/closed mouth, painted
eyes: 24in (61cm) at auction   **$2,800**
#1286, molded hair with blue ribbon,
glass eyes, open smiling mouth:
   16in (41cm) toddler   **$4,000****
Mark:

   1295
F. S. & Co.
Made in
Germany
    30

****Not enough price samples to compute a
reliable range.

FACTS
Franz Schmidt & Co., doll factory,
Georgenthal near Waltershausen,
Thüringia, Germany.
Heads by Simon & Halbig,
Gräfenhain, Thüringia, Germany.
1890-on.

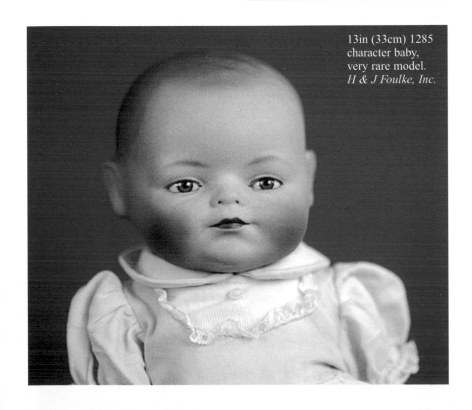

13in (33cm) 1285
character baby,
very rare model.
H & J Foulke, Inc.

Schmitt

Marked Schmitt Bébé: Ca. 1879. Perfect bisque socket head with skin or good wig, large paperweight eyes, closed mouth, pierced ears; Schmitt-jointed composition body with flat bottom; appropriate clothes; all in good condition.

Long face, (For photograph, see *13th Blue Book*, page 179.):

    16-18in (41-46cm) **$15,000-$16,000**
    23-25in (58-64cm) **$20,000-$22,000**
    30in (76cm) **$26,000-$28,000**

Short face (parted lips):

    14-16in (36-41cm) **$11,000-$12,500**
    22in (56cm) **$15,500-$17,500**

Oval/round face, (For photograph, see *11th Blue Book,* page 321.):

    11-13in (28-33cm)
            $9,000-$10,000**
    15-17in (38-43cm)
            $12,000-$14,000**

Cup and saucer neck: 17in (43cm) at auction   **$17,050**

Open/closed mouth, two rows of teeth:

    24in (61cm)   **$25,000****

Wax-over papier-mâché head:

    16in (41cm)   **$2,200-$2,600**
    23in (58cm) all original, with extra dresses, at auction   **$5,750**

**Not enough price samples to compute a reliable range.

FACTS
Schmitt & Fils, Paris, France, 1854-1891.
Mark: On both head and body:

16in (41cm) bébé. *Richard Wright Antiques.*

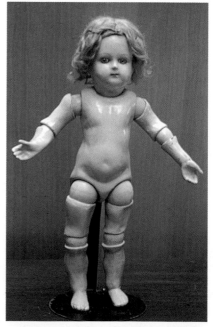

13in (33cm) bébé with wax-over papier-mâché head. *Private Collection.*

Schoenau & Hoffmeister

Child Doll: Perfect bisque head, original or good wig, sleep eyes, open mouth; ball-jointed body; original or good clothes; all in nice condition.

#1906, 1909, 5700, 5800:

14-16in (36-41cm)	**$350-$400**
21-23in (53-58cm)	**$450-$500**
28-30in (71-76cm)	**$750-$850**
33in (84cm)	**$1,100-$1,200**
39in (99cm)	**$2,200-2,400**

#4000, 4600, 5000, 5500:

15-17in (38-43cm)	**$425-$450**
22in (56cm)	**$550-$600**
26in (66cm)	**$800-$850**

Künstlerkopf:

24-26in (61-66cm)	**$850-$950**

Shoulder head, kid body:

18-20in (46-51cm)	**$275-$350**
13-15in (33-38cm) hinged pink kid body	**$425-$475**

FACTS
Schoenau & Hoffmeister, Porzellanfabrick Burggrub, Burggrub, Bavaria, Germany, porcelain factory, 1901-on. Arthur Schoenau also owned a doll factory. 1884-on.
Trademarks: Hanna, Burggrub Baby, Bébé Carmencita, Viola, Künstlerkopf, Das Lachende Baby.
Mark:

A S   S ☆(PB) H   4600   Germany

Right: 12in (31cm) A.S. child. *H & J Foulke, Inc.*

Below: 24in (61cm) 1909 child. *H & J Foulke, Inc.*

11in (28cm)
pouty baby.
*H & J
Foulke, Inc.*

Character Baby: 1910-on. Perfect bisque socket head, good wig, sleep eyes, open mouth; composition bent-limb baby body; all in good condition. **#169, 769** "Burggrub Baby" or "Porzellanfabrik Burggrub."

13-15in (33-38cm)	**$325-$425**
18-20in (46-51cm)	**$475-$575**
23-24in (58-61cm)	**$700-$750**
28in (71cm)	**$900-$1,000**

Painted bisque: 14in (36cm) toddler, factory original   **$325-$350**

Hanna:
Baby:

14-16in (36-41cm)	**$650-$750**
20-22in (51-56cm)	**$900-$1,000**

Toddler:

14-16in (36-41cm)	**$900-$1,000**

Brown: See page 56.

OX: 15in (38cm) toddler   **$1,400-$1,500****
Das Lachende Baby, 1930:
   23-24in (58-61cm) **$2,200-$2,500****

Princess Elizabeth, 1929, chubby five-piece body:

17in (43cm)	**$1,700-$1,900**
20-23in (51-58cm)	**$2,000-$2,200**

Pouty Baby: Ca. 1925. Perfect bisque solid dome head with painted hair, tiny sleep eyes, closed pouty mouth; cloth body with composition arms and legs; dressed; all in good condition.
   11-12in (28-31cm)   **$600-$700**

**Not enough price samples to compute a reliable range.

Schoenhut

Salesman's Cutaway Sample
$800-$1,000
Original Stand   **$75-$100**
Original Shoes: very good condition
$200-$250
Character: 1911-1930. Wooden head and spring-jointed body, marked head and/or body; original or appropriate wig, brown or blue intaglio eyes, open/closed mouth with painted teeth or closed mouth; original or suitable clothing; original paint may have a few scuffs.
14-21in (36-53cm):
  Excellent condition **$1,700-$2,100***
  Good, some wear **$1,150-$1,350***

Character with carved hair: Ca. 1911-1930. Wooden head with carved hair, comb marks, possibly a ribbon or bow, intaglio eyes, mouth usually closed; spring-jointed wooden body; original or suitable clothes; original paint may have a few scuffs.
14-21in (36-53cm):
  Excellent condition **$2,200-$2,500**
  Good, some wear **$1,600-$1,800**
  Early style **$5,000-$8,000**
Tootsie Wootsie: 15in (38cm) at auction **$4,900**

*Allow extra for rare faces and exceptional original condition.

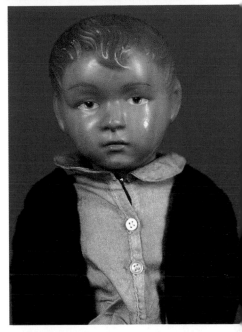
14in (36cm) 204 character with walking body. *Private Collection.*

FACTS
Albert Schoenhut & Co., Philadelphia, PA, U.S.A. 1872-on. Wood, spring-jointed, holes in bottom of feet to fit metal stand. 11-21in (28-53cm).
Designer: Early: Adolph Graziana and Mr. Leslie; later: Harry E. Schoenhut.
Mark: Paper label:

Incised:

SCHOENHUT DOLL
PAT. JAN. 17, '11, U.S.A.
& FOREIGN COUNTRIES

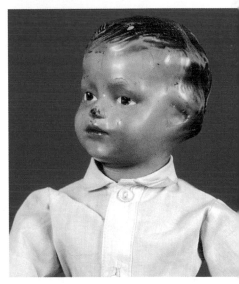
17in (43cm) 205 character. *Private Collection.*

Snickelfritz: 15in (38cm) with wear
                                $3,500**

Carved hat, at auction $9,100**
Mannekin Man: 20in (51cm) $2,500

Baby Face: Ca. 1913-1930. Wooden
head and fully-jointed toddler or bent-
limb baby body, marked head and/or
body; painted hair or mohair wig, painted eyes, open or closed mouth; suitably
dressed; original paint; all in good
condition, with some wear.
Mark:

Baby:	
12in (31cm)	$550-$600
15-16in (38-41cm)	$700-$800
Toddler:	
11in (28cm)	$800-$900
14in (36cm)	$800-$850*
16-17in (41-43cm)	$850-$950*

Mama Doll: 1924-1927. Wood head
and hands, cloth body:
   14-17in (36-43cm) **$1,100-$1,200**

Walker: Ca. 1919-1930. All-wood with
"baby face," mohair wig, painted eyes;
curved arms, straight legs with "walker" joint at hip; no holes in bottom of
feet; original or appropriate clothes; all
in good condition; original mint.
   13-17in (33-43cm) $700-$900+

Miss Dolly: Ca. 1915-1930. Wooden
head and spring-jointed wooden body;
original or appropriate mohair wig,
decal eyes, open/closed mouth with
painted teeth; original paint; original or
suitable clothes.
14-21in (36-53cm):
   Excellent condition $750-$850
   Good condition, some wear
                                $550-$650
Sleep Eyes:
   Excellent condition $1,000-$1,200
   Mint, all original, at auction $1,600

All-Composition: Ca. 1924. Molded
blonde curly hair, painted eyes, tiny
closed mouth; original or appropriate
clothing; in good condition.
Paper label on back:

   13in (33cm) $500-$600**

+Allow $100 additional for original shoes
with "wedge" sole.
*Allow more for mint condition.
**Not enough price samples to compute a
reliable range.

16in (41cm) character, copy of K & R
114. *Private Collection.*

Right: 16in (41cm) mama doll. *Private Collection.*

Below: 19in (48cm) *Miss Dolly. Private Collection.*

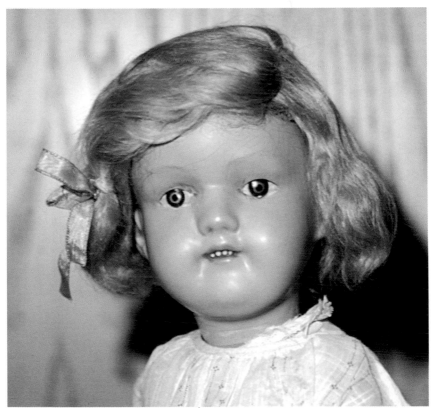

Simon & Halbig

Shoulder head with molded hair: Ca. 1870s. Perfect bisque shoulder head, painted or glass eyes, closed mouth, molded hair; cloth body, bisque lower arms; appropriately dressed; all in good condition.

Mark: *S 7 H*

on front shoulder plate

18-20in (46-51cm) **$1,500-$2,000**
9in (23cm) painted eyes, swivel neck **$1,250**
12in (31cm) glass eyes, swivel neck **$1,500**

Fashion Doll (*Poupée*): Ca. 1870s. Perfect bisque socket head on bisque shoulder plate, good mohair wig or molded blonde hair, glass eyes, closed mouth; gusseted kid lady body; appropriately dressed; all in good condition. No marks. (For face, see *12th Blue Book* page 330.)
15-16in (38-41cm) **$2,500-$3,000**
Twill over wood body:
9-10in (23-25cm) **$3,300-$3,800**
15-16in (38-41cm) **$5,200-$5,700**
With bisque feet: 9½in (24cm) at auction **$4,620**

Child doll with closed mouth: Ca. 1879. Perfect bisque socket head on ball-jointed wood and composition body; good wig, glass set or sleep eyes, closed mouth, pierced ears; dressed; all in good condition. (See *Simon & Halbig Dolls, The Artful Aspect* for photographs of mold numbers not shown here.)
#719: 20-23in (51-58cm) **$5,500-$6,500**
#749: 20-22in (51-56cm) **$3,800****
#905, 908: 14-17in (36-43cm) **$3,500-$4,500****

FACTS
Simon & Halbig, porcelain factory, Gräfenhain, Thüringia, Germany, purchased by Kämmer & Reinhardt in 1920. 1869-on.
Mark:

S 13 H
949
1079-2
DEP
S H
Germany

19in (48cm) 908 closed-mouth child. *Ann Lloyd.*

#929:
17-18in (43-46cm)   **$3,800- $4,200**
27in (69cm) at auction   **$7,250**
#939:
14-15in (36-38cm)   **$2,500-$2,700**
26in (66cm)   **$4,000**
#949:
15-16in (38-41cm)   **$2,100-$2,500**
22-23in (56-58cm)   **$2,900-$3,100**
27-28in (69-71cm)   **$3,800-$4,200**
#979: 15-16in (38-41cm)   **$3,000****
Kid or Cloth Body:
   #720, 740, 940, 950:
9-10in (23-25cm)   **$550-$650**
16-18in (41-46cm)   **$1,200-$1,400**
22in (56cm)   **$1,600-$1,800**
   #949: 18-21in (46-53cm)
     $1,800-$2,200
   #920: 16-20in (41-51cm)
     $2,000-$2,500**

All-Bisque Child: 1880-on. All-bisque child with swivel neck, pegged shoulders and hips; appropriate mohair wig, glass eyes, open or closed mouth; molded stockings and shoes.
#886, over-the-knee black or blue stockings, low orange or blue stockings; open mouth:
4½in (11cm)   **$750-$800***
5½-6in (14-15cm)   **$1,100-$1,300***
7-7½ (18-19cm)   **$1,600-$2,000***
8½-9in (22-23cm)   **$2,500-$3,500***
#890, over-the-knee black stockings; open mouth:
3¾in (9cm)   **$500**
5-5½in (13-14cm)   **$725-$825**
7-7½in (18-19cm)   **$1,100-$1,250**
Closed mouth, round face:
6-6½in (15-16cm)   **$1,850-$2,150**
Jointed knees   **$5,500****
Closed mouth, five-strap bootines:
7½-8in (19-21cm)   **$3,600-$4,400****

*Allow extra for strap bootines and square cut teeth.
**Not enough price samples to compute a reliable range.

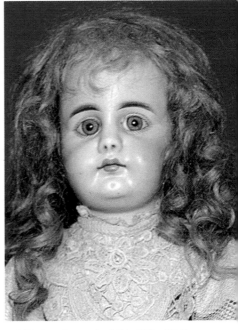

949 closed-mouth child. *Elliot Zirlin.*

4¾in (11cm) all-bisque with long blue stockings. *H & J Foulke, Inc.*

Above: 15in (38cm) 1009 child on original French body. *H & J Foulke, Inc.*

Below: 35in (89cm) 1079 child. *H & J Foulke, Inc.*

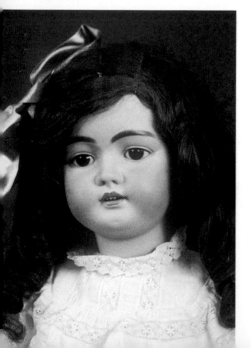

Child doll with open mouth and composition body: Ca. 1889 to 1930s. Perfect bisque head, good wig, sleep or paperweight eyes, open mouth, pierced ears; original ball-jointed composition body (may be French); very pretty clothes; all in nice condition. (See *Simon & Halbig Dolls, The Artful Aspect* for photographs of mold numbers not shown here.)

#719, 739, 749, 759, 769, 939, 979:
17-19in (43-45cm)	**$1,900-$2,300**
22-23in (56-58cm)	**$2,600-$3,100**

#719: 23in (58cm) Edison, operating
$4,800

#905, 908: 12-14in (31-36cm)
$1,500-$1,800

#929: 23in (58cm) at auction   **$3,800**

#939: 30in (76cm)   **$3,500**

#949:
16-18in (41-46cm)	**$1,600-$1,800**
28-29in (71-74cm)	**$2,600-$2,900**
36in (91cm) at auction	**$5,500**

#1009:
15-16in (38-41cm)	**$800-$900**
19-21in (48-53cm)	**$1,100-$1,300**
24-25in (61-64cm)	**$1,500-$1,800**

#1039:
16-18in (41-46cm)	**$800-$1,000***
23-25in (58-64cm)	**$1,150-$1,350***

#1039, key-wind walking body, (R.D.):
16-22in (41-56cm)	**$1,700-$1,800**

#1039, walking, kissing:
20-22in (51-56cm)	**$1,050-$1,250**

#1078, 1079:
7-10in (18-26cm) five-piece body	**$425-$500**
8in (20cm)	**$750-$800**
10-12in (25-31cm)	**$800-$900**
14-15in (36-38cm)	**$625-$650**
17-19in (43-48cm)	**$725-$750**
22-24in (56-61cm)	**$800-$900**
28-30in (71-76cm)	**$1,000-$1,200**
34-35in (86-89cm)	**$1,800-$2,000**
42in (107cm)	**$3,800-$4,200**

#1109:
14in (36cm)	**$850**
18in (46cm)	**$1,100**

#1139: 26in (66cm)   **$1,850****

*Allow $100 extra for flirty eyes.
**Not enough price samples to compute a reliable range.

#1248, 1249, Santa:

13-15in (33-38cm)	**$900-$1,000**
21-24in (53-61cm)	**$1,300-$1,500**
26-28in (66-71cm)	**$1,700-$1,900**
32in (81cm)	**$2,200-$2,300**
38in (96cm)	**$3,200**
Head only: 5in (13cm)	**$715**

#540, 550, 570, Baby Blanche:

22-24in (56-61cm)	**$700-$800**

#176, (A. Hülss), Flapper:

18in (46cm)	**$750-$850**

Child doll with open mouth and kid body: Ca. 1889 to 1930s. Perfect bisque swivel head on shoulder plate or shoulder head with stationary neck, sleep eyes; well costumed; all in good condition.

#1010, 1040, 1080, 1260:

14-16in (36-41cm)	**$500-$600**
21-23in (53-58cm)	**$700-$800**

#1009, 1039:

17-19in (43-48cm)	**$850-$950**

#1250, 1260: with pink kid body and composition arms:

14-16in (36-41cm)	**$550-$650**
22-24in (56-61cm)	**$800-$900**
29in (74cm)	**$1,000-$1,100**

#949, 19-21in (48-53cm)

	$1,200-$1,400

So-called "Little Women" type: Ca. 1900. Mold number **1160**. Shoulder head with fancy mohair wig, glass set eyes, closed mouth; cloth body with bisque limbs, molded boots; dressed; all in good condition.

5½-7in (14-18cm)	**$350-$400**
10-11in (25-28cm)	**$425-$475**
14in (36cm)	**$650-$750**

Character Child: Ca. 1909. Perfect bisque socket head with wig or molded hair, painted or glass eyes, open or closed mouth, character face; jointed composition body; dressed; all in good condition. (See *Simon & Halbig Dolls, The Artful Aspect* for photographs of mold numbers not shown here.)

#120: 18-19in (46-48cm)

	$3,200-$3,400

#150:

11in (28cm)	**$5,500-$6,000**
14in (36cm)	**$12,000**

20in (51cm)	**$23,000**
24in (61cm)	**$30,000**

#151:

14-15in (36-38cm)	**$5,000-$5,500**
18in (46cm)	**$7,500**
24in (61cm)	**$13,000**

#153:

14in (36cm)	**$18,000-$22,000**
17in (43cm)	**$35,000-$40,000**

#174: 21in (53cm)   **$1,750-$1,950**

#600: 19in (48cm) toddler

	$1,500-$1,650

#1279:

14-17in (36-43cm)	**$2,000-$2,400**
19-21in (48-53cm)	**$2,700-$3,200**
27in (69cm)	**$5,500-$6,000**
33in (84cm)	**$6,500**

#1299: 14-17in (36-43cm)

	$1,200-$1,600

17in (43cm) 1249 *Santa* child. *H & J Foulke, Inc.*

#1339:
　18in (46cm)　　$1,000-$1,100**
　28-32 (71-81cm)　$1,900-$2,100**
#1388, 23in (58cm)　　$30,000**
#1398, 23in (58cm)　　$20,000**
IV, #1448:
　13-14in (33-36cm)
　　　　　$16,000-$18,000**
　17-18in (43-46cm)　$24,000**
　25in (63cm) at auction　$33,000

Character Baby: Ca. 1909 to 1930s. Perfect bisque head, molded hair or wig, sleep or painted eyes, open or open/closed mouth; composition bent-limb baby or toddler body; nicely dressed; all in good condition. (See *Simon & Halbig Dolls, The Artful Aspect* for photographs of mold numbers not shown here.)

#156 (A. Hülss):
　Baby:
　　15-17in (38-43cm)　$600-$700
　　23in (58cm)　$1,000-$1,100
　Toddler, five-piece body:
　　15in (38cm)　　$750-$800
　　29in (73cm)　　$2,400**

#1294:
　Baby:
　　17-19in (43-48cm)　$700-$800

　23-25in (58-64cm)　$1,100-$1,300
　28in (71cm) with clockwork eyes
　　　　　　$2,500**
　Toddler: 20in (51cm)　$1,500-$1,600
#1428:
　Baby:
　　10-11in (25-28cm)　$1,000-$1,200
　　13-14in (33-36cm)　$1,500-$1,800
　　21in (53cm)　$2,700-$3,000
　Toddler:
　　11in (28cm)　　$1,600
　　15-18in (38-46cm)　$2,400-$2,600
　　24in (61cm)　$3,750-$4,250
#1488:
　15in (38cm)　　$4,000-$4,200
　Baby: 20in (51cm)　　$5,500
　Toddler: 16-18in (41-46cm)
　　　　　　$4,500-$5,000
#1489 Erika, baby:
　21-22in (53-56cm)　$3,700-$4,200**
#1498:
　Baby: 16in (41cm)　　$2,500**
　Toddler: 22in (56cm)　　$4,600**
#172, baby:
　14-15in (36-38cm)　　$3,500**

Lady doll: Ca. 1910. Perfect bisque socket head, good wig, sleep eyes,

**Not enough price samples to compute a reliable range.

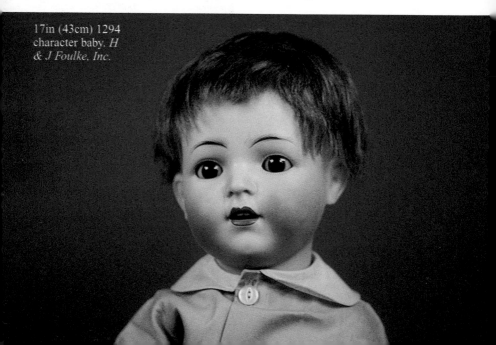

17in (43cm) 1294 character baby. *H & J Foulke, Inc.*

pierced ears; lady body, molded bust, slim arms and legs; dressed; all in good condition.

#1159 (may have an H. Handwerck body):

12in (31cm)	**$1,100-$1,200**
19-20in (48-51cm)	**$2,100-$2,400**
25-27in (64-69cm)	**$3,000-$3,500**

#1468, 1469:

13-15in (33-38cm) naked	
	$2,500-$3,000
Original clothes	**$3,500-$4,300**

#1303 lady:

20in (51cm)	**$18,000-$20,000****
16in (41cm) Candy Container	
Marquis, at auction	**$13,500**

#152 lady: 24in (61cm) at auction
                                    $47,000**
#1308 man: 13in (33cm)   **$13,000****
#1307: 21in (53cm)   **$12,500**
#1303 Indian: 21in (53cm) **$17,000****
#1305: 18in (46cm)   **$12,500**

**Not enough price samples to compute a reliable range.

16in (41cm) 1488 character toddler. *Mary Barnes Kelley Collection.*

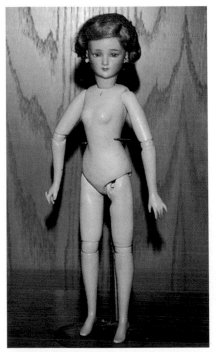

14in (36cm) 1469 lady. *Private Collection.*

22½in (57cm) 1498 character. *Mary Barnes Kelley Collection.*

Snow Babies and Santas

Snow Babies: All-bisque immobile figures with snowsuits and caps of pebbly-textured bisque; painted features; various positions.

Standing: 1½in (4cm)	**$55-$65**
2½in (6cm)	**$150-$160**
4¾in (12cm)	**$400-$450**
Sitting:	
1½in (4cm)	**$50-$60**
3-3½in (8-9cm)	**$250-$300**
Jointed arms and legs:	
3½in (9cm)	**$350-$400**
5¼in (13cm)	**$450-$500**
Shoulder head on cloth body:	
4½in (11cm)	**$185-$210**
10in (25cm)	**$300-$350**
Fine early quality with high hood:	
2in (5cm)	**$185-$210**
With musical instrument:	
2in (5cm)	**$125-$150**
Twins: 2in (5cm)	**$150-$160**
Snowman: 2½in (6cm)	**$100-$125**
Snow bear: 1½in (4cm)	**$60-$75**

Action Figures:

Huskies pulling sled with snow baby: 3in (9cm)	**$300**
Reindeer pulling sled with snow baby: 2in (5cm)	**$275**
Snow baby riding reindeer: 2½in (6cm)	**$325**
Snow baby riding snow bear: 3in (9cm)	**$350**
Tumbling snow baby: 2½in (6cm)	**$175-$185**
Snow baby on sled:	
1½in (4cm)	**$125**
3in (8cm)	**$225**
Three snow babies on sled	**$225**
Santa on snow bear	**$400-$450**
Snow babies sliding on cellar door: 2½in (6cm)	**$275-$325**
Snow dog and snowman on sled: 2in (5cm)	**$275-$325**
Santa going down chimney	**$375**
Santa on train	**$425**
Snow Children:	
Seated girl: 1½in (4cm)	**$135**
Boy or girl on sled	**$185-$210**

"No Snows:"

Boy and girl on sled: 2in (5cm)	**$165-$185**
Skiing boy: 2½in (6cm)	**$110**
Santa:	
3in (9cm)	**$125-$135**
2in (5cm)	**$95**

Group of German Santa figurines. *H & J Foulke, Inc.*

Steiff

Steiff Doll: Felt, plush or velvet, jointed; seam down middle of face, painted features, button eyes; original clothes; most are character dolls, many have large shoes to enable them to stand; all in excellent condition.

Children (Character Dolls):
11-12in (28-31cm)	**$1,000-$1,250**
16-17in (41-43cm)	**$1,500-$1,650**
Black child: 17in (43cm)	**$2,100**
Adults:*	**$2,000 up**
Gnome: 12in (31cm)	**$700-$900**

*Fewer women are available than men.

U.S. Zone Germany: 12in (31cm) child with glass eyes **$500-$600**

Collector's Note: To bring the prices quoted, Steiff dolls must be clean and have good color. Faded and dirty dolls bring only one-third to one-half of these prices.

FACTS
Fräulein Margarete Steiff, Würtemberg, Germany. 1894-on.
Mark: Metal button in ear.

12in (31cm) Gnome.
Nancy A. Smith Collection.

Jules Steiner

Round face: Ca. 1870s. Perfect very pale bisque socket head, appropriate wig, bulgy paperweight eyes, round face, pierced ears; jointed composition body; dressed; all in good condition. **Mark:** None, but sometimes body has a label.

Two rows of pointed teeth:
16-19in (41-48cm)   **$6,000-$7,000**
Closed mouth: 18-22in (46-56cm)
$10,000-$12,000

Gigoteur: Kicking, crying bébé, mechanical key-wind body with composition arms and lower legs:
17-18in (43-46cm)   **$2,100-$2,300**
23in (58cm)   **$2,600-$2,750**
21in(53cm) all original and boxed, at auction   **$4,800**

Täufling-type body: Bisque shoulders, hips and lower arms and legs:
18-21in (46-53cm)   **$6,500**
Swivel neck   **$7,500**

Marked C or A Series Steiner Bébé: 1880s. Perfect socket head, cardboard pate, appropriate wig, sleep eyes with wire mechanism or bulgy paperweight eyes with tinting on upper eyelids, closed mouth, round face, pierced ears with tinted tips; jointed composition body with straight wrists and stubby fingers (sometimes with bisque hands); appropriately dressed; all in good condition. Sizes 4/0 (8in) to 8 (38in). Series "C" more easily found than "A."
Mark: (incised)

$S^{IE} \; A \; 0$

(red script)

J Steiner ... B^té S.g.D.g J Bourgoin S^té

(incised)

$S^{IE} \; C \; 4$

(red stamp)

J. STEINER B. S. G.D.G.

8-10in (20-25cm)   **$6,000-$7,000**
15-16in (38-41cm)   **$6,500-$7,000**
21-24in (53-61cm)   **$8,000-$9,000**
28in (71cm)   **$12,000**

Wax pate with inset hair:
15½in (39cm)   **$25,000****

Series G, closed mouth:
15in (38cm)   **$17,000**
18in (46cm)   **$21,000**
28in (71cm)   **$32,000**

**Not enough price samples to compute a reliable range.

FACTS
Jules Nicolas Steiner and successors, Paris, France. 1855-1908.

8in (20cm) Sie C *Bébé Steiner. H & J Foulke, Inc.*

16in (41cm) Fire A
Bébé Steiner.
Private Collection.

17in (43cm)
A-10 *Le Petit*
Parisien. Linda
Kellerman.

8in (20cm) Fire A *Bébé Steiner. Private Collection.*

Figure A Steiner Bébé: Ca. 1887-on. Perfect bisque socket head, cardboard pate, appropriate wig, paperweight eyes, closed mouth, pierced ears; jointed composition body; appropriately dressed; all in good condition. Figure "A" more easily found than "C."

Mark: (incised) J. STEINER
B^TE S.G.D.G.
PARIS
F^IRE A 15

Body and/or head may be stamped:
"Le Petit Parisien
BÉBÉ STEINER
MEDAILLE d'OR
PARIS 1889"
or paper label of doll carrying flag
Mark: head (incised):
1892 on   A-19
PARIS
(red stamp):
"LE PARISIEN"
body (purple stamp):
"BÉBÉ 'LE PARISIEN'
MEDAILLE D'OR
PARIS"

8-10in (20-25cm) five-piece body
$3,000-$3,500
8-10in (20-25cm) fully-jointed
$4,000-$5,000
15-16in (38-41cm)   **$5,000-$5,600**
22-24in (56-61cm)   **$6,000-$6,800**
28-30in (71-76cm)   **$7,500-$8,000**
38in (96cm)   **$11,000-$12,000**

Open mouth:
17in (43cm)   **$2,500**
22in (56cm)   **$2,900**
23in (58cm) all original and boxed,
at auction   **$3,900**

Figure B, open mouth with two rows of teeth:
16in (41cm)   **$3,500-$3,700**
23-25in (58-64cm)   **$5,000-$6,000**
32in (81cm) at auction   **$7,000**
Figure C, closed mouth:
19-23in (48-58cm)   **$6,000-$7,500**
Figure D, closed mouth: 25in (64cm)
at auction   **$38,000**

Swaine & Co.

Swaine Character Babies: Ca. 1910-on. Perfect bisque head; composition baby body with bent limbs; dressed; all in good condition. (See previous *Blue Books* for photographs of specific models.)

Incised Lori, molded hair, glass eyes, open/closed mouth:
22-24in (56-61cm)   **$2,500-$2,700**
#232, (open-mouth **Lori**):
8½in (21cm)   **$700-$750**
12-14in (31-36cm)   **$1,000-$1,250**
20-22in (51-56cm)   **$1,600-$1,700**
DIP (wig, glass eyes, closed mouth):
8½–9½2in (21-24cm)   **$700-$750**
11in (28cm)   **$850-$900**
14-16in (36-41cm)   **$1,300-$1,500**
14in (36cm) toddler   **$1,800**
DV (molded hair, glass eyes, open/closed mouth):
13in (33cm)   **$1,300-$1,350**
16in (41cm)   **$1,500-$1,550**
DI (molded hair, intaglio eyes, open/closed mouth):
12-13in (31-33cm)   **$800-$850**

B.P., B.O. (smiling character):
16-18in (41-46cm)   **$5,000-$5,500****
F.P.: 8-9in (20-23cm)   **$1,050-$1,250****
A.P. (wig, painted eyes, closed mouth):
15in (38cm) at auction   **$5,200**
Blonde Molded Curly Hair Boy (intaglio eyes, closed mouth):
17in (43cm) at auction   **$1,800**

**Not enough price samples to compute a reliable range.

FACTS
Swaine & Co., porcelain factory, Hüttensteinach, Sonneberg, Thüringia, Germany. Ca. 1910-on for doll heads.
Mark: Stamped in green:

Pair of Swaine toddlers with painted and glass eyes. *Jensen's Antique Dolls.*

Thuillier

Marked A.T. Child: Perfect bisque head, cork pate, good or appropriate old wig, paperweight eyes, pierced ears, closed mouth; body of wood, kid or composition; appropriate old clothes, excellent quality; in good condition.

Early face, soft features and decoration:
   12-13in (31-33cm) **$30,000-$35,000**
   16-18in (41-46cm) **$40,000-$45,000**
   24in (61cm)   **$55,000-$60,000**

Later face, heavier features and decoration:
   16-18in (41-46cm) **$23,000-$25,000**
   26in (66cm)   **$32,000-$35,000**

Open mouth, two rows of teeth:
   20-22in (51-56cm) **$9,000-$12,000**
   36in (91cm)   **$25,000**

Approximate size chart:
   1 = 9in (23cm)
   3 = 12in (31cm)
   7 = 15½in (39cm)
   9 = 18in (46cm)
   12 = 22-23in (56-58cm)
   15 = 36-37in (91-93cm)

FACTS
A. Thuillier, Paris, France.
Some heads by F. Gaultier. 1875-1893.
Mark:

A.8.T.

21in (53cm)
A.T. *Private Collection.*

Unis

Unis Child Doll: Perfect bisque head, good wig, sleep eyes, open mouth; wood and composition jointed body; pretty clothes; all in nice condition.
#301 or **60** (fully-jointed body):

8-10in (20-25cm)	**$425-$475**
15-17in (38-43cm)	**$650-$700**
23-25in (58-64cm)	**$825-$875**
28in (71cm)	**$950-$1,150**

Five-piece body:

5in (13cm) painted eyes	**$160-$185**
6½in (17cm) glass eyes	**$275-$300**
11-13in (28-33cm)	**$350-$375**

Black or brown bisque:

11-13in (28-33cm)	**$375-$425**
Bleuette: 11in (28cm)	**$950-$1,000**

Princess: See page 112.

#251 character toddler:

14-15in (36-38cm)	**$1,300-$1,500**
28in (71cm)	**$2,200-$2,400**

Composition head **#301** or **#60**:

11-13in (28-33cm)	**$150-$175**
20in (51cm)	**$350-$400**

Composition head **#251** or **#247** toddler:

22in (56cm)	**$650-$750**

FACTS
Société Française de Fabrication de Bébés et Jouets. (S.F.B.J.) of Paris and Montreuil-sous-Bois, France. 1922 on.
Mark:

4in (10cm) all original Unis child. *H & J Foulke, Inc.*

Izannah Walker

Izannah Walker Doll: Stockinette, pressed head, features and hair painted with oils, applied ears; treated limbs; muslin body; appropriate clothes; in very good condition.

Pre-patent dolls:

    17-19in (43-48cm) **$18,000-$22,000**
    Fair condition   **$8,500-$9,500**
    Very worn   **$3,000-$4,000**
1873 patent dolls, molded ears:
    18in (46cm)   **$4,000-$6,000**

FACTS
Izannah Walker, Central Falls, RI, U.S.A. 1873, but probably made as early as 1840s.
Mark: Later dolls are marked:

Patented Nov. 4th 1873

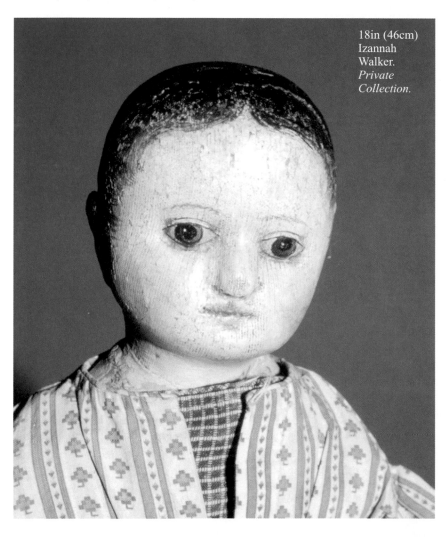

18in (46cm) Izannah Walker. *Private Collection.*

Wax Dolls
(Poured)

English Poured Wax Doll: Various firms in London, England, such as Peck, Montanari, Pierotti, Meech, Marsh, Morrell, Cremer and Edwards. 1850s through the early 1900s. Head, lower arms and legs of wax; cloth body; sometimes stamped with maker or store; set-in hair, glass eyes; lovely elaborate original clothes or very well dressed; all in good condition.

Baby:
  17-19in (43-48cm)
  $1,250-$1,650
  23-24in (58-61cm)
  $1,900-$2,200
Child:
  6in (15cm) all original
  $650-$750
  17-18in (43-46cm)
  $1,700-$2,000
Baby or child, lackluster ordinary face:
  20-22in (51-56cm)
  $800-$1,000
Lady: 22-24in (56-61cm)
  $2,500-$3,000
Man: 19in (48cm)
at auction   **$2,420**

French Fashion Lady, Ca. 1930. Wax head, couturier outfit: 13in (33cm)
  $400-$600

Mechanical Baby in satin-lined wood box, musical: 12in (31cm)   **$350-$450**

Wax (Reinforced)

Reinforced Poured Wax Doll: Poured wax shoulder head lined on the inside with plaster composition, glass eyes (may sleep), closed mouth, open crown, pate, curly mohair or human hair wig nailed on (may be partially inset into the wax around the face); muslin body with wax-over-composition lower limbs (feet may have molded boots); appropriate clothes; all in good condition, but showing some nicks and scrapes.

Child or baby:
  11in (28cm)   **$250-$275**
  14-16in (36-41cm)   **$375-$425**
  19-21in (48-53cm)   **$500-$550**
Lady: 23in (58cm)   **$800-$1,000**
  with molded shoulder plate   **$2,500****
  with molded gloves, all original   **$2,500****
Socket head on ball-jointed composition body (Kestner-type):
  13in (33cm)   **$700-$800**
  19in (48cm)   **$1,200-$1,300**

**Not enough price samples to compute a reliable range.

18½in (47cm) English poured wax child, all original. *H & J Foulke, Inc.*

FACTS
Various firms in Germany. 1860-1890.
Mark: None.

Wax-Over-Composition

English Slit-head Wax: Ca. 1830-1860. Round face, human hair wig, glass eyes (may open and close by a wire), faintly smiling; all in fair condition, showing wear.

18-22in (46-56cm)	**$900-$1,100**
28-30in (71-76cm)	**$1,500-$1,800**

Molded Hair Doll: Ca. 1860-on. German wax-over-composition shoulder head; nice old clothes; all in good condition, good quality.

14-16in (36-41cm)	**$325-$375**
22-25in (56-64cm)	**$550-$650**

Alice hairdo: 16in (41cm) early model, squeaker torso **$650-$750**

Wax-over Doll with Wig: Ca. 1860s to 1900. German. Original clothing or suitably dressed; entire doll in nice condition.
Standard quality:

11-12in (28-31cm)	**$225-$250**
16-18in (41-46cm)	**$300-$350**
22-24in (56-61cm)	**$400-$450**

Superior quality (heavily waxed):

16-18in (41-46cm)	**$425-$475**
25-26in (64-66cm)	**$675-$775**

"Blinking" eye doll, eyes open and close with bellows in torso:
16in (41cm) all original **$1,000**

Molded Bonnet Wax-over Doll: Ca. 1860-1880. German. Nice old clothes; all in good condition.
16-17in (41-43cm), common model **$450-$500**
13½in (35cm) baby with bonnet and real curls **$750-$800**
20-24in (51-61cm) lady with real curls and unusual hat **$2,000-$3,000**

Double-Faced Doll: 1880-on. Fritz Bartenstein. One face crying, one laughing, rotating on a vertical axis by pulling a string, one face hidden by a hood. Body stamped "Bartenstein."
15-16in (38-41cm) **$850**

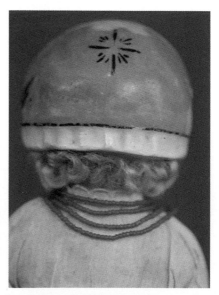

13½in (35cm) wax-over-composition baby with molded bonnet and applied curls, all original. *H & J Foulke, Inc.*

Norah Wellings

Wellings Doll: All-fabric, stitch-jointed shoulders and hips; molded fabric face (also of papier-mâché, sometimes stockinette covered), painted features; all in excellent condition. Most commonly found are sailors, Canadian Mounties, Scots and Black Islanders.

Characters (floppy limbs):

8-10in (20-25cm)	**$75-$100**
13-14in (33-36cm)	**$150-$200**
Glass eyes: 14in (36cm) black	
	$250-$300

Children:

12-13in (31-33cm)	**$400-$500**

16-18in (41-46cm)	**$600-$700**
23in (58cm)	**$900-$1,000**
11½in (29cm) chubby toddler	**$350**
Glass eyes: 16-18in (41-46cm)	
	$700-$800

Boudoir Doll: 22-24in (56-61cm)
$300-$400

Old Couple: 26in (66cm)
$1,200-$1,500 pair

Bobby: 16in (41cm) glass eyes
$800-$1,000

Harry the Hawk: 10in (25cm)	**$200**
Nightdress Case	**$400**
Baby: 11in (28cm)	**$350-$400**
Rabbit: 9in (23cm)	**$350**

FACTS
Victoria Toy Works, Wellington, Shropshire, England, for Norah Wellings. 1926-Ca. 1960.
Designer: Norah Wellings
Mark: On tag on foot: "Made in England by Norah Wellings."

22in (56cm) *Miss Smith*, all original. *H & J Foulke, Inc.*

Wood, American
(Springfield Dolls)

Joel Ellis Wooden Doll: Co-operative Manufacturing Co., Springfield, Vermont. 1873-1874. All wood with mortise and tenon joints; carved hair painted black (a few blondes), painted eyes; metal hands and feet painted black (a few bright blue). Marked only with a black paper band around waist with 1873 patent date. Fair condition, most have paint chips on the face.

12in (31cm)	**$1,200-$1,500**
15in (38cm)	**$1,800-$2,000**

Martin, Sanders & Johnson Wooden Doll: Jointed Doll Co., Springfield, Vermont. 1879-1885. Composition head over wood core (usually blonde); fully-jointed wood body; metal hands and feet painted blue. Marked only with a black paper band around waist with "Improved Jointed Doll" and patent dates ('79, '80 and '82). Fair condition.

12in (31cm)	**$850-$950**

Mason & Taylor Wooden Doll: D.M. Smith Co., Springfield, Vermont. 1879-1885. Composition head over wood core (usually blonde); fully-jointed wood body; early dolls had wooden spoon-type hands; blue metal feet. Fair condition.

12in (31cm)	**$850-$950**

15in (38cm) Joel Ellis jointed wood doll. *Private Collection.*

Wood, English

William & Mary Period: Ca. 1690. Carved wooden face, painted eyes, tiny lines comprising eyebrows and eyelashes, rouged cheeks, flax or hair wig; wood body, cloth arms, carved wood hands (fork shaped), wood-jointed legs; appropriate clothes; all in fair condition.

    12-17in (31-43cm)   **$40,000**

Queen Anne Period: Ca. early 1700s. Carved wooden face, dark glass eyes (sometimes painted), dotted eyebrows and eyelashes; jointed wood body, cloth upper arms; appropriate clothes; all in fair condition.

    18in (46cm)   **$18,500**
    24in (61cm)   **$25,000**

Georgian Period: Mid to late 1700s. Round wooden head with gesso covering, inset glass eyes (later sometimes blue), dotted eyelashes and eyebrows, flax or hair wig; jointed wood body with pointed torso; appropriate clothes; all in fair condition.

    12-13in (31-33cm)   **$2,500-$3,200**
    16-18in (41-46cm)   **$4,500-$5,000**
    24in (61cm)   **$6,000**

Early 19th Century: Wooden head, gessoed, painted eyes, flax or hair wig; pointed torso; old clothes (dress usually longer than legs); all in fair condition.

    13in (33cm)   **$1,300-$1,600**
    16-21in (41-53cm)   **$2,000-$3,000**

19in (48cm) Queen Anne, Ca. 1725. *Private Collection.*

Wood, German
(Peg-Woodens)

Early to Mid 19th Century: Delicately carved head, varnished, carved and painted hair and features, with a yellow tuck comb in hair, painted spit curls, sometimes earrings; mortise and tenon peg joints; old clothes; all in fair condition.

4in (10cm)	**$450-$550**
6-7in (15-18cm)	**$650-$750**
12-13in (31-33cm)	**$1,350-$1,450**
17-18in (43-46cm)	**$1,800-$2,000**

28in (71cm) exceptional carving, naked, at auction **$16,200**
Fortune tellers: 17-20in (43-51cm)
$2,500-$3,000
Shell dolls: 8½in (28cm)
$1,200-$1,300 pair
Peddler with lovely old wares:
8in (20cm) **$2,400**

Late 19th Century: Wooden head with painted hair, carving not so elaborate as previously, sometimes earrings, spit curls; dressed; all in good condition.

1in (2½cm)	**$100-$125**
4in (10cm)	**$125-$135**
7-8in (18-20cm)	**$175-$225**

12in (31cm)	**$350-$375**
16in (41cm)	**$450-$500**
21in (53cm)	**$1,000-$1,100**

Turned red torso: 10in (25cm)
$150-$200
Wood shoulder head, carved bun hairdo, cloth body, wood limbs:

9in (23cm) all original	**$350-$400**
17in (43cm)	**$500-$550**
24in (61cm)	**$800-$900**

Early 20th Century: Turned wood head, carved nose, painted hair; peg-jointed; painted white lower legs, painted black shoes.
11-12in (28-31cm) **$60-$80**

FACTS
Craftsmen of the Grödner Tal, Austria, and Sonneberg, Germany, such as Insam & Prinoth (1820-1830), Gorden Tirol and Nürnberg verlegers of peg-wooden dolls and wood doll heads. Late 18th to 20th century. **Mark:** None.

11½in (29cm) peg-wooden with yellow tuck comb. *Sweetbriar.*

Wood, German
(20ᵀᴴ Century)

Wood, Swiss

"Bébé Tout en Bois" (Doll All of Wood): All of wood, fully jointed; wig, inset glass eyes, open mouth with teeth; appropriate clothes; all in fair to good condition.

Child:

13in (33cm)	**$425-$475**
17-19in (43-48cm)	**$650-$750**
22-24in (56-61cm)	**$950**
18in (46cm) mint, all original	**$1,100**
Baby: 16½in (42cm)	**$400-$500**

Swiss Linden Wood Doll: Wooden head with hand-carved features and hair with good detail (males sometimes have carved hats); all-carved wood-jointed body; original regional attire; excellent condition.

9-10in (23-25cm)	**$275-$375**
12in (31cm)	**$450-$550**
15in (38cm)	**$750-$850**
17-18in (43-46cm)	**$1,000-$1,200**
12in (31cm) boy with carved hat	**$600-$650**
13in (33cm) wood and cloth babies	**$450**

FACTS
Various companies, such as
Rudolf Schneider and Schilling,
Sonneberg, Thüringia, Germany.
1901-1914.
For French trade.
Mark: Usually none; sometimes
Schilling "winged angel" trademark.

FACTS
Various craftsmen, Brienz, Switzerland.
20th century.
Mark: Usually a paper label on
wrist or clothes.

16in (41cm) *Tout en Bois. H & J Foulke, Inc.*

15in (38cm) Swiss Wood, all original. *H & J Foulke, Inc.*

Worsted Dolls

Worsted or **Woolen Doll:** Stockinette face, wool hair, black bead eyes, embroidered features; stockinette or cloth body; original crocheted or knitted wool clothes; sometimes a knotted wool fabric was used; all original clothing; excellent condition.

11in (28cm)	**$100-$100**
15in (38cm)	**$165-$185**

FACTS
Emil Wittzack, Gotha, Thüringia, Germany, and probably others. 1830s-1917. Unmarked.

11in (28cm) worsted doll, all original. *H & J Foulke, Inc.*

Modern & Collectible Dolls

Dolls in this section are listed alphabetically by manufacturer, by material or sometimes by trade name. Dolls are arranged in chronological order by date within a main entry.

Unless otherwise indicated, values given in this section are retail prices for clean dolls in excellent overall condition, with good complexion color, perfect hair in original set and original unfaded clothing, including underwear, shoes and socks. Dolls in crisp mint condition will bring 25 to 50 percent more. Dirty and faded dolls that have been heavily played with are worth 10 to 30 percent of these values

13½ (34cm) American Character *Toni*. For additional information, see page 225. *Rosemary Kanizer.*

Madame Alexander

CLOTH DOLLS: Original tagged clothing.
Characters: Ca. 1933-1940. All-cloth with molded felt or flocked mask face, painted eyes to the side. **Little Women, David Copperfield, Oliver Twist, Edith, Babbie, Alice** and others.
16in (41cm) only:

Fair	$200-$300
Good	$350-$450
Excellent	$750-$850

Alice: 19-20in (48-51cm) good
$400-$500
Playmates: 1940s, 28in (71cm) fair to good **$400**
Bunny Belle:
12in (31cm) excellent **$750**
Cloth Baby, Ca. 1936:

13in (33cm) very good	$300-$350
17in (43cm) very good	$475-$525
24in (61cm)	$625

Cloth Dionne Quintuplet, Ca. 1935:
17in (43cm) very good **$850-$900****
24in (61cm)very good
$1,200-$1,300**
Susie Q. & Bobby Q., Ca. 1938:
12-16in (31-41cm) excellent with purse or book strap **$800-$850**
15in (38cm) **$1,000-$1,100**
Little Shaver: 1942. Yarn hair, very good condition:

7in (18cm)	$475-$500
10-12in (25-31cm)	$450-$500
20in (51cm)	$750

Kamkins-type: (hard felt face), very good condition,
20in (51cm) **$650-$750****
Funny: 1963-1977,
18in (46cm) **$65-$75**
Muffin: 1963-1977, 14in (36cm) **$95**

**Not enough samples to compute a reliable range.

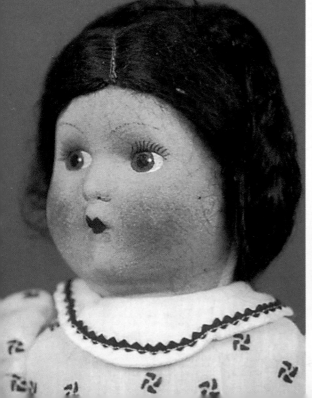

FACTS
Alexander Doll Co., Inc., New York, NY, U.S.A. 1923 - on, but as early as 1912, the Alexander sisters were designing doll clothes and dressing dolls commercially.
Mark: Dolls themselves marked in various ways, usually "ALEXANDER." Clothing has a white cloth label with blue lettering sewn into a seam which says "MADAME ALEXANDER" and usually the name of the specific doll. Cloth and other early dolls are unmarked and identifiable only by the clothing label.

16in (41cm) cloth *Meg* from *Little Women*, all original. *H & J Foulke, Inc.*

COMPOSITION DOLLS: All in original tagged clothing; excellent condition, with bright color and perfect hair; faint crazing acceptable.

Dionne Quintuplets, 1935 (each Quint has her own color for clothing: **Yvonne** - pink; **Annette** - yellow; **Cecile** - green; **Emelie** - lavender; **Marie** - blue):

7-8in (18-20cm)	$275-$325
Matched set	$2,200
In bed	$2,500-$2,600
In basket with extra outfits	$3,350
With five pieces of wooden Dionne furniture	$3,750
10-11in (25-28cm) baby	$350-$375
11-12in (28-31cm) toddler	$400-$450
14in (36cm) toddler	$500-$550
16in (41cm) baby with cloth body	$450
20in (51cm) toddler	$700-$750
23-24in (58-61cm) baby with cloth body	$650-$75
Pins: each	$90-$100
Tagged dress and bonnet:	$150

Above: 8in (20cm) *Dionne Quintuplet,* all original. *H & J Foulke, Inc.*

Left: 7in (18cm) *December Birthday Doll,* all original. *H & J Foulke, Inc.*

Small dolls: 1935-1945.

   7-9in (18-23cm):

Foreign Countries	**$175-$225**
Storybook Characters	**$250-$300**
Special Outfits	**$400-$500**
Birthday Dolls	**$325-$375**
Bride and Bridesmaids	
	$225-$250 each
Little Women	**$275 each**

Little Colonel: 1935.

   8½in (22cm)   **$600-$700****

   3in (33cm)   **$650-$700**

Unnamed Girl: Ca. 1935. dimples, sleep eyes, 13in (33cm)   **$400-$450**

Nurse: Ca. 1935.

   13in (33cm)   **$800-$900**

Betty: Ca. 1935. painted or sleep eyes, wigged or molded hair:

   13in (33cm)   **$425-$475**

   19in (48cm)   **$700-$750**

Baby Jane: 1935.

   16in (41cm)   **$900-$1,000**

Topsy Turvy: Ca. 1936.

   7½in (19cm)   **$210-$235**

Dr. DaFoe: 1936.

   14in (36cm)   **$1,500-$1,600**

Three Little Pigs: 1938-1939.

   12-13in (31-33cm)   **$750-$800 each**

**Not enough price samples to compute a reliable range.

20in (51cm) *Baby McGuffey*, all original. *H & J Foulke, Inc.*

20in (51cm) *McGuffey Ana*, all original. *H & J Foulke, Inc.*

15in (38cm) *Flora McFlimsey*, all original. *H & J Foulke, Inc.*

16in (41cm) *Snow White*, all original. *H & J Foulke, Inc.*

14in (36cm) *Scarlett O'Hara*, all original. *Rosemary Kanizer.*

Marionettes: 1935. Character faces, 10-12in (25-30cm):

Tony Sarg	**$250-$275**
Disney	**$350-$400**

Babies: 1936-on. **Little Genius, Baby McGuffey, Precious, Butch, Bitsey;** composition head, hands and legs, cloth bodies:

11-12in (28-31cm)	**$250-$300**
16-18in (41-46cm)	**$400-$450**
24in (61cm)	**$550**
Pinky:	
16-18in (41-46cm)	**$450-$550**

Princess Elizabeth Face: Original tagged clothes; all in excellent condition.
Princess Elizabeth: 1937.

13in (33cm) closed mouth	
	$400-$500

16-18in (41-46cm)	**$550-$650**
22-24in (56-61cm)	**$750-$850**
27in (69cm)	**$950-$1,000**
8in (20cm) Dionne head	**$600**

McGuffey Ana: 1937. Braids:

9in (23cm) painted eyes	**$425-$475**
11in (28cm) closed mouth	
	$475-$525
15-16in (38-41cm)	**$525-$625**
20-22in (51-56cm)	**$750-$850**

Snow White: 1937. Closed mouth, black hair:

13in (33cm)	**$500-$550**
16-18in (41-46cm)	**$700-$750**

Flora McFlimsey: 1938.

13in (33cm)	**$550-$650**
15in (38cm)	**$700-$800**
22in (56cm)	**$1,000-$1,100**

Kate Greenaway: 1938.

13in (33cm)	**$600-$650**
16-18in (41-46cm)	**$800-$850**

Wendy Ann Face: Original tagged clothes; all in excellent condition.

Wendy Ann: 1936.

9in (23cm) painted eyes	**$350-$375**
14in (36cm) swivel waist	**$450-$550**
21in (53cm)	**$800-$900**
14in (36cm) molded hair	
	$600-$650*

Scarlett O'Hara: 1937. Black hair, blue or green eyes:

11in (28cm)	**$950**
14in (36cm)	**$950-$1,000**
18in (46cm)	**$1,450**
21in (53cm)	**$1,850**

Madelaine du Bain: 1938.

14in (36cm)	**$550-$650**

Miss America: 1939.

14in (36cm)	**$850****

Bride & Bridesmaids: 1940.

14in (36cm)	**$400-$450**
18in (46cm)	**$600-$650**
21in (53cm)	**$750-$850**

Portraits: 1940s.

21in (53cm)	**$2,500 up**

**Not enough price samples to compute a reliable range.

Above: 16in (41cm) *Jane Withers*, all original. *H & J Foulke, Inc.*

Top Left: 20in (51cm) *Bride*, all original. *H & J Foulke, Inc.*

Left: 13in (33cm) *Jeannie Walker*, all original, with box. *H & J Foulke, Inc.*

Sleeping Beauty, Cinderella:
Ca. 1941, 14in (36cm)   **$550-$650**
Carmen (Miranda), 1942, (black hair):
9in (23cm) painted eyes   **$350-$375**
14-15in (36-38cm)   **$550-$650**
21in (53cm)   **$1,200-$1,400****
Fairy Princess or Fairy Queen: 1942.
14in (36cm)   **$650-$700**
18in (46cm)   **$750-$800**
Armed Forces Dolls: 1942.
WAAC, WAVE, WAAF, Soldier,
Marine: 14in (36cm)   **$1,000**

Special Faces: Original tagged clothes;
all in excellent condition.
Jane Withers: 1937.
13in (33cm) closed mouth
$1,100-$1,300
15-16in (38-41cm)   **$1,250-$1,350**
21in (53cm)   **$1,650-$1,850**
Sonja Henie: 1939.
14in (36cm) swivel waist **$800-$900**
15in (38cm) gift set, boxed   **$3,200**
18in (46cm)   **$1,000**
21in (53cm)   **$1,200-$1,400**
Jeannie Walker: 1941.
13-14in (33-36cm)   **$850**
18in (46cm)   **$1,200****
13in (33cm) boxed, at auction
$1,732.50
14in (36cm) non-walker **$550-$650**
Special Girl: 1942. cloth body:
22in (56cm)   **$550-$650****

Margaret Face: Original tagged
clothes; all in excellent condition with
perfect hair and pretty coloring.
Margaret O'Brien: 1946. With dark
braided wig:
14in (36cm)   **$1,100**
18in (46cm)   **$1,350-$1,500**
Karen Ballerina: 1946. With blonde
wig in coiled braids:
14in (36cm)   **$850-$950**
18in (46cm)   **$1,250**
21in (53cm)   **$1,650-$1,850**
Alice-in-Wonderland: 1947.
14in (36cm)   **$525-$575**
18in (46cm)   **$650-$750**
21in (53cm)   **$1,000**

**Not enough price samples to compute
reliable range.

17in (43cm) *Margaret O'Brien,* all original. *H & J Foulke, Inc.*

14in (36cm) *Sonja Henie,* all original. *H & J Foulke, Inc.*

HARD PLASTIC DOLLS: 1948-on. Original tagged clothes; excellent condition with bright color and perfect hair.

Margaret Face: 1948-1956.
Alice in Wonderland: 1949-1952.
14in (36cm) $600-$650
Babs: 1948-1949.
14in (36cm) $1,000
18in (46cm) $1,200
Bride: 1948.
14in (36cm) $650-$700
20in (51cm) $1,200-$1,400
Bride: Pink gown, 1950.
14in (36cm) $1,000
18in (46cm) $1,200
Cinderella: 1950.
Ball gown:
14in (36cm) $850
18in (46cm) $1,250
"Poor" dress: 14in (36cm) $650
Cynthia (black): 1952-1953.
14in (36cm) $850
18in (46cm) $1,150-$1,300

Fairy Queen: 1947-1948.
14in (36cm) $750
18in (46cm) $950
Fashions of the Century: 1954.
18in (46cm) at auction $3,400
Glamour Girls: 1953.
18in (46cm) $1,450-$1,650
Godey Ladies: 1950.
14in (36cm) $1,400-$1,600
Groom: 18in (46cm) $650-$850
Margaret O'Brien: 1948.
14in (36cm) $1,000-$1,100
18in (46cm) $1,300
Margaret Rose: 1948-1953.
14in (36cm) $750-$800
18in (46cm) $850-$900
18in (46cm) **Beaux Arts Series,**
1953 $1,650
Mary Martin: 1950, Sailor suit:
14in (36cm) $850
18in (46cm) $1,000
McGuffey Ana: 1949.
14in (36cm) $1,100-$1,200
18in (46cm) $1,300-$1,400

14in (36cm) *Margot Ballerina*, all original. *H & J Foulke, Inc.*

14in (36cm) *Maggie*, all original. *Rosemary Kanizer.*

Nina Ballerina: 1949-1951. Blonde:
14in (36cm)	**$850**
18in (46cm)	**$1,100**
21in (53cm)	**$1,600**

Peggy Bride: Ca. 1950.
20in (51cm)	**$1,200**

Prince Charming: 1950.
14in (36cm)	**$775**
18in (46cm)	**$875**

Prince Philip: Ca. 1950.
18in (46cm)	**$800-$850**

Queen Elizabeth II: 1953.
18in (46cm) with long velvet cape
	$1,600
No cape	**$1,000**

Snow White: 1952.
14in (36cm)	**$750-$800**
18in (46cm)	**$1,100**

Story Princess: 1954-1956.
14in (36cm)	**$650-$700**
18in (46cm)	**$750-$800**

Wendy-Ann: 1947-1948.
14in (36cm)	**$750-$800**
18in (46cm)	**$850-$950**

Wendy Bride: 1950.
14in (36cm)	**$600-$650**
18in (46cm)	**$850**

Wendy (from **Peter Pan** set): 1953.
14in (36cm)	**$550-$600**

Maggie Face: 1948-1956.
Alice in Wonderland: 1949-1952.
14in (36cm)	**$600-$650**
18in (46cm)	**$750-$800**

Annabelle: 1952.
15in (38cm)	**$650-$750**
18in (46cm)	**$850-$900**

Glamour Girls: 1953.
18in (46cm)	**$1,500-$1,800**

Godey Man: 1950. 14in (36cm)**$1,200**
John Powers Models:
14in (36cm)	**$1,500-$1,600**

Kathy: 1951.
14in (36cm)	**$725**
18in (46cm)	**$875**

Margot Ballerina: 1953.
14in (36cm)	**$700-$800**
18in (46cm)	**$900**

Maggie: 1948-1953.
14in (36cm)	**$550-$600**
17in (43cm)	**$700-$750**
20in (51cm) Bridesmaid	**$850**

Me and My Shadow: 1954.
18in (46cm)	**$1,600-$2,000**

Peter Pan: 1953.
15in (38cm)	**$700-$800**

Polly Pigtails: 1949.
14in (36cm)	**$550-$600**
17in (43cm)	**$700-$750**

Rosamund Bridesmaid: 1953.
15in (38cm)	**$650-$700**
18in (46cm)	**$800-$850**

Little Women: 1948-1956.
Floss hair, 1948-1950:
14-15in (36-38cm)	**$475-$525 each**
Amy, loop curls	**$525-$550**
Dynel hair	**$375-$425 each**

Little Men: 1952, (**Nat, Stuffy, Tommy Bangs**) **$900-$1,000**

Babies: 1948-1951. Cloth body, hard plastic or vinyl limbs (**Baby Genius, Bitsey, Butch**):
12in (31cm)	**$250-$300**
16-18in (41-46cm)	**$400-$450**

Winnie and Binnie: 1953-1955.
15in (38cm)	**$350-$400**
With trunk and trousseau, at auction	**$4,600**
18in (46cm)	**$500-$550**
25in (64cm)	**$650**

14in (36cm) *Meg* from *Little Women.*
Rosemary Kanizer.

Skating outfit
15in (38cm)   **$700-$750**
Mary Ellen: 31in (79cm) **$625-$675**
Sweet Violet:
18in (46cm) fully-jointed body
$1,000 up
All original, boxed, at auction
$1,700
Victoria (black, green-and-white
dress): 15in (38cm)   **$600-$650**
Flower Girl:
15in (38cm)   **$650**
18in (46cm)   **$1,050**

Cissy: 1955-1959. 21in (53cm):
Street clothes   **$500-$600**
Basic underwear, shoes, stockings
$400
Cocktail dresses   **$650-$750**
Ball gowns   **$950-$1,250**
Queen   **$1,000-$1,200**
Bride   **$800-$1,100**
Bridesmaid   **$850-$900**
Cissy at auction:

Lady in Red #2285, 1958   **$2,300**
Lace Gown #2172, 1957   **$1,400**

Alexander-Kins: 1953-to present. All-hard plastic; original tagged clothes; all in excellent condition with perfect hair and rosy cheeks. A played-with doll having partial or faded costume will bring 25% of quoted prices.
Wendy:
7½-8in (19-20cm):
1953, straight-leg
non-walker   **$450 up**
nude   **$300**
1954-1955, straight-leg
walker   **$400 up**
nude   **$275**
1956-1964, bent-knee
walker   **$350 up**
nude   **$185**
1965-1972, bent-knee
non-walker   **$275-$325**
nude   **$90**

21in (53cm) *Cissy*, all original. *H & J Foulke, Inc.*

16in (41cm) *Pinky*, with music box. *H & J Foulke, Inc.*

Wendy: basic (panties, shoes and socks), boxed **$325-$375**
Quizkin: 1953 **$500-$600**
Wendy in Special Outfits:
  Agatha: 1953 **$900-$1,000**
  American Girl: 1962-1963 **$350**
  Amish Boy or **Amish Girl:** 1966-1969 **$350**
  Aunt Pitty Pat: 1957 **$1,600**
  Baby Clown: 1955 **$1,200**
  Bible Characters **$7,000-$10,000**
  Billy or **Bobby:** 1955-1963 **$450-$500**
  Bride: 1956-1961 **$350-$450**
  Bridesmaid: pink 1955 **$900**
  Cherry Twin: 1957 **$900 each**
  Cousin Grace: 1957, boxed **$1,600**
  Cousin Marie: 1963 **$900**
  Davy Crockett Boy or **Girl:** 1955 **$600-$700**
  Easter Wendy: 1953 **$1,000**
  Edith: 1958 **$650-$700**
  Groom: 1956-1963 **$400-$450**
  Guardian Angel: 1954 **$650-$750**
  Hiawatha: 1967-1969 **$350**
  Little Madeline: 1953 **$775**
  Little Southern Girl: 1953 **$850-$950**
  Little Victoria: 1954 **$1,300**
  Maypole Dance: 1954, boxed **$650**
  McGuffey Ana: 1964-1965 **$350**
  Miss USA: 1966-1968, boxed **$425**
  My Shadow: 1954 **$1,500**
  Nurse: 1956-1965 **$450-$500**
  Parlour Maid: 1956 **$1,000**
  Pocahontas: 1967-1969 **$350**
  Prince Charles: 1957 **$800**
  Princess Anne: 1957 **$800**
  Priscilla or **Colonial Girl:** 1962-1970 **$350**
  Scarlett: 1965-1972 **$400**
  Southern Belle: 1963 **$450-$500**
  Wendy Can Read: 1957, boxed **$950**
  Wendy Does Highland Fling: 1955 **$400**
  Wendy Dude Ranch: 1955 **$600**
  Wendy in Easter Egg: 1965 **$1,700**
  Wendy Ice Skater: 1956 **$450**
  Wendy Loves to Waltz: 1955 **$625**
  Wendy in Riding Habit: 1965, boxed **$550**

International Costumes:
  Bent-knee walker **$150-$200**
  Bent-knee non-walker, 1965-1972 **$75-$100**
  Korea, Africa, Hawaii, Vietnam, Eskimo, Morocco, Ecuador, Bolivia **$250-$300**
  Straight-leg, rosy cheeks, 1973-1976 **$60**
  Straight-leg, pinched lips, 1982-1987 **$40-$45**
  Current face, 1988-on **$40-$50**
Storybook, Ballerinas & Brides:
  Bent-knee non-walker **$75-$100**
  Straight-leg, rosy cheeks, 1973-1976 **$60-$70**

8in (20cm) #600 *Wendykin*, bent-knee walker, all original. *Rosemary Kanizer.*

8in (20cm) *Japan*, #770, with bent knees and *Maggie* face, all original. *H & J Foulke, Inc.*

Straight-leg, pinched lips,
1982-1987   **$40-$45**
Current face, 1988-on   **$45-$55**
Little Women, set of five:
Straight-leg walker, 1955   **$1,500**
Bent-knee walker, 1956-1964**$1,200**
Bent-knee non-walker   **$650-$750**
Straight legs   **$300-$350**
1994 FAO Schwarz Movie outfits
                                        $600
Exclusive and Special Editions:
Enchanted Doll House:
1980-1981   **$250-$275**
Wendy: 1989, MADC exclusive
                                        $175
Navajo Woman: 1994,
MADC Convention   **$300-$350**
Bobbie Sox: 1990, Disney   **$175**
David & Diana: 1989, FAO
Schwarz, set   **$175-$200**
Mouseketeer: 1991, Disney
                                  $100-$125
Easter Bunny: 1991, Child at
Heart   **$300-$350**
Cowboy: 1987, MADC Convention
                                  $400-$450
Little Miss Magnin: 1992,
I. Magnin with tea set and teddy
bear   **$150**
Tippi Ballerina: 1988,
CU Gathering   **$350-$400**
Little Emperor: 1992,
UFDC Luncheon   **$500-$600**
Anne of Green Gables: 1994,
trunk set, Neiman-Marcus
                                  $225-$275
Sailor Boy: UFDC, 1990   **$750**

Little Genius: 1956-1962. Baby with short curly wig, 8in (20cm):
Basic or simple outfit   **$225**
Fancy outfit   **$275**
Christening outfit   **$350**

Lissy Face: 1956-1958.
Lissy: 12in (31cm)   **$400-$500**
Boxed with trousseau **$1,200-$1,500**
F.A.O. Schwarz exclusive   **$950**
Bridesmaid   **$600**
Kelly: 1959   **$400-$500**
Little Women: 1957-1959   **$250**
Southern Belle: 1963   **$1,200**
McGuffey Ana: 1963   **$1,600**
Katie: 1962   **$1,200**

8in (20cm) *United States,* #516, all original, with *Maggie* face. *H & J Foulke, Inc.*

Tommy: 1962   **$1,000**
Cinderella: 1966   **$850**
  Boxed set   **$1,250**
Laurie: 1967   **$400**
Pamela: 1962-1963
  Boxed with wigs   **$1,000**
  Suitcase gift set   **$1,500**
Columbian Sailor: UFDC 1993
    $225

Elise: 1957-1964. 16½in (42cm):
  Basic undergarment, shoes,
    stockings   **$250-$275**
  Street clothes   **$400-$425**
  Ball gowns   **$650-$850**
  Bride: **$425-$475**
  Sleeping Beauty:
    Disney   **$600-$700**
    Bridesmaid   **$500-$550**
    Ballerina   **$550**
  Vinyl head: 1964
    (Kelly Face)   **$325-$375**
    Riding Outfit, boxed   **$475**

Cissette Face: 1957-1973.
  Cissette, 1957-1963: 10in (25cm)
  Basic doll, mint-in-box   **$350-$400**

8in (20cm) *Little Genius*, original tagged dress and matching hat. *H & J Foulke, Inc.*

Above: 16½in (42cm) *Elise*, all original. *Kathy & Terri's Dolls.*

Left: 12in (31cm) *Columbian Sailor*, UFDC 1993, all original. *H & J Foulke, Inc.*

Day dresses	**$375-$425**	**Godey:** 1968-1970	**$300-$350**
Cocktail dresses	**$500-$600**	**Scarlett:** 1968-1973	**$300-$350**
Evening gowns	**$650-$800**	**Renoir:** 1968-1970	**$325-$375**
Queen: 1957-1963	**$400-$450**	**Agatha:** 1968	**$350-$375**
Gold Ballerina: 1959	**$450-$500**	**Southern Belle:**	
Denmark: 1962	**$500-$600**	1968-1973	**$300-$350**
Gibson Girl	**$700-$800**	**Melinda:** 1968-1970	**$300-$350**
Jacqueline: 1962	**$750-$850**	**Jenny Lind:** 1969	**$500-$550**
Margot: 1961	**$600-$700**	**Melanie:** 1969-1970	**$375-$400**
Klondike Kate:		**Queen:** 1972-1973	**$250-$350**
1962	**$1,250-$1,500**		
Sleeping Beauty:		**Shari Lewis:** 1959.	
1959-1960	**$375-$425**	14in (36cm)	**$550-$650**
Mardi Gras:		21in (53cm)	**$750-$850**
1992, Spiegel	**$60-$125**		
Diamond Lil:		**Maggie Mixup:** 1960-1961.	
1993, MADC	**$190-$300**	16½in (42cm)	**$400-$450**
Lady Hamilton: #975, 1957	**$1200**	8in (20cm)	**$450-$550**
Cinderella: 1989, Disney	**$650-$750**	8in (20cm) angel	**$800-$1,000**
Miss Unity: 1991, UFDC	**$350-$400**	**Little Lady**	**$350**
Portrettes, 1968-1973:		**Little Lady Gift Set**	**$1,000**

10in (25cm) *Cissette*, all original and boxed. *Rosemary Kanizer.*

8in (20cm) *Maggie Mixup & Her Dog Danger,* all original. *Private Collection.*

VINYL DOLLS. Original tagged clothing; excellent never-played-with condition, bright color.

Kelly Face: 1958-1965. 15in (38cm):
Kelly	**$300-$350**
Pollyana	**$300-$350**
Marybel: complete case	**$325-$375**
Edith	**$325-$375**
Elise	**$325-$375**

Jacqueline, 1961-1962:
21in (53cm) suit	**$650-$700**
Riding habit	**$700-$750**
Brocade gown #2130, 1962	**$900-$1,000**
10in (25cm)	**$750-$850**

Portraits: 1962-current. 21in (53cm):
Scarlett,	
Cotton print, 1968	**$900-$1,000**
Green velvet or taffeta, 1975-1982	**$350-$400**
Satin print, 1978	**$500**
Red gown, 1989	**$400**
Melanie: 1967-1974	**$400-$500**
Queen: 1968	**$700-$750**
Godey: 1969	**$500-$550**
Bride: 1969	**$650-$700**
Madame Pompadour: 1970	**$900-$1,000**
Mimi: 1971	**$450-$500**
Gainsborough: 1973	**$350-$400**
Madame Alexander: 1984-1990	**$300**
Sarah Bernhardt: 1987	**$300**

Caroline: 1961-1962.
15in (38cm)	**$300-$400**
Riding habit	**$375-$425**

Melinda: 1963.
14in (36cm)	**$350-$400**

Janie Face: 1964-1990. 12in (31cm):
Janie: 1964-1966	**$225-$275**
Lucinda: 1969-1970	**$250-$300**
Rozy: 1969	**$275-$325**
Suzy: 1970	**$275-$325**
Muffin: 1989-1990	**$50-$60**

Brenda Starr: 1964.
12in (31cm)	**$225-$250**
Yolanda: 1965	**$225-$250**

Betty: 1960, smiling face, walker, 30in (76cm)   **$350**

Patty: 1965, 18in (46cm)   **$250-$275**

Chatterbox: 1961, battery-operated talker, 24in (61cm)   **$250-$275**

Smarty Face: 1962-1965. 12in (31cm):
Smarty: 1962-1963	**$225-$275**
With baby	**$325-$350**
Brother	**$225-$275**
Katie: (black), 1965	**$350-$400**

Polly Face: 1965-1971. 17in (43cm):
Polly: 1965	**$225-$275**
Mary Ellen Playmate	**$275**
Leslie: (black) 1965-1971	**$300-$325**

Mary Ann Face: 1965-current.
14in (36cm):
Mary Ann: 1965	**$225**
Orphant Annie: 1965-1966	**$300**
Gidget: 1966	**$275**
Little Granny: 1966	**$150**
Riley's Little Annie: 1967	**$175**
Renoir Girl: 1967-1971	**$150-$175**
Disney Snow White: 1967-1977	**$350-$375**
Easter Girl: 1968	**$650-$750**
Scarlett: flowered gown, 1968	**$450-$500**
Madame: 1967-1975	**$150-$175**
Jenny Lind & Cat: 1969-1971	**$225**
Gone with the Wind: 1969-1986	**$75-$95**

14in (36cm) *Melinda*, all original. *Rosemary Kanizer.*

Jenny Lind: 1970 **$275-$300**
Grandma Jane: 1970 **$150-$175**
Goldilocks: 1978-1982 **$75**
Bonnie Blue: 1989 **$100-$110**
Discontinued dolls: 1982-1995
$50-$90
Babies: 1963-present. Cloth and vinyl:
Littlest Kitten: 1963, 8in (20cm):
Basic or simple outfit **$200-$225**
Fancy outfit **$250-$275**
Sugar Tears: 1964,
14in (36cm) **$75-$100**
Fischer Quints: 1964,
7in (18cm) set **$300-$350**
Sweet Tears: 1965-1982.
14in (36cm) **$55-$65**
Layette sets **$125-$175**
Baby Ellen: (black), 1965-1972,
14in (36cm) **$100-$110**

14in (36cm) *Mary, Mary,* 1994, all original. *H & J Foulke, Inc.*

Little Bitsey: 1967-1968,
9in (23cm) **$130**
Pussy Cat: (black), 1970-1984,
20in (51cm) **$100-$125**
Mary Cassatt Baby: 1969-1970,
20in (51cm) **$200-$250**
Happy: 1970,
20in (51cm) **$200-$250**
Smiley: 1971,
20in (51cm) **$200-$250**
Baby Lynn: 1973-1976,
20in (51cm) **$100-$125**
Baby Brother: 1977-1979,
20in (51cm) **$75-$100**
Baby McGuffey: 1971-1976,
20in (51cm) **$200-$250**
Mommy's Pet: 1977-1986,
20in (51cm) **$75-$100**
Mary Mine: 1977-1989 **$125-$150**
Sound of Music, small set,
1965-1970:
Friedrich: 8in (20cm) **$150**
Gretl: 8in (20cm) **$150**
Marta: 8in (20cm) **$150**
Brigitta: 10in (25cm) **$200**
Louisa: 10in (25cm) **$200**
Liesl: 10in (25cm) **$200**
Maria: 12in (31cm) **$225**
Sound of Music, large set, 1971-1973
(allow 100% more for sailor outfits):
Friedrich: 11in (28cm) **$175-$200**
Gretl: 11in (28cm) **$150-$165**
Marta: 11in (28cm) **$150-$165**
Brigitta: 14in (36cm) **$125-$150**
Louisa: 14in (36cm) **$125-$150**
Liesl: 14in (36cm) **$125-$150**
Maria: 17in (43cm) **$275**
Kurt: 11in (28cm) sailor suit **$350**
Coco: 1966, right leg bent slightly at
knee:
21in (53cm) **$1,800-$2,000**
Portrait Dolls: 1966 **$1,800-$2,200**
Scarlett: #2061, white gown **$2,500**
Elise Face: 1966-1991, redesigned
vinyl face, 17in (43cm):
Elise Portrait Doll:
1972-1973 **$125-$150**
Ballerinas **$75-$85**
Brides **$65-$75**
Formals **$65-$75**
Marlo: 1967 **$550-$650**
Maggie: 1972-1973 **$175-$200**

Peter Pan Set: 1969.

   Peter Pan: 14in (36cm)   **$200-$225**

   Wendy: 14in (36cm)   **$200-$225**

   Michael: 11in (28cm)   **$250**

   Tinker Bell: 10in (25cm)

                      $300-$350

Nancy Drew Face: 1967-1994.

  12in (31cm):

   Nancy Drew: 1967   **$200-$225**

Renoir Child: 1967   **$125-$150**

Pamela: with wigs, late 1960s

                      $550-$650

Poor Cinderella: 1967   **$125-$150**

Little Women: 1969-1989   **$60-$65**

Romantic Couples   **$75 pair**

Discontinued dolls   **$30-$35**

First Ladies: 1976-1989.

  14in (36cm) each   **$50-$75**

14in (36cm) *Pussy Cat*, all original. *H & J Foulke, Inc.*

12in (31cm) *Rozy*, all original. *H & J Foulke, Inc.*

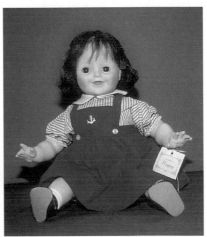

20in (51cm) *Happy*, all original. *Rosemary Kanizer.*

American Character

Marked Petite or American Character Mama Dolls: 1923-on. Composition/cloth; original clothes; all in good condition.

16-18in (41-46cm)	**$225-$265**
24in (61cm)	**$325-$375**

Baby Petite: 12in (31cm) **$200**

Puggy: 1928, all-composition, frowning face; original clothes; all in good condition, 12in (31cm) **$525-$575**

Marked Petite Girl Dolls: 1930s. All-composition; original clothes; all in good condition with nice coloring and perfect hair.

16-18in (41-46cm)	**$325-$350**
24in (61cm)	**$400-$425**
Petite Toddler: 13in (33cm)	**$250**

George Washington: 19in (48cm) all original, at auction **$1,000**

Sally: 1930. All-composition; painted eyes, molded hair or wigged with sleep eyes; original clothes; all in good condition with nice coloring.

12in (31cm)	**$225-$250**
16in (41cm)	**$275-$325**

Sally-Joy: 1930. Composition, cloth.

18in (46cm)	**$350-$375**
21in (53cm)	**$375-$400**

FACTS
American Character Doll Co.,
New York, NY, 1919-on.
Trademark: Petite.

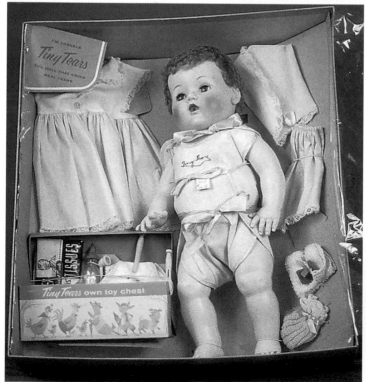

18in (46cm) *Tiny Tears*, boxed with layette. *H & J Foulke, Inc.*

Carol Ann Beery: 1935. All-composition "Two-Some Doll" with special crown braid, matching playsuit and dress.

13in (33cm)	**$500-$600**
16½in (42cm)	**$700-$800**

Toodles: 1956. Hard rubber baby, drink-and-wet baby; original clothes; excellent condition.

18-22in (46-56cm)	**$250-$300**

Toodles Toddler: 1960. Vinyl and hard plastic, "Peek-a-Boo" eyes.

24in (61cm)	**$275-$300**
30in (76cm)	**$350-$375**

Tiny Tears: 1950s. Hard plastic head with tear ducts; drink-and-wet baby; original clothes; excellent condition. Rubber body:

12in (31cm)	**$175-$225**
18in (46cm)	**$250-$300**

Original box and accessories:

13in (33cm)	**$400-$450**
18in (46cm)	**$750**

All-vinyl, 1963:

12in (31cm)	**$65-$75**
15in (38cm)	**$85-$95**
Boxed with accessories	**$200**
Teenie Weenie: boxed, at auction	**$128**

Sweet Sue: 1953. All-hard plastic or hard plastic and vinyl, some with walking mechanism, some fully-jointed including elbows, knees and ankles; original clothes; all in excellent condition, with perfect hair and pretty coloring.

14in (36cm)	**$275-$300**
18-21in (46-53cm)	**$325-$350**
24in (61cm)	**$325-$375**
17in (43cm) boxed bride	**$450**

Annie Oakley: 1955,

14in (36cm)	**$450**

Alice in Wonderland:

18in (46cm)	**$550**

Sweet Sue Sophisticate: vinyl head,

20in (51cm)	**$275-$325**

Toni: vinyl head, 1958.

10½in (26cm)	**$190-$210**
20in (51cm)	**$275-$325**
boxed	**$400**

Ricky, Jr.: 1955, all-vinyl:

14in (36cm)	**$110-$125**
21in (53cm)	**$200-$225**

Eloise: Ca. 1955. All-cloth; yellow yarn hair; original clothing; in excellent condition. Designed by Bette Gould from the fictional little girl "Eloise" who lived at the Plaza Hotel in New York City.

21in (53cm)	**$450-$500**

24in (61cm) *Sweet Sue*, all original. *H & J Foulke, Inc.*

Whimsies: 1960. Characters; original clothing; excellent condition. **Hedda Get Bedda** (three faces), **Wheeler the Dealer, Lena the Cleaner, Polly the Lady, Bessie the Bashful Bride, Dixie the Pixie** and others:

19-21in (48-53cm)	**$125-$150**
Mint-in-box with tag	**$225**

Little Miss Echo: 1962. Recorded voice; original clothing, excellent condition.

30in (76cm) boxed	**$250-$300**
Out of box	**$150**

Tressy: 1963-1965. Growing hair:

12½in (32cm) boxed	**$125-$150**
Doll only	**$70-$80**
Black	**$400**

Pre-teen Tressy: 1963. Growing hair:

14in (36cm) boxed	**$100-$125**
Cricket: 1965, boxed	**$75**
Mary Make-up: 1965, boxed	**$125**

10½in (26cm) *Toni*, all original. *Rosemary Kanizer.*

Arranbee

My Dream Baby: 1924, bisque head, cloth body,

15-16in (38-41cm)	**$325-$350**

Storybook Dolls: 1930s. All-composition; original storybook costumes; all in excellent condition, with perfect hair and pretty coloring.

9-10in (23-25cm)	**$175-$195**
Boxed	**$275**

Bottletot: 1926, all-composition; molded celluloid bottle in hand; appropriate clothes; all in good condition,

13in (33cm)	**$195**

Nancy: 1930. All-composition; original clothes; all in good condition, with pretty coloring.

12in (31cm) molded hair, painted eyes	**$250-$275**
12in (31cm) with trousseau in wardrobe trunk	**$500-$550**
16in (41cm) sleep eyes, wig, open mouth	**$400-$425**

Debu'Teen and Nancy Lee: 1938-on. All-composition; original clothes; all in good condition with perfect hair and pretty coloring.

11in (28cm)	**$225**
14in (36cm)	**$350**
18in (46)	**$425**
21in (53cm)	**$500**
Skating Doll: 18in (46cm)	**$500**
Brother: 14in (36cm)	**$350-$375**
WAC: 18in (46cm)	**$500**

Little Angel Baby: 1940s. Composition, cloth; original clothes; all in good condition.

16-18in (41-46cm)	**$300-$350**
Hard plastic: 18in (46cm)	**$350**

FACTS
Arranbee Doll Co.,
New York, NY, U.S.A. 1922-1960.
Mark: "ARRANBEE" or "R & B."

Nanette and Nancy Lee: 1950s. All-hard plastic; original clothes; all in excellent condition, with rosy cheeks.

14in (36cm)	**$400-$450**
17in (43cm)	**$500-$550**
20in (51cm) Skater	**$650**
Cinderella:	
14in (36cm)	**$500-$600**
Floss wig, evening gown:	
14in (36cm)	**$400-$450**

Littlest Angel: 1956. All-hard plastic, jointed knees, walker; original clothes; all in excellent condition.

10-11in (25-28cm)	**$130-$165**
Boxed	**$200-$250**
Boxed outfits	**$45-$65**
Little Angel: 1950s,	
12in (31cm)	**$125-$150**
Coty Girl: 1958, all-vinyl, fashion body, high-heeled feet,	
10½in (27cm) boxed	**$175-$200**

16in (41cm) *Nancy,* all original. *H & J Foulke, Inc.*

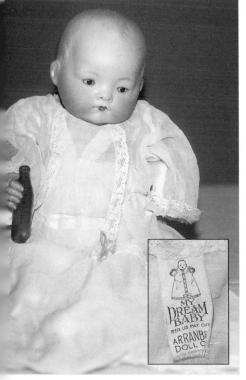

16in (41cm) *My Dream Baby* with bottle and label. *H & J Foulke, Inc.*

14in (36cm) *Nancy Lee,* all original. *H & J Foulke, Inc.*

Artist Dolls, Traditional

Traditional Artists: Many members of NIADA or ODACA. All dolls original and excellent.

Armstrong-Hand, Martha: porcelain, babies and children **$2,500**

Barrie, Mirren: cloth historical characters, 11½in (30cm) **$110-$125**

Beckett, Bob & June: carved wooden children **$275-$325**

Blakeley, Halle: high-fired clay lady dolls **$550-$750**

Brandon, Elizabeth: porcelain children - **Theola, Joshua, Joi Lin, Jael** **$300-$500**

Bringloe, Frances: carved wooden **American Pioneer Children,** 6¼in (16cm) **$600 pair**

Bruyere, Muriel: biscuit-fired clay **Little Vie,** 8in (31cm) **$125**

Bullard, Helen: carved wood **Holly, Barbry Allen** **$135-$150**

21in (53cm) Emma Clear china head lady. *H & J Foulke, Inc.*

Hitty **$350**
American Family Series: (16 dolls) **$300 each**

Clear, Emma: porcelain, china and bisque shoulder head dolls **$350-$500**
Danny **$450**
George & Martha Washington **$500-$600 pair**
Gibson Girl **$350-$400**

DeNunez, Marianne: Bru Jne:
10in (25cm) **$300**
19in (49cm) **$350**

Florian, Gertrude: ceramic composition dressed ladies **$300**
Mother and Baby **$400**

Heizer, Dorothy: cloth sculpture
Fashion Pair of 1770s **$2,800**
Queens: 10-13in (25-33cm) **$1,100-$1,500**
Mary, Mary: 16in (41cm) **$3,100**

Hale, Patti:
carved wood heads **$200-$300**
Hitty: all-wood **$300**

Johnson, Sharon: porcelain children **Elizabeth, Lil Jewel** **$125**

Kane, Maggie Head: porcelain **Gypsy Mother** **$400-$450**

Ling, Tita: Phillipines, carved wood, 12in (30cm) **$650**

Oldenburg, Maryanne: porcelain children **$200-$250**

Park, Irma: wax-over-porcelain miniatures, depending upon detail **$175 up**

Parker, Ann:
historical characters **$275-$300**

Redmond, Kathy:
embellished porcelain shoulder heads:
Victoria Set: four dolls **$1,500**
Henry VIII **$600**
Henry's Wives **$450 each**
Elizabeth I & Edward **$250 each**
Medieval Ladies **$450**
Children **$350-$400**

Saucier, Madeline: cloth
15in (38cm) **$450**

Getrude Florian *Mother & Baby in Rocking Chair. H & J Foulke, Inc.*

Lewis Sorensen *Toymaker. H & J Foulke, Inc.*

Shreve Island Plantation: flat wood, painted underwear, **Julie Ann,**
3¾in (9cm)   **$45-$50**
Smith, Sherman: carved wood
  5-6in (13-15cm)   **$250-$300**
  Pinocchio:
    7½in (19cm)   **$350-$400**
  Hitty   **$300**
  Miss Unity: 12½in (31cm)   **$550**
Sorensen, Lewis: wax
  Father Christmas   **$1,200**
  Toymaker   **$800**
  Gibson Girls   **$350-$375**
Sweet, Elizabeth: 18in (46cm) **Amy,**
  1970   **$250**
Thompson, Martha: porcelain
  **Princess Caroline, Prince
  Charles, Princess Anne**
    $800-$900 each
  Little Women   **$600-$700**
  Betsy   **$800-$900**
  McKim Child (not bisque)   **$800**

Royal Ladies   **$1,500 up**
The Eisenhowers   **$2,300 pair**
Tuttle, Eunice:
  miniature porcelain children
    $500-$600
  Angel Baby   **$400-$425**
Vargas: Black wax characters   **$400**
Walters, Beverly: porcelain, miniature
  fashions   **$500 up**
Wyffels, Berdine: porcelain,
  6in (15cm) girl, glass eyes   **$195**
Zeller, Fawn: porcelain
  One-of-a-kind dolls   **$2,000 up**
  Angela   **$800-$900**
  Jeanie   **$600-$800**
  Jackie Kennedy   **$800**
  Polly Piedmont: 1965   **$600-$800**
  Holly: U.S. Historical Society
    $500-$600
  Polly II: 1989, U.S. Historical
  Society   **$200-$225**

Artist Dolls, UFDC

U.F.D.C. National & Regional Souvenir Dolls: Created by doll artists in limited editions and distributed to convention attendees as souvenirs. Before 1982, most dolls were given as kits; after 1982, most dolls were fully made up and dressed. Except as noted, dolls have porcelain heads, arms and legs; cloth bodies. A few are all-porcelain.

Alice in Wonderland: Yolanda Bello, 1990 Region 10, complete doll **$165**

Alice Roosevelt: Kathy Redmond, 1990 National, complete doll **$150-$165**

   Eleanor, companion doll **$225-$250**

Baby Stuart: Pat Robinson; 1996 National; complete doll **$135**

Bo-Peep: Fred Laughton, 1989 Region 15; carved wood with staff and sheep **$85**

Charity: Fred Laughton, 1995 National, peg-wooden **$100-$125**

Cookie: Linda Steele, 1987 Regional, complete doll **$225**

Crystal Faerie: Kazue Moroi and Lita Wilson, 1983 Midwest Regional, complete doll **$85**

Emma: Rappahannock Rags, 1993 National, cloth **$95**

Father Christmas: Beverly Walters, 1980 National, (kit) fully made up **$400**

Gibson Girl Bathing Beauty: Phyllis Wright,. 1993 Regional, with bathing costume and beach chair **$85**

Janette: Fawn Zeller, 1991 National, complete doll, undressed **$300-$350**

Kate: Anili, 1986 National, all-cloth, with original box **$165-$185**

Ken-Tuck: Janet Masteller, 1972 Regional, (kit) fully made up **$65-$75**

Laurel: Lita Wilson and Muriel Kramer, 1985 Regional, fully made up **$75-$85**

Li'l Apple: Faith Wick, 1979 National, fully made up with romper suit **$50**

   Apple Lil, companion doll **$75**

Lindbergh: Faith Wick, 1981 National, complete doll **$85**

Lissette: Kathy Hansen, 1998 National, all-bisque doll with trunk **$330**

13in (33cm) *Sunshine,* UFDC 1983 National Convention souvenir doll, all original. *H & J Foulke, Inc.*

Little Miss Sunshine: Diana Lence
Crosby, 1974 Florida Regional,
(kit) fully made up   **$65-$75**
Louise: Marilyn Stauber, 1997
National, complete doll   **$135**
Mary: Linda Steele, 1987 National,
fully made up   **$90-$100**
Lewis, companion doll **$125-$150**
Miami Miss: Fawn Zeller, 1961
National,
(kit) fully made up   **$200-$250**
dressed   **$300-$350**
Nellie Bly: Muriel Kramer, 1985
Pittsburgh Regional, complete doll
                             $85-$95
Osceola: X. Kontis, 1954 National,
composition   **$125-$150**
PaPitt: X. Kontis, 1953 National,
composition   **$125-$150**
Pinky: Linda Cheek, California
Regional, complete doll **$250-$300**
Portrait of a Young Girl: Jeanne
Singer, 1986 Rochester Regional,
complete doll   **$200**
Precious Lady: Maori Kazue, 1972
National, fully made up   **$95**
Princess Kimimi: Lita Wilson, 1977
Ohio Regional, (kit) fully made up
                             $85-$95
Queen Victoria: Virginia Orenyo,
1994 National, complete doll **$135**
Rose O'Neill: Lita Wilson, 1982
National, complete doll **$150-$165**
Scarlett: Beverly Walters, 1976
Regional, half-doll, fully made up
                             $135
Scarlett: Lita Wilson and Muriel
Kramer, 1989 Florida Regional,
half-doll, fully made up **$125-$135**
Sunshine: Lucille Gerrard, 1983
National, complete doll   **$75-$85**
Wain, companion doll   **$90-$100**
Tammy: Jeanne Singer, 1989 Western
New York Doll Club, complete doll
                             $85
Trick or Treat: Dana Martindale, 1991
Regional, complete doll with "Nose"
                             $125

Artist Dolls, Commercial

Commercial Doll Artists: Prices are
for a factory perfect doll, never-played-
with, including all accessories, wrist
tag, certificate and box, if any.

Anri, carved wood:
  Ferrandiz, Gabriel, Marie:
    14in (36cm)   **$350**
    Sarah Kay: 13½in (34cm) **$350**
Dolfi, carved wood: 13in (33cm)
                           $175-$225
Good-Krüger, Julie, vinyl:
    Children: 21in (53cm) **$125-$175**
    Anne with an E   **$200-$300**
    Sew Much Love (Club Doll) **$200**
    Dolls of Many Lands, Germany
                               $300
Gunzel, Hildegard:
Wax over porcelain:
    Mara Lee: 1998, 30in (76cm)
                             $2,000
    Lillibeth: 1997   **$1,900**
Vinyl:
    For Alexander Doll Co., 1990-1993:
      17in (43cm)   **$80-$90**
      27in (69cm)   **$200**
    Sahra Richel & Patti: 2000,
      29in (73cm)   **$800-$900**
    Binella   **$550-$650**
    Uda Jane: 27in (69cm) **$700-$800**
    Chipie Baby: 1998, 21in (53cm)
                           $250-$300
    Lamponi: 22in (56cm) **$320-$360**
    Darleen: 31in (78cm) **$650-$750**
    Piccolina II: 1998, 25in (63cm)
                               $450
    Ilse: 1996, 26in (56cm) **$395**
    Gunzel Kids: 1992, 13in (33cm)
                             $35-$40
Porcelain:
    Melody and Friend: 1992,
      25in (63cm)   **$350**
Hartmann, Sonya:
    Children   **$150-$250**
    Lucinda: 1999, Disney **$350**
Heath, Philip:
    Lauren: 40in (102cm)   **$650**
    Steven & Felicia: 1993, red hair,
      24in (61cm)   **$500-$600 pair**

World of Children Collection
$300-$400
Heller, Karin, all-cloth: Children
$250-$300
Iacono, Maggie, all-cloth: Children,
fully-jointed $800-$900
Kish, Helen:
Ballerinas: 12in (33cm) $95-$105
Nanette: fully-jointed   **$185**
Alice in Wonderland: 1996,
16in (41cm)   **$325**
Lawton, Wendy:
Lotta Crabtree, 1992 (12 dolls):
13in (33cm) at auction   **$690**
With travel trunk, at auction   **$931**
Patricia & Her Patsy: 1993   **$495**
Tish: 1991, Disney   **$350**
The Blessing: 1990   **$330**
Storybook Collection $65-$75
Baa Baa Black Sheep: 1990   **$460**
Middleton, Lee, vinyl:
Sugar Britches, Honey Love, other
babies and toddlers $65-$85
Forever Cherish: 1987,
at auction   **$530**
Roche, Lynne & Michael, porcelain
and wood: 20-22in (51-56cm)
$1,000-$1,200
Schrott, Rotraut, for Gadco:
Martina, porcelain, 1988:
28in (71cm)   **$400**
Vinyl $200-$250

Marlene, porcelain:
28in (71cm)   **$400**
Vinyl $200-$250
Puyi: 1989, 26in (66cm)   **$150**
Suzi: 1989, 28in (71cm)   **$150**
Laura: 28in (71cm)   **$250**
Spanos, FayZah, vinyl:
Babies $75-$125
Hershey Kisses & Hugs:
18in (46cm)   **$50**
Tonner, Robert:
Models: 19in (48cm) $175-$200
Chloe: (500), 1996   **$250**
Tyler: Santa Fe 2000, package
$275
Tyler: UFDC 2000   **$425**
Treffeisen, Ruth:
Porcelain Children:
25-30in (64-76cm) $1,700-$2,200
Vinyl Children: $250-$350
Ilsa: 23in (58cm)   **$200**
Olivia & Oliver: babies, 1999
$350-$400 pair
Turner, Judith, vinyl for Hasbro:
Real Baby: 1984 $55-$65
Sleeping version   **$95**
Turner, Virginia, vinyl:
Large Children: 30-32in (76-81cm)
$250-$280
Small Children: 21in (53cm)
$110-$125
Woods, Robin, vinyl:
Camelot Collection: 14in (36cm)
$75-$125
Let's Play Dolls (Alexander Doll
Co.):
13in (33cm) $75-$95
Trunk set $140-$160
Dancer's Recital: trunk and
wardrobe   **$125**
Scarlett Christmas: 1989 $75-$100
Dee Dee: 1989, (Disney)   **$150**
Fantasia Fairy: 1994   **$190**
Children:
8in (21cm) $25-$30
12-14in (31-36cm) $50-$75

*Helen Kish 1995-1996 Nanette and 1996
McKenzie in Sunday Best. Rae-Ellen
Koenig, The Doll Express.*

Ashton-Drake Galleries

Prices are for dolls in mint condition with certificates and boxes.

Designer - Yolanda Bello:
Picture Perfect Babies:
  Jason: (1st) — $250-$300
  Heather: (2nd) — $65-$85
  Jennifer: (3rd) — $70-$90
  Matthew: (4th) (1987) — $75-$85
  Amanda: (1988) — $50-$60
  Sarah: (1989) — $40-$50
  Jessica: (1989) — $40-$50
  Lisa: (1990) — $40-$50
  Michael: (1990) — $65
  Emily: (1991) — $40-$50
  Danielle: (1991) — $40-$50
Playtime Babies:
  Lindsey: (1994) — $40
  Shawna: (1994) — $40
  Todd: (1994) — $40
Lullaby Babies — $25-$30
Moments to Remember:
Jill: (1993) — $45-$55
Justin: (1991) — $45-$55
Magical Moments of Summer:
Whitney: (1995) — $35-$45
Heaven Scent Babies:
  Megan Rose: (1994) — $45
  Sweet Carnation — $45

Designer - Wendy Lawton:
  Little Women: Set of five — $250-$300

Designer -Joan Ibarolle:
  Little House on the Prairie characters: (1992-1995) — $85-$115 each

Designer - Dianna Effner:
  Heroines from the Fairy Tale Forest:
    Goldilocks, Cinderella, Snow White, Red Riding Hood, Rapunzel: 16in (41cm) — $45-$55
    What Little Girls Are Made Of, 15in (38cm):
      Sunshine & Lollipops: (1997) — $50
      Peaches & Cream — $40

Christmas & Candy Canes: (1999) — $40
Mother Goose Series, 14in (36cm):
  Mary, Mary: (1991) — $40-$45
  Girl with curl: (1992) — $40-$45
  Curly Locks: (1993) — $40-$45
  Snips & Snails: (1993) — $40-$45
Classic Collection: Hillary, (1995) 15in (38cm) — $50-$55
Babies: Sugar Plum, (1994) 8in (20cm) — $60

Designer - Julie Good-Krüger:
  Amish Blessings: Rebeccah, Rachael — $50 -$60 each
  All I Wish for You: (Angel Series) (1994-1997) — $30-$40
  Oh Holy Night Set: (nine dolls) — $350
Baby Talk:
  Night, Night: (1995) — $35
  Bye, Bye: (1995) — $35

Dianna Effner *Sugar Plum. Rae-Ellen Koenig, The Doll Express.*

Titus Tomescu *Eternal Love* bride. *Rae-Ellen Koenig, The Doll Express.*

Gene in *Crème de Cassis. Sidney Jeffrey.*

Designer - Mary Tretter:
Wizard of Oz: Dorothy, Scarecrow, Cowardly Lion, Tinman
                                      $50-$65 each

Designer - Brigette Duval:
Fairy Tale Princesses:
   18in (46cm)   **$40-$50**
Cinderella, Prince and Coach
   8in (21cm)   **$65**

Designer - Titus Tomescu:
From This Day Forward: (Brides)
1994   **$60-$70**
Miracles of Jesus: Ascension $150
Barely Yours (Babies):
   Snug as a Bug   **$45**
   Cute as a Button   **$45**
Snow Babies   **$40**

For Walt Disney:
Snow White   **$60-$70**
Dopey   **$60**

Designer - Mel Odom:
Gene:
   Premiere: 1996   **$300-$350**
   Holiday Magic: 1996, First
      Christmas outfit only **$150-$225**
   Atlantic City 1996 Convention
   Package: bathing outfit and all
      handouts given at the
      convention   **$800-$1,200**
   My Favorite Witch: 1997
      Convention doll   **$1,800**
   Midnight Romance: 1997 FAO
      Schwarz exclusive   **$125-$150**
   Night at Versaille: 1997 FAO
      Schwarz exclusive   **$150-$200**
   Broadway Medley: 1998
      Convention doll   **$225-$275**
   King's Daughter   **$135-$180**
   Warm Wishes: 2000 FAO
      Schwarz exclusive   **$110**
   Tea Time at the Plaza: 1999
      FAO Schwarz exclusive   **$90**

Barbie®

FACTS
Mattel, Inc., Hawthorne, CA, U.S.A.
1959 to present. Hard plastic and vinyl.
11½–12in (29-31cm).
Mark: 1959-1962: "Barbie TM/Pats. Pend./© MCMLVIII/by/Mattel, Inc."
1963-1968: "Midge TM/© 1962/Barbie®/© 1958/by/Mattel, Inc."
1964-1966:"© 1958/Mattel, Inc./U.S. Patented/U.S. Pat. Pend."
1966-1969: "© 1966/Mattel, Inc./U.S. Patented/U.S. Pat. Pend./ Made in Japan."

First BARBIE®: 1959. Vinyl, solid body; very light complexion, white irises, pointed eyebrows, gold hoop earrings, ponytail; black and white striped bathing suit; holes in feet to fit stand; mint condition.

11½in (29cm) boxed **$6,500-$8,500***

Doll only, no box or accessories:

Mint	**$3,500-$4,500**
Very good	**$2,500**
Stand	**$1,200**
Shoes	**$50**
Hoop earrings	**$65**

Dressed display boxed doll: **#862**

Barbie-Q **$13,500**

Second BARBIE®: 1959-1960. Vinyl, solid body; very light complexion; same as above, but no holes in feet; some wore pearl earrings; mint condition. Made three months only.

11½in (29cm) boxed **$6,000-$7,000***

Doll only, no box or accessories,

Very good **$3,000-$4,000**

*Brunette harder to find than blonde.

BARBIE® #1, boxed. McMasters Premier Doll Auctions.

BARBIE® #2. McMasters Premier Doll Auctions.

Third BARBIE®: 1960. Vinyl, solid body; very light complexion; same as #2, but with blue irises and curved eyebrows; no holes in feet; mint condition.

11½in (29cm) boxed	**$900-$1,200**
Doll only, mint	**$500-$600**
Dressed display boxed doll: #892	
Golden Elegance	**$4,400**

Fourth BARBIE®: 1960. Vinyl; same as #3, but with solid body of flesh-toned vinyl; mint condition.

11½in (29cm) boxed	**$650-$750**
Doll only, mint	**$350**
Dressed display boxed doll:	
#881 Busy Gal	**$2,800**

Fifth BARBIE®: 1961. Vinyl; same as #4; ponytail hairdo of firm Saran; mint condition.

11½in (29cm) boxed	**$450-$550**
Doll only, mint	**$275-$325**

BARBIE® #5, boxed. McMasters Premier Doll Auctions.

Other BARBIES®: All prices are for mint-in-box dolls unless otherwise noted.

Bubble Cut BARBIE®,	
1961 on	**$300-$325***
Doll only, mint	**$150-$175***
Bubble side part: Doll only,	
mint	**$300**
Fashion Queen BARBIE®: 1963	**$500**
Doll only with three wigs	**$125-$135**
Miss BARBIE®: 1964	**$1,300**
Swirl Ponytail BARBIE®:	
1964	**$550-$650***
Doll only, mint	**$250-$350***

Bendable Leg BARBIE®, 1965 and 1966:

American Girl, center part	
	$1,500-$2,400
Side part	**$3,500-$4,500**
High color face	**$3,400**
Color Magic BARBIE®, 1966:	
Brunette	**$1,600-$2,200**
Blonde	**$1,200-$1,800**
Doll only, mint:	
Brunette	**$1,300**
Blonde	**$850**
Twist & Turn BARBIE®:	
1967	**$375-$425**
Titian	**$425-$475**
Trade-In box, mint	**$700**
Talking BARBIE®: 1970	**$225-$250**
Living BARBIE®: 1970	**$225**
Hair Happenin's BARBIE®:	
1971	**$1,200**
Montgomery Ward BARBIE®:	
1972, Mint doll	**$250-$300**
Growin' Pretty Hair: 1971-1972	**$375**

Gift Sets, mint-in-box:

Fashion Queen BARBIE® & Ken:	
1964	**$1,200**
Wedding Party, 1964	**$1,900**
On Parade (BARBIE®, Ken and	
Midge): 1964	**$1,100**
Skipper Party Time: 1964	**$550**
Little Theatre: 1964	**$7,500**
Pep Rally (no dolls): 1964	**$800**

*Allow 25% extra for platinum or white ginger hair.

Bubblecut *BARBIE®*, dressed and boxed doll. *McMasters Premier Doll Auctions.*

Bubblecut *BARBIE®*, boxed. *McMasters Premier Doll Auctions.*

Outfits: All never-removed-from-package. Deduct 50% for *complete* but out-of-package outfits.

Roman Holiday	$3,000 up
Gay Parisienne	$2,000 up
Easter Parade	$2,500 up
Shimmering Magic	$1,500 up
Here Comes the Bride	$950 up
Pan Am Stewardess	$2,000 up
BARBIE® Baby Sits	$300 up
Dogs & Duds	$300 up
Enchanted Evening	$400 up
1600 Series and Jacqueline Kennedy-style outfits	$295 up
Dinner at 8	$250
Commuter Set	$1,500
Picnic Set	$295

Midnight Blue	$500 up
Miss Astronaut	$750 up
Silken Flame	$145
Senior Prom	$275
Plantation Belle	$400
Open Road	$350
Registered Nurse	$250

Accessories, Mint-in-package:

BARBIE® doll's First Car	$250-$300
BARBIE® doll's First Dreamhouse	$150
Fashion Shop	$300
Little Theatre	$500
Cases	$25 up
BARBIE® doll's Bed	$100

Above: German *American Girl BARBIE®*, boxed. *McMasters Premier Doll Auctions.*

Right: *Dramatic New Living BARBIE®*, boxed. *McMasters Premier Doll Auctions.*

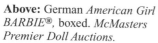

Other Dolls: All prices are for mint-in-box dolls unless otherwise noted.

Ken #1: 1961	**$225**
Bendable legs	**$300-$325**
Dressed boxed doll	**$275 up**
Midge: 1963	**$195**
1966, Bendable legs	**$550**
Allan, 1964-1966:	
Bendable legs	**$350**
Straight legs	**$175**
Skipper: 1964, straight legs	**$175**

Dramatic New Living Skipper	**$150**
Bendable Legs	**$200**
Ricky: 1965	**$200**
Scooter: 1965, straight legs	**$200**
Francie, 1966-1967:	
Doll only, bendable legs, mint	**$185**
Straight legs	**$200**
Twist 'n Turn	**$260-$285**
Black: 1967, mint-in-package	**$1,500**
Doll only, mint	**$850**
"No Bangs," 1970	**$1,500**
Doll only, mint	**$900 up**
Growin' Pretty Hair	**$270**

Hair Happenin's: 1970	**$275**
Casey: 1967	**$275-$300**
Twiggy: 1967	**$325-$375**
Christie: 1968-1972, (Black)	
Twist 'n Turn	**$350**
Stacey: 1968-1971, Twist 'n Turn	**$350**
P.J.: 1969-1971, Twist 'n Turn	
	$225-$275
Live Action on Stage	**$215**
Truly Scrumptious: 1969	**$525**
Doll only, mint	**$300**
Julia: 1969	**$300**
Talking	**$200**
Tutti: 1967-1970	**$150**
Chris: 1967-1970	**$210**
Todd: 1967-1970	**$200**
Pretty Pairs:	
Angie 'N Tangie	**$250-$300**
Nan 'N Fran	**$225-$250**
Lori 'N Rori	**$250-$275**

Bob Mackie BARBIE® Dolls:

1990 Gold	**$450**
1991 Platinum	**$425**
1991 Starlight Splendor (black)	
	$400
1992 Empress Bride	**$550**
1992 Neptune Fantasy	**$600-$700**
1993 Masquerade Ball	**$300**
1994 Queen of Hearts	**$200**
1995 Goddess of the Sun	**$175**

Christmas BARBIE® Dolls

1988, English language box	**$550**
1989	**$200**
1990	**$175**
1991	**$150**
1992	**$100**
1993	**$120**
1994	**$100**
1995	**$55**
1996	**$50**
1997	**$35-$45**
1998	**$25**

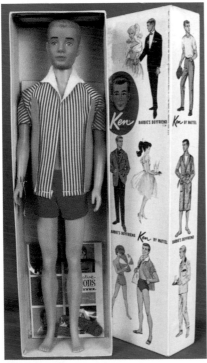

Ken, boxed. *McMasters Premier Doll Auctions.*

Midge with lifelike bendable legs, boxed. *McMasters Premier Doll Auctions.*

Skipper with lifelike bendable legs, boxed. *McMasters Premier Doll Auctions.*

Dramatic New Living Skipper, boxed. *McMasters Premier Doll Auctions.*

Exclusive Store Specials:

1990 Winter Fantasy
(FAO Schwarz)   **$125**
1993 Little Debbie   **$40-$50**
1993 Rockettes
(FAO Schwarz)   **$125**
1994 Nicole Miller
(Bloomingdales)   **$65-$75**
1994 Victorian Elegance
(Hallmark)   **$75**
1994 Silver Screen
(FAO Schwarz)   **$125**
1994 Tooth Fairy (WalMart)   **$20**
1995 Shopping Chic
(Speigel)   **$75-$85**
1995 Jeweled Splendor
(FAO Schwarz)   **$150**
1995 Circus Star
(FAO Schwarz)   **$100**
1995 Donna Karan
(Bloomingdales)   **$80-$90**
1995 Royal Enchantment
(J.C. Penney)   **$40**

1995 Statue of Liberty
(FAO Schwarz)   **$75-$80**
1997 Pink Ice (Toys R Us) **$75-$80**

Timeless Creations (now BARBIE®
Collectibles):

Stars and Stripes Collection:
1990 Air Force BARBIE®   **$55**
1991 Navy BARBIE®   **$50**
1992 Marine BARBIE®   **$50**
1992 Marine Gift Set   **$85**
1993 Army Gift Set   **$75**
1994 Air Force Gift Set   **$60**
Classique Collection:
1992 Benefit Ball   **$125**
1993 Opening Night   **$65**
1993 City Style   **$70**
1994 Uptown Chic   **$70**
1994 Evening Extravaganza **$60**
1994 Evening Extravaganza
(black)   **$75**
1995 Midnight Gala   **$65**

Nostalgia Series:

1994 35th Anniversary:

(blonde)	$45
(brunette)	$60
1994 Gift Set	$100-$125
1994 Solo in the Spotlight	$35
1995 Busy Gal	$65
1996 Enchanted Evening	$35
1996 Poodle Parade	$30
1997 Fashion Luncheon	$40

Scarlett Series, 1994 & 1995:

Green Velvet	$75
Red Velvet	$75-$85
Barbecue	$75
Honeymoon	$85
Ken as Rhett Butler	$60

Great Eras:

1993 Gibson Girl	$100
1993 1920s Flapper	$125
1994 Egyptian Queen	$100
1994 Southern Belle	$90-$100
1995 Medieval Lady	$60
1996 Grecian Goddess	$50
1997 Chinese Empress	$50

Other BARBIE® Dolls:

1986 Blue Rhapsody (porcelain)	$700
1988 Mardi Gras	$80
1989 Pink Jubilee	$1,500 up
1990 Wedding Fantasy	$50
1992 My Size	$125
1994 Snow Princess	$125
1994 Gold Jubilee	$600-$700
1994 Evergreen Princess	$75
1994 Evergreen Princess (red hair)	$300
1995 Peppermint Princess	$65
1995 Starlight Waltz	$75
1995 Dior, First	$90-$100
1995 50th Anniversary (porcelain)	$350
1996 Pink Splendor	$500
1996 Jewel Princess	$35
1996 Jewel Princess (Disney brunette)	$125-$150
1996 Escada	$65-$75
1996 Dior, Second	$85
1997 Bill Blass	$60
1997 Midnight Princess	$45-$50
1997 Midnight Princess (Disney, brunette)	$100-$110

Twiggy, boxed. *McMasters Premier Doll Auctions.*

Twist 'n Turn Casey, boxed. *McMasters Premier Doll Auctions.*

Betsy McCall

American Character Doll Co.: 1957. All-hard plastic, jointed knees; molded eyelashes, rooted Saran hair on wig cap; original clothes; excellent with rosy cheeks.

8in (20cm) basic, (undergarment, shoes and socks) **$200-$250**

Mint-in-box, basic **$375-$425**
In dresses **$250-$300**
In gowns **$300-$400**
Designer Studio Set **$925**

Clothes, clean and in very good condition:

Dresses **$30-$50**
Shoes and socks **$35-$40**
Boxed outfits **$100-$125**

American Character: 1960. All-vinyl, slender limbs; lashed sleep eyes; original clothes; excellent condition.

14in (36cm) **$350-$375**
20in (51cm) **$450-$500**
30in (76cm) **$550-$600**
36in (91cm) **$650-$750**

20in (51cm) American Character *Betsy McCall* bride, all original. *Rosemary Kanizer Collection.*

Boxed, all original:
14in (36cm) **$650-$750**
20in (51cm) **$850-$950**

Jointed at wrists, waist, knees and ankles:
22in (56cm) **$400-$450**
30in (76cm) **$625-$675**

Ideal Novelty & Toy Co.: 1948. Vinyl head, hard plastic body; original clothes; excellent condition
14in (36cm) **$250-$300**
Mint-in-box **$725**

Ideal Novelty & Toy Co.: 1959. All-vinyl; original clothes; excellent condition.
Betsy McCall:
36in (91cm) **$550-$650**
Sandy McCall:
38in (96cm) **$500-$600**

Uneeda: 1959-1961.
All-vinyl, 11½in (29cm) **$125-$135**
Boxed **$275-$300**

Horsman: 1974.
All-vinyl, 29in (73cm)
boxed **$225-$275**

Tomy: 1984. Porcelain/cloth, all original and boxed, Four Seasons, 16in (41cm) **$40-$50**

Tonner, Robert: All original.
"Stamp Doll," 1997
Porcelain,
11in (28cm) **$75-$80**
50th Anniversary, 2000
8in (20cm) **$165-$175**
Second Betsy McCall
Convention **$125**
Disney Mousketeer, 1997
$275-$300
Disney Snow White, 1999
$145-$150
"Hello Portland," 2001
8in (20cm) **$90-$100**

Boudoir Dolls

Boudoir Doll: Head of composition, cloth or other material, painted features, mohair wig; composition or cloth stuffed body, unusually long extremities; usually high-heeled shoes; original clothes elaborately designed and trimmed; all in excellent condition.

FACTS
Various French, U.S. and Italian firms.
Early 1920s into the 1940s.

Cloth Face, 1920s:
   Exceptional quality art doll: silk
   hair, 28-30in (71-76cm)
                   $400-$500

Standard quality: dressed
   28-30in (71-76cm)   **$200-$250**
   Naked   **$90-$110**
Composition Head:
   1920s Smoking Doll,
     25in (64cm)   **$450-$500**
   1940s, dressed   **$125**
Lenci: See page 145.
Poured Wax: 22in (56cm)   **$600**

21in (53cm) leather boudoir doll. *Private Collection.*

Buddy Lee

Burgarella

Marked Buddy Lee: Molded hair, painted eyes to side; jointed at shoulders, stiff hips, legs apart; dressed in original Lee clothes; all in very good condition.

Composition, 1920-1948:	
13in (33cm)	**$450-$550**
Hard Plastic, 1949-1962:	
13in (33cm)	**$450-$550**
Coca Cola uniform	**$650-$750**
John Deere	**$600**
Gasoline Station Uniform	**$600-$800**

Burgarella Child: Excellent quality; all-composition; jointed at neck, shoulders, elbows, hips and knees; human hair or mohair wig, short face with chubby cheeks, dramatic painted eyes, small mouth; all in excellent condition.

All original clothing:	
16-18in (41-46cm)	**$500-$600**
22in (56cm)	**$650-$750**
Sexed boy, all original	**$750-$800**

Hard plastic *Buddy Lee*, all original. *Rae-Ellen Koenig, The Doll Express.*

22in (56cm) Burgarella child, original dress. *Sweetbriar.*

FACTS
H.D. Lee Co., Inc.,
garment manufacturers of
Kansas City, MO. 1920-1962.
Mark: "Buddy Lee" embossed on back

FACTS
Gaspare Burgarella, Rome, Italy. Ca.
1925 until World War II.
Designer: Ferdinando Stracuzzi
Mark: Cloth label sewn on clothes
"BURGARELLA Made in Italy"

Cameo Doll Company

Kewpie: 1913. See page 131.

Bundie: 1918-1925, all-composition,
11in (28cm)   **$300****

Scootles: 1925. Designed by Rose O'Neill. All-composition; appropriate clothes; all in very good condition.

7-8in (18-20cm)	**$400-$500**
12-13in (31-33cm)	**$450-$500**
15-16in (38-41cm)	**$600-$650**
20in (51cm)	**$1,000-$1,200**

Sleep eyes:

12in (31cm)	**$700-$750**
20in (51cm)	**$1,250-$1,500**

Black: 13-14in (33-36cm) **$650-$750**

All-bisque (Japan):

4½in (11cm)	**$325-$375**
6-7in (15-18cm)	**$500-$550**

FACTS

Cameo Doll Company, New York, NY, later Port Allegany, PA. Original owner: Joseph L. Kallus.
1922-on.

Baby Bo Kaye: 1925. See page 42.

Wood Segmented Characters: Designed by Joseph L. Kallus. Composition head, segmented wood body; undressed; all in very good condition.

Margie, 1929:

10in (25cm)	**$225-$250**
15in (38cm)	**$400-$450**
17in (43cm)	**$550**

Pinkie: 1930, 10in (25cm)
$250-$275

Joy, 1932:

10in (25cm)	**$250-$275**
15in (38cm)	**$375-$400**

Betty Boop, 1932:

12in (31cm)	**$650-$750**

With molded bathing suit and composition legs; wearing a cotton print dress   **$750-$850****

**Not enough price samples to compute a reliable range.

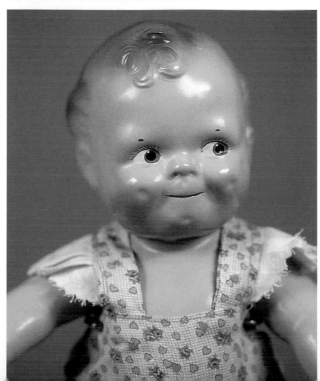

12in (31cm)
Scootles, all original.
H & J Foulke, Inc.

12in (31cm) *Giggles*, all original. *H & J Foulke, Inc.*

10in (25cm) Cameo *Margie* variation. *H & J Foulke, Inc.*

Pop-Eye: 1935   **$300****
Hotpoint Man: 16in (41cm)   **$800****
RCA Radiotron: 16in (41cm) **$800****
Bandy: General Electric, 18in (46cm)
                                        $800**
Pete the Pup: 9in (23cm)   **$400-$425**

Giggles: 1946. Designed by Rose O'Neill. All-composition; original romper; all in very good condition.
     14in (36cm)   **$450-$500****
     Boxed   **$650-$750**

Little Annie Rooney: 1925. Designed by Jack Collins. Composition; painted eyes, yarn wig; all original.
     16in (41cm)   **$700****

Baby Blossom: 1927, composition and cloth, 19-20in (48-51cm) **$550-$650****

Champ: 1942, composition, molded hair, freckles, all original,
     16in (41cm)   **$500-$600****

Vinyl Dolls:
  Miss Peep: 1957. All original:
     16-18in (41-46cm)   **$75-$85**
     Boxed   **$125-$135**
  Newborn Miss Peep: 1962,
     14in (36cm) boxed   **$65**
  Baby Mine: 1961, all original,
     20in (51cm) boxed   **$175-$225**
  Margie: 1958, all original,
     17in (43cm) boxed **$175-$225****
  Scootles, all original:
     1964, 14in (36cm)   **$165-$185**
     1973 Ltd. Ed. (Maxines),
        16in (41cm)   **$200-$225**
     1980s, (Jesco), all original:
        12in (31cm)   **$40-$60**
        16in (31cm)   **$75**
  Lee Middleton Stamp Doll:
     12in (31cm)   **$40**

**Not enough price samples to compute a reliable range.

Campbell Kids

E.I. Horsman Co.: 1910-1914. Designed by Grace G. Drayton. Composition head, molded and painted bobbed hair; original cloth body; appropriate or original clothes; all in good condition.
Mark: On head:

E.I.H. © 1910

Cloth label on sleeve:

> The Campbell Kids
> Trademark by
> Joseph Campbell.
> Mfg. by E.I. Horsman Co

10-13in (25-33cm)	**$275-$325**
16in (41cm)	**$400-$450**

American Character & E.I. Horsman Co.: 1923. Designed by Grace G. Drayton, sometimes called *Dolly Dingle*. All-composition; molded bobbed hair, painted eyes to side; original clothes; all in good condition.
12in (31cm)	**$550-$650**

E. I. Horsman Co.: 1948. All-composition; molded bobbed hair, painted eyes to side, watermelon mouth; original clothes; all in good condition.
12in (31cm)	**$450-$475**
With Campbell Soup outfit and label	**$600**

All-Vinyl: 1950 on. Original clothes, bright color, unplayed-with condition.
8in (20cm)	**$25-$30**
11in (28cm)	**$40-$45**

All-Cloth, Knickerbocker: 1973,
12in (31cm) boxed	**$38-$42**

Porcelain: 1997, Soup Can box,
11½in (29cm)	**$50-$60**

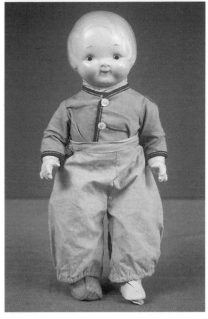

13in (33cm) Horsman 1920s *Campbell Kid,* all original. *H & J Foulke, Inc.*

12in (31cm) Horsman 1948 *Campbell Kid,* all original. *H & J Foulke, Inc.*

Dewees Cochran

Dewees Cochran Doll: Latex with jointed neck, shoulders and hips; human hair wig, painted eyes, character face; dressed; all in good condition.
Cindy: 1947-1948
15-16in (38-41cm) **$800-$900**
Grow-up Dolls: Stormy, Angel, Bunnie, J.J. and **Peter Ponsett** each at ages 5, 7, 11, 16 and 20, 1952-1958
$2,200-$2,500
Look-Alike Dolls: (six different faces)
$2,200-$2,500
Individual Portrait:
Children **$2,500-$4,500**
Baby, 9in (23cm) **$1,500**
American Children: See page 262.

10in (25cm) Dewees Cochran portrait doll, all original. *H & J Foulke, Inc.*

FACTS
Dewees Cochran, Fenton, CA, 1940-on.
Mark:
Signed under arm or behind right ear.

Composition (American)

Condition: Unless otherwise noted, all dolls should be all original with perfect hair, good coloring, original clothes; light crazing acceptable.

All-Composition Child Doll: 1912-1920. Various firms, such as Bester Doll Co., New Era Novelty Co., New Toy Mfg. Co., Superior Doll Mfg. Co., Artcraft Toy Product Co., Colonial Toy Mfg. Co. Ball-jointed composition body; appropriate clothes; all in good condition. These are patterned after German bisque-headed dolls.
22-24in (56-61cm) **$275-$325**
Character baby, all-composition
19in (48cm) **$250-$300**

Early Composition Character Doll: Ca. 1912. Composition head with molded hair or wig and painted features; cloth body; appropriate clothes.
12-15in (31-38cm) **$150-$175**
18-20in (46-51cm) **$225-$275**
24-26in (61-66cm) **$325-$350**
Two-face toddler, 14in (36cm)
$275-$300

Molded Loop Dolls: Ca. 1930s. Composition head with molded bobbed hair and loop for tying on a ribbon; quality is generally mediocre.
12-15in (31-38cm) **$150-$175**

Patsy-type Girl: Ca. 1930s. All-composition with molded bobbed hair; of good quality.
9-10in (23-25cm) **$165-$185**
14-16in (36-41cm) **$250-$300**
20in (51cm) **$350**

Mama Dolls: Ca. 1920-on. Composition head with hair wig; composition lower limbs, cloth body.
16-18in (41-46cm) **$225-$250**
20-22in (51-56cm) **$325-$350**
24-26in (61-66cm) **$400-$450**

Above: 13in (33cm) early composition toddler, all original. *H & J Foulke, Inc.*

Top Right: 23in (58cm) *Shirley Temple*-type composition child, all original. *H & J Foulke, Inc.*

Right: 13½in (34cm) *Nibur* composition toddler, all original. *H & J Foulke, Inc.*

15in (38cm)
composition
bride, all
original.
*Private
Collection.*

Babies and Infants: Ca. 1920 on. Composition head with molded hair; composition lower arms, cloth body (may have composition lower legs).

14-16in (36-41cm)	**$175-$225**
18-20in (46-51cm)	**$250-$300**

Dionne-type Doll: Ca. 1935. All-composition with molded hair or wig; of good quality.

7-8in (18-20cm) baby	**$135**
13in (33cm) toddler	**$225-$250**
18-20in (46-51cm) toddler	**$300-$325**

Alexander-type Girl: Ca. 1935. All-composition; of good quality.

13in (33cm)	**$225-$250**
16-18in (41-46cm)	**$300-$350**
22in (56cm)	**$350-$400**

Shirley Temple-type Girl: Ca. 1935-on, all-composition; of good quality.

16-18in (41-46cm)	**$400-$500**

Storybook or International Costume Doll: Ca. 1940. All-composition.
11in (28cm)

Excellent quality	**$150-$175**
Standard quality	**$65-$75**

Miscellaneous Specific Dolls:
Carmen (Miranda): Eegee.

14in (36cm)	**$225**
20in (51cm)	**$350**

Cat, Rabbit or **Pig head:** naked,

10-11in (25-28cm)	**$350-$400**

David: Bible Doll Co. of America,

11in (28cm) boxed	**$285**

Famlee: 1921, boxed with six heads and six costumes   **$1,000**
Grace G. Drayton:

14in (36cm)	**$400-$500**

Hedwig/DiAngeli:
Elin, Hannah, Lydia, Suzanne:

14in (36cm)	**$625-$675**

Indian child: 1940s,

8in (21cm) boxed	**$60**

Jackie Robinson:

13½in (34cm)	**$700-$800**

Jerry Mahoney: Juro Novelty.

24in (61cm)	**$275-$325**

Kewpie-type characters:

12in (31cm)	**$65-$75**

Little Miss Movie: Eegee.

27in (69cm)	**$700-$800**

Lone Ranger: with hat, holster and gun, 16in (41cm)   **$750-$800**
Miss Curity: 18in (46cm)   **$450-$500**
Monica: 1941-1951, inset human hair, 17-18in (43-46cm)   **$450-$550**

Right: 14in (36cm) Hedwig/DiAngeli *Elin*, all original. *H & J Foulke, Inc.*

Below Left: 17in (43cm) *Monica*, all original. *H & J Foulke, Inc.*

Below Right: 11in (38cm) rabbit head composition, re-dressed. *H & J Foulke, Inc*

19in (48cm) *Santa Claus,* re-dressed. *H & J Foulke, Inc.*

14in (36cm) *Trudy,* all original. *H & J Foulke, Inc.*

P.D. Smith: 22in (56cm)   **$2,600****

Paris Doll Co. Peggy:
  28in (71cm) walker   **$350-$400**

Puzzy: 1948, H. of P.
  15in (38cm)   **$350-$400**

Royal "Spirit of America:"
  15in (38cm) with original box and
  outfits   **$300-$350**

Santa Claus: 19in (48cm)   **$400-$450**

Sizzy: 1948, H. of P.
  14in (36cm)   **$250-$300**

Sterling Doll Co. Sports Dolls:
  29in (74cm) all original   **$300-$350**

Trudy: three faces, 1946, 14in (36cm),
  all original   **$225-$250**

Three Pigs and Wolf: boxed set, all
  original   **$800-$1,000**

Black Composition Dolls: Ca. 1930.
Original or appropriate clothes; some
have three yarn tufts of hair on either
side and on top of the head; all in good
condition.

"Topsy" Baby:
  10-12in (25-31cm)   **$160-$175**
  16in (41cm)   **$250-$275**

Toddler:
  15-16in (38-41cm)   **$300-$350**

Girl: 17in (43cm)   **$350-$400**

1910 character:
  13½in (34cm)   **$300-$350**

Patsy-type:
  13-14in (33-36cm)   **$300-$350**

Tony Sarg Mammy with Baby:
  17in (43cm)   **$1,000-$1,100**

Ming Ming Baby: Quan-Quan Co.,
Los Angeles and San Francisco,
California. Ca. 1930. All-composition
baby; original Oriental costume of
colorful taffeta with braid trim; feet
painted black or white for shoes.
  10-12in (25-31cm)   **$200-$225**

**Not enough price samples to compute a
reliable range.

Composition
(German)

All-Composition Child Doll: Socket head with good wig, sleep (sometimes flirty) eyes, open mouth with teeth; jointed composition body; appropriate clothes; all in good condition; of excellent quality.

12-14in (31-36cm)	**$225-$275**
18-20in (46-51cm)	**$375-$425**
22in (56cm)	**$450-$500**

Character face:

18-20in (46-51cm)	**$425-$525**

Double-Face Googly:

14in (36cm)	**$425-$475**

Black Composition Doll: All-composition; molded hair or wig, glass eyes (sometimes flirty); appropriate clothes; all in good condition.

11in (28cm)	**$350**
16-18in (41-46cm)	**$650-$750**
Patsy-type: 11in (28cm) all original	**$650**

Dora Petzoldt Child: 1919 on. Molded composition (sometimes cloth) head, closed mouth, pensive character face, painted eyes, mohair wig; cloth body, sometimes with long arms and legs; original clothing; all in very good condition.

19-22in (48-56cm)	**$850-$950**
Moderate wear, re-dressed	**$400-$450**

Character Baby: Composition head with good wig, sleep eyes, open mouth with teeth; bent-limb composition baby body or hard-stuffed cloth body; appropriate clothes; all in good condition; of excellent quality.

All-composition baby:

16-18in (41-46cm)	**$375-$425**
Cloth body: 18-20in (46-51cm)	**$300-$350**

All-composition toddler:

16-18in (41-46cm)	**$450-$500**

FACTS
Various German firms such as König & Wernicke, Kämmer & Reinhardt and others. Ca. 1920s on.

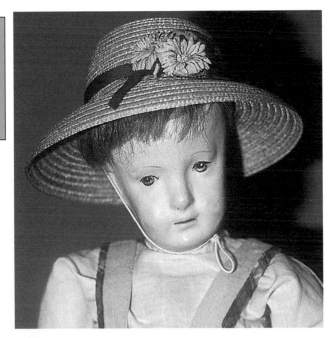

19in (48cm) Dora Petzoldt child. *Jensen's Antique Dolls.*

Composition
(Japanese)

Cosmopolitan

Japanese Composition Doll: All-composition with molded hair, painted features; original rayon panties with "Japan" stamp or naked; all in excellent condition.

Dionne Quintuplets:

Baby: 7in (18cm)	**$165-$185**
Baby: 9in (23cm)	**$250-$300****
Toddler: 7½in (19cm)	**$165-$185**
9in (23cm)	**$250-$300**

Choir Boy: with book molded in hands, 10in (25cm) **$135-$150**
Toddler: 8in (20cm), all original
$125-$135
Shirley Temple: See page 302.

**Not enough price samples to compute a reliable range.

8in (20cm) *Little Miss Ginger. Rosemary Kanizer.*

7½in (19cm) *Shirley Temple. H & J Foulke, Inc.*

FACTS
Unidentified Japanese Companies, 1920-1940.
Mark: "Japan" incised or stamped on back torso.

8in (20cm) *Ginger Mouseketeer*, all original. *Kathy & Terri's Dolls.*

Ginger: 1954 on. All-hard plastic walker; sleep eyes; original clothes; excellent condition with good color and perfect hair.

Unmarked, 8in (20cm)	**$150-$175**
Mint-in-box	**$225**
Roundup, Mouseketeer or **Davy Crockett**	**$225-$250**
Disneyland Costumes	**$300-$350**
Girl Scout or **Brownie**	**$175-$225**
Boxed outfits	**$30-$60**
Boxed wig	**$135**
Dresser	**$190**
Vinyl head, all original	**$50-$60**

Miss Ginger: 1957 on. Vinyl head; hard plastic body with adult figure, high-heeled feet; original clothes; excellent condition. **Mark**: "GINGER" on head.

10½in (27cm)	**$190-$210**
Dresses	**$20-$30**
Boxed outfits	**$75**

Little Miss Ginger: 1958 on. Vinyl head; rigid vinyl body, adult figure with high-heeled feet; original clothes; excellent condition; eyes not askew. **Mark**: "GINGER" on head.

8in (20cm)	**$75-$85**
Shoes	**$20**
Dresses	**$20-$30**

FACTS
Cosmopolitan Doll & Toy Corp.,
Jackson Heights, NY.

Deluxe Reading

Bride Dolls: 1958. All-vinyl, fashion doll; complete original bride clothes.

24-29in (61-74cm)	**$75-$85**

Candy: 1962. All-vinyl fashion doll, three extra costumes, hats and accessories; boxed.

20in (51cm)	**$150-$175**

Penny Brite: 1963. All-vinyl child doll, with accessories and wardrobe sold separately.

8in (20cm) original dress	**$20-$25**
Boxed doll	**$40**
Boxed outfit	**$15-$40**
Beauty Salon	**$45**
Vinyl Carrying Case	**$25-$30**
Kitchen Set	**$45**
Three Rooms Boxed Set, at auction	**$360**

Dawn: 1969 on. Topper. All-vinyl play doll with accessories, wardrobe and friends.

6in (15cm)	**$30-$40**
Boxed doll	**$65-$75**
Boxed or packaged outfit	**$40-$60**
Flower Fantasy: boxed	**$200-$250**
Dancing Glori: (no bangs)	**$165**
Kip Majorette	**$75-$85**
Gary	**$65-$75**

Suzy Homemaker: 1964, vinyl and hard plastic, jointed knees,

21in (53cm)	**$65**

Right: *Kip Majorette, Dawn's friend. Rosemary Kanizer.*

Far Right: *Gary, Dawn's friend. Rosemary Kanizer.*

EFFanBEE

Metal Heart Necklace or Bracelet with chain **$45-50**
Metal Pinback Button **$65-$75**

COMPOSITION DOLLS

Early Characters: Composition character face, molded painted hair; cloth stuffed body; appropriate clothes; in good condition. Some marked "Deco." 12-16in (30-41cm).

Baby Grumpy: 1912, molds **172, 174** or **176** **$375-$425**
Miss Coquette, Naughty Marietta: 1912 **$400-$425**
Pouting Bess: 1915, **162** or **166** **$350-$375**
Billy Boy: 1915 **$350-$375**
Whistling Jim: 1916 **$350-$375**
Harmonica Joe: 1924 **$400-$450**
Katie Kroose: 1918 **$400-$450**

Buds: 1915-1918
7in (18cm) **$175-$195**
Black **$200-$225**
Aunt Dinah: 1915, 16in (41cm) **$600**
Johnny Tu-Face: 1912 **$400-$450**
Betty Bounce: 1913 **$350-$400**
Baby Huggins: 1915 **$300**

FACTS
EFFanBEE Doll Co., New York, NY, 1912-on.
Marks: Various, but nearly always marked "EFFanBEE" on torso or head, sometimes with doll's name.
Wore a metal heart-shaped bracelet; later a gold paper heart label.

15in (38cm) shoulder head *Patsy. H & J Foulke, Inc.*

12in (31cm) all-composition baby with early script mark. *H & J Foulke, Inc.*

Shoulder Head Dolls: Composition shoulder head; cloth torso, composition arms and legs; original clothes; all in good condition.

Baby Grumpy: 1925-1939.

12in (31cm) white	**$300-$325**
Black	**$375-$400**

Pennsylvania Dutch Dolls: 1936-1940, all original and excellent   **$225**

Baby Dainty: 1912-1922.

15in (38cm)	**$250-$275**

Patsy: 1925.

15in (38cm)	**$350-$400**
30in (76cm) at auction	**$3,000**

Rosemary, 1925; **Marilee,** 1924; and other name dolls:

14in (36cm)	**$275-$300**
17in (43cm)	**$350-$400**
25in (64cm)	**$450-$550**
30in (76cm)	**$650-$750**
Marilee: 30in (76cm) mint, at auction	**$3,300**

Mary Ann: 1928.

19-20in (48-51cm)	**$375-$425**
All-composition	**$450-$500**

Mary Lee: 1928.

16-17in (41-43cm)	**$325-$375**
All-composition	**$375-$425**

Mae Starr: Phonograph doll, 1928.

30in (76cm)	**$600-$700**
Mint, with six records, at auction	**$950**

Babies: Composition head, light crazing acceptable; perfect hair and good coloring; cloth body; original clothes; all in good condition.

Bubbles: 1924.

Mark: 19 © 24

EFFANBEE
DOLLS
WALK-TALK-SLEEP
MADE IN USA

EFFANBEE
BUBBLES
COPYR 1924
MADE IN U.S.A.

16-18in (41-46cm)	**$400-$450**
20-22in (51-56cm)	**$500-$550**
25-26in (63-66cm)	**$650-$750**
20in (51cm) redressed	**$325-$350**

Baby Evelyn: 18in (46cm)   **$250-$275**

Lovums: 1928.

Mark: EFFAN BEE
LOVUMS
©
PAT N⁰. 1,283,558

16-18in (41-46cm)	**$350-$400**
22-24in (56-61cm)	**$500-$550**
28in (71cm)	**$650-$700**

11in (28cm) *Brethren Lady* Pennsylvania Dutch doll. *H & J Foulke, Inc.*

12in (31cm) *Baby Grumpy,* all original. *H & J Foulke, Inc.*

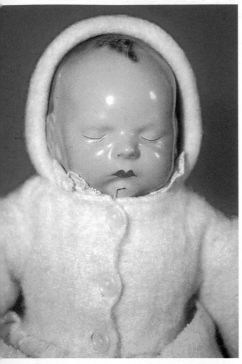

13in (33cm) *Babyette*, all original. *H & J Foulke, Inc.*

Mickey, Baby Bright Eyes, Tommy Tucker, Katie: 1939-1949.

16-18in (41-46cm)	**$350-$385**
22-24in (56-61cm)	**$450-$500**
Twins in Boxed Set,	
14in (36cm)	**$900**

Sweetie Pie: 1942.

16-18in (41-46cm)	**$350-$385**
22-24in (56-61cm)	**$450-$500**
Boxed, with layette,	
23in (58cm)	**$750**

Baby Effanbee: 1925. 12in (31cm)

$160-$180

Lambkin: 1930s.

16in (41cm)	**$450-$475**
Boxed, with pillow	**$650-$700**

Sugar Baby: caracul wig, 1936.

16-18in (41-46cm) **$300-$350**

Babyette: eyes closed, 1943.

13in (33cm) boxed with pillow

$550-$600

Pat-O-Pat: (clap hands), 1925.

13in (33cm) **$150-$165**

Patsy Family: 1928-on. All-composition; original or appropriate old clothes; may have some light crazing.
Marks:

Bracelet

EFFANBEE
PATSY JR.
DOLL

EFFANBEE
PATSY
DOLL

EFFANBEE
PATSY
BABY KIN

Wee Patsy: 6in (15cm)	**$475-$500**
Boxed	**$550-$600**
Boxed with extra outfits	**$750-$850**
Sewing set, boxed set	**$650**
Storybook Doll, all original	**$600**
Black maid	**$1,000**

Baby Tinyette:

7in (18cm) **$325-$350**

Quintuplets: set of five, boxed, all original **$2,500**

9in (23cm) *Patsy Babyette,* all original. *H & J Foulke, Inc.*

9in (23cm) *Patsyette,* all original and boxed. *H & J Foulke, Inc.*

Tinyette Toddler:

8in (20cm)	$325-$350
Doctor, boxed with tag	$950
Boxed trousseau set	$1,200

Patsy Babyette: 9in (23cm) $325-350

Patsyette:

9in (23cm)	$425-$450
Brown	$650
Hawaiian	$650

King and Queen: at auction
$3,000 pair
George and Martha Washington:
$650 pair
Mint and boxed, at auction
$1,500 pair

Patsy Baby:

11in (28cm)	$375-$425
Boxed	$650-$675
Brown	$650-$750

In three-tiered trunk with accessories
$1,300

Patsy Jr., Patsy Kins, Patricia Kin:

11in (28cm)	$425-$475
Brown, at auction	$1,050-$1,250

Movie **Anne Shirley:** red wig
$600-$700
White Horse Inn pair, at auction
$1,500

Patsy:

14in (36cm)	$550-$600
Oriental: at auction	$1,850
1946, unmarked	$400-$450
Boxed	$550
Brother: boxed	$950

On "Patricia" body, magnetic hands
$800-$900

Patsy:

Patricia:

15in (38cm)	$525-$575
Movie **Anne Shirley:** red wig	$700
Martha Washington	$650

11in (28cm) *Patsy Jr.,* all original. *H & J Foulke, Inc.*

Patsy Joan:

16in (41cm)	$525-$575
Boxed, fur coat and hat	$850
1946 (different mold)	$475-$525
Brown	$675

Patsy Ann:

19in (48cm)	$575-$625
Brown	$1,250
Boxed, early wig, fur coat and hat	
	$1,250

Patsy Lou: 22in (56cm) $575-$675

Patsy Ruth:

26in (66cm)	$1,500-$1,600

Patsy Mae:

30in (76cm)	$1,500-$1,600

Skippy: 1929. 14in (36cm)

Soldier, Sailor	$450-$500
Boy's Suit	$650
White Horse Inn, at auction	$1,100
Cowboy: at auction	$1,200
Aviator	$1,500
Fireman: at auction	$3,400
Re-dressed	$350-$400
Brown, at auction	$3,000

16in (41cm) *Patsy Joan*, all original. *H & J Foulke, Inc.*

W.C. Fields: 1930, composition head, hands and feet; cloth body; original clothes, 19in (48cm) at auction **$1,425**

Dy-Dee Baby: 1933-on.
Mark:

"EFF-AN-BEE
DY-DEE BABY
US PAT.-1-857-485
ENGLAND-880-060
FRANCE-723-980
GERMANY-585-647
OTHER PAT PENDING"

Hard rubber head with applied rubber ears, soft rubber body; appropriate old clothes; good condition.

9in (23cm)	$275-$300
11in (28cm)	$175-$200
13in (33cm)	$200-$225
15in (38cm)	$250-$275
20in (51cm)	$375-$400
24in (61cm)	$450

With box and layette:

13in (33cm)	$525
15in (38cm)	$575

Carded five-piece nursery set with

Dy-Dee booklet	$150
Dy-Dee pajamas	$32
Bottle, bubble pipe	$25
Book: **Dy-Dee Dolls Days**	$75

Hard plastic head with applied ears, soft rubber body; appropriate old clothes; good condition.

11in (28cm)	$125-$150
15in (38cm)	$225-$250
20-21in (51-53cm)	$325-$350

All-Composition Children: 1933-on. Original clothes; all in very good condition; nice coloring and perfect hair.

Anne Shirley, 1935-1940; **Little Lady,** 1940-1949:

14-15in (36-38cm)	$275-$300
17-18in (43-46cm)	$300-$325
21in (53cm)	$400-$450
27in (69cm)	$500-$550

Boxed with trousseau:

18in (46cm)	$700
WAAC outfit: 14in (36cm)	$650
Little Eva: 15in (38cm)	$1,400

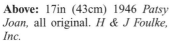

Above: 17in (43cm) 1946 *Patsy Joan,* all original. *H & J Foulke, Inc.*

Top Right: 22in (56cm) *Patsy Lou* with wig. *H & J Foulke, Inc.*

Right: 15in (38cm) *Dy-Dee Baby. H & J Foulke, Inc.*

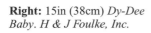

American Children: 1936-1939. Dewees Cochran. Closed mouth, 19-21in (48-53cm) marked "American Children" head on "Anne Shirley" body:

Peggy Lou and others: painted eyes **$2,200**

Gloria Ann and others: sleep eyes **$2,000**

Gloria Ann: boxed, at auction **$4,500**
17in (43cm) boy, unmarked, painted eyes **$1,800****

Open mouth, unmarked:

Barbara Joan:
15in (38cm)   **$700-$750**
Ice Queen (skater)   **$750**

Barbara Ann:
17in (43cm)   **$750-$800**

Barbara Lou:
21in (53cm)   **$900-$950**
Birthday Doll: music box in torso,
17in (43cm)   **$1,050**

Suzette: 1939, painted eyes,
11½in (29cm)   **$350-$400**
Suzanne: 1940, 14in (36cm) **$350-$400**
Portrait Dolls: 1940, Ballerina, Bo-Peep, Gibson Girl, bride, groom, dancing couple, colonial,
11in (28cm)   **$300-$350**
Candy Kid: 1946. Toddler, molded hair:
12in (31cm)   **$350-$400**
"The Champ:" at auction   **$630**
Betty Brite: 1933, caracul wig,
16½in (42cm)   **$325-$375**

Betty Bounce: 1933, "Lovums" head, caracul wig, 19in (48cm)   **$375-$425**
Butin-Nose, 1939:
9in (23cm)   **$275-$300**
Oriental   **$500**
Brother and Sister: 1943, yarn hair, 16in (41cm) and 12in (31cm)
$250-$300 each

Charlie McCarthy: 1937. Strings at back of head to operate mouth; original clothes; all in very good condition.
17-20in (43-51cm)   **$650-$750**
Mint-in-box with button   **$850-$950**

Historical Dolls: 1939. All-composition. Three each of 30 dolls portraying the history of American fashion, 1492-1939. "American Children" heads with elaborate human hair wigs and painted eyes; elaborate original costumes using velvets, satins, silks and brocades; all in excellent condition.

Mark: On Head:
"EFFanBEE AMERICAN CHILDREN"

21in (53cm)   **$1,500-$1,800**
Historical Doll Replicas, 1939:
14in (36cm)   **$500-$600**
Boxed   **$700-$750**

**Not enough price samples to compute a reliable range.

20in (51cm)
American Child.
H & J Foulke, Inc.

Top Left: 17in (43cm) *Barbara Ann*, all original. *H & J Foulke, Inc.*

Top Right: 14in (36cm) *Suzanne*, all original. *H & J Foulke, Inc.*

Bottom Right: 12in (31cm) *Candy Kid*, all original. *H & J Foulke, Inc.*

Bottom Left: 11½in (29cm) *Suzette*, all original. *H & J Foulke, Inc.*

21in (53cm) 1740 original historical doll. *H & J Foulke, Inc.*

14in (36cm) 1908 historical doll replica. *H & J Foulke, Inc.*

HARD PLASTIC DOLLS

Howdy Doody: 1949-1950. Hard plastic or composition head and hands; molded hair, sleep eyes; cloth body; original clothes; all in excellent condition.

19-23in (48-58cm)	**$300-$400**
Mint-in-box	**$525-$575**

Noma, the Electronic Doll: 1950. Battery operated talking mechanism.

28in (71cm)	**$325-$375**
Boxed	**$500**

Honey: 1949-1955. All-hard plastic; original clothes; all in excellent condition. Later dolls have walking mechanism.

Mark: "EFFANBEE"

14in (36cm)	**$325-$350**
18in (46cm)	**$375-$425**
24in (61cm)	**$500**
In Schiaparelli outfits:	
18in (46cm)	**$500**
Prince Charming	**$500-$600**
Cinderella	**$500-$600**
Alice	**$400-$450**

Tintair Honey:

14in (36cm)	**$400-$450**
In original box with accessories	**$600-$650**

VINYL DOLLS: All original and excellent condition.
Mickey: 1956, 10-11in (25-28cm)
$90-$100
Champagne Lady: 1959,
19in (48cm) $250-$300
Fluffy*: 1957 on,
8in (20cm) $35-$40
11in (28cm) $40-$50
Boxed Outfits $20-$25
Patsy Ann: 1960 on,
15in (38cm) $100-$125
Suzette:* 1962, 15in (38cm) $75-$100
Melodie: 1953-1956, battery operated singing talking doll, all original,
27in (69cm) $325-$375
Mary Jane: 1959 on,
32in (81cm) $225-$275
Nurse $275-$325
Little Lady: 1958, 19in (48cm) $200

*For girl scouts, see page 271.

Fashion Lady: Ca. 1958,
19in (48cm) $250
Most Happy Family: 1958, (Mother, Sister, Brother, Baby), boxed,
8-21in (20-53cm) $250-$300
Alyssa: Ca. 1960, 23in (58cm) $225
Bud: Ca. 1960, 24in (61cm) $200-$225
Happy Boy: 1961,
10½in (27cm) $50-$60
Half Pint: 1982 on,
11in (28cm) toddler $25-$35
Boudoir Lady: 1961,
30in (76cm) boxed $275
Dy-Dee Darlin': 1971,
18in (46cm) $100
Baby Lisa: 1980, designed by Astry Campbell, in basket with accessories,
11in (28cm) $100
Disney Dolls: 1977, 14in (36cm) $175
Alice in Wonderland
Cinderella
Snow White
Sleeping Beauty
Cinderella & Prince Charming Set:
1985, 12in (31cm) $95
Hagara, Jan, 1984, 15in (38cm):
Christina with teddy $125
Laurel $100
Hibel, Edna, 1984:
Flower Girl of Brittany $85
Contessa Isabella $85

Suzie Sunshine: 1961-1979, designed by Eugenia Dukas,
18in (46cm) boxed $110
Sugar Pie: 1962-1964,
18in (46cm) boxed $125

Effanbee Club Limited Edition Dolls:
1975 **Precious Baby** $200-$300
1976 **Patsy** $200-$225
1977 **Dewees Cochran** $75-$100
1978 **Crowning Glory** $50-$60
1979 **Skippy** $200-$225
1980 **Susan B. Anthony** $60-$65
1981 **Girl with Watering Can**
$65-$75
1982 **Princess Diana** $100-$125
1983 **Sherlock Holmes** $75-$85
1984 **Bubbles** $55-$65
1985 **Red Boy** $55-$60
1986 **China Head** $25-$35

10in (25cm) *Mickey* football player. *H & J Foulke, Inc.*

17in (43cm) Lady in Orange, all original. *Emma Vann.*

Legend Series, Mint-in-box:

W.C. Fields: 1980		**$200**
John Wayne: (cowboy), 1981		**$250**
John Wayne: (cavalry), 1982		**$250**
Mae West: 1982		**$95**
Groucho Marx: 1983		**$95**
Judy Garland: 1984		**$125**
Lucille Ball: 1985		**$125**
Liberace: 1986		**$250**
James Cagney: 1987		**$65**
Humphrey Bogart: 1988		**$65**
George Burns: 1996		**$50-$60**
Gracie Allen: 1996		**$50-$60**
Carol Channing		**$50**

Presidents, Mint-in-box:

Abraham Lincoln: 1983	**$75**
George Washington: 1983	**$75**
Teddy Roosevelt	**$95**
Franklin D. Roosevelt	**$75**
Andrew Jackson: 1989	**$75**

Personalities: Mint-in-box.

Mark Twain: 1984	**$60**
Louis Armstrong: 1984-1985	**$95**
Sir Winston Churchill: 1984	**$75**
Eleanor Roosevelt	**$75**
Babe Ruth	**$200**

Pride of the South: 1981-1983,
13in (33cm) mint-in-box   **$50-$60**
Grandes Dames: 1976-1983,
15in (38cm) mint-in-box   **$50-$60**
Gigi: 1979-1980, 11in (28cm) mint-in-box   **$40**
International & Storybook: 1976 on,
11in (28cm) mint-in-box   **$20-$30**
Wizard of Oz: 1994, six-doll set **$125**
Mary Poppins: 1985   **$35-$40**
Heidi: 1984   **$40-$50**
Peter Pan: 1994, three-doll set   **$50**

17in (43cm) *Andrew Jackson*, all original. *Emma Vann*

Freundlich

General Douglas MacArthur: Ca. 1942. All-composition portrait doll; molded hat, original khaki uniform; all in good condition.
Mark: Cardboard tag: "General MacArthur"

18in (46cm)	**$450-$500**

Military Dolls: Ca. 1942. All-composition with molded hats, original clothes; **Soldier, Sailor, WAAC** and **WAVE;** all in good condition.

15in (38cm)	**$275-300**

Baby Sandy: 1939-1942. All-composition; appropriate clothes; all in good condition.

8in (20cm)	**$200-$225**
12in (31cm)	**$300-$350**
14-15in (36-38cm)	**$450-$500**
20in (51cm) boxed	**$850**

Other Composition Dolls:
Orphan Annie & Sandy: 12in (30cm) pair with tags **$575-$625**

Red Ridinghood, Wolf & Grandmother Set: all original,

9in (23cm)	**$800-$900**
Dionne Quints and Nurse Set: all original	**$650-$750**
Dummy Dan: 15in (38cm)	**$125**
Goo Goo Eva and others:	
20in (51cm)	**$90-$110**
Goo Goo Topsy: (black),	
20in (51cm)	**$110-$135**
Pig Baby: 9in (23cm)	**$400**
Wolf: 11in (28cm) naked	**$250-$350**

FACTS

Freundlich Novelty Corp., New York, NY, U.S.A. 1923-on.

9in (23cm) baby pig. *H & J Foulke, Inc.*

12in (31cm) *Baby Sandy,* all original with button. *H & J Foulke, Inc.*

G.I. Joe®

Marked G.I. Joe: Molded and painted hair and features, scar* on right cheek; fully-jointed body; complete original outfit; all in perfect condition. Dolls less than perfect sell for considerably less.

*All **G.I. Joe** dolls have a scar on the right cheek except **Foreign** dolls and the **Nurse**.

Action Soldier: all original, boxed
$285-$300
Action Sailor: (painted hair), boxed
$450-$500
Action Marine: boxed $350
Action Pilot: boxed $600
Action Soldier Black: (painted hair), boxed $1,500
Naked Dolls:
Action Soldier: (painted hair) $95
Adventure Team: (flocked hair*)
$75
Adventure Team: (flocked hair and beard**) $70
Black Action Soldier: (painted hair) $450

Action Soldiers of the World (painted hair, no scars):

German Soldier:
Boxed, large box   **$1,200**
Boxed, small box   **$600**
Dressed doll only, no accessories
$225-$250
Russian Infantry Man:
Boxed, large box   **$1,200**
Boxed, small box   **$600**
Dressed doll only, no accessories
$225-$250
British Commando:
Boxed, large box   **$1,250**
Boxed, small box   **$500**
Dressed doll only, no accessories
$200-$225

**Hair must be in excellent condition.

FACTS
Hasbro (Hassenfeld Brothers, Inc.)
Pawtucket, RI, U.S.A. 1964 - 1979.
Hard plastic and vinyl.
12in (31cm) fully-jointed.
Mark: "G.I. Joe®." After 1967, added:
"Copyright 1964
Pat. No. 3,277,602
By Hasbro
Patent Pending
Made in U.S.A."

G.I. Joe Action Marine and Action Soldier, boxed. *McMasters Premier Doll Auctions.*

French Resistance Fighter:
Boxed, large box   **$900**
Boxed, small box   **$500**
Dressed doll only, no accessories
                                 $200-$225
Australian Jungle Fighter:
Boxed, large box   **$750**
Boxed, small box   **$400**
Dressed doll only, no accessories
                                 $150-$175
Japanese Imperial Soldier (unique model used only for this type):
Boxed, large box   **$1,300**
Boxed, small box   **$800**
Dressed doll only, no accessories
                                 $275-$300
Talking Action Soldier: boxed   **$400**
Talking Action Sailor: boxed   **$600**
Talking Action Marine: boxed   **$475**
Talking Action Pilot: boxed   **$800**
Nurse Action Girl:
Boxed   **$3,000**
Dressed doll only   **$1,200**
Naked doll   **$350**
Adventurer: (lifelike hair), Black, boxed   **$300**
Man of Action: (lifelike hair), boxed   **$250**
Man of Action with Kung-Fu Grip: (lifelike hair), boxed   **$225**
Talking Man of Action: (lifelike hair), boxed   **$225-$250**
Land Adventurer: (lifelike hair and beard), boxed   **$185-$200**
Air Adventurer: (lifelike hair and beard), boxed   **$240-$265**
Sea Adventurer: (lifelike hair and beard), boxed   **$225-$250**
Talking Astronaut, (lifelike hair):
Boxed   **$400-$425**
Dressed doll   **$275-$300**
Accessories:
Footlocker: green   **$40**
Space Capsule: boxed   **$350**
Five Star Jeep: boxed   **$500-$550**
Desert Patrol Jeep: boxed   **$1,900**
Motorcycle: boxed   **$250**

Outfits in unopened packages:
#7532 Green Beret Special Forces
                                 $600
#7521 Military Police (brown)   **$400**
#7521 Military Police (aqua)   **$1,350**

#7531 Ski Patrol   **$250**
#7620 Deep Sea Diver   **$300**
#7710 Dress Parade Set   **$225**
#7824 Astronaut Suit   **$250**
#7537 West Point Cadet   **$1,500**
#7624 Annapolis Cadet   **$1,400**
#7822 Air Cadet   **$1,400**
#7612 Shore Patrol   **$300**
#7807 Scramble Set   **$275**

G.I. Joe Action Pilot, boxed. *McMasters Premier Doll Auctions.*

G.I. Joe Sea Adventurer, boxed accessories. *McMasters Premier Doll Auctions.*

Ginny-Type Dolls*

Prices are for dolls in excellent overall condition with perfect hair, pretty coloring and original outfits. All dolls are hard plastic and about 7-8in (18-20cm) tall. Ca. 1950-1960.

A & H Doll Mfg. Corp.:
Gigi	$45-$50
Boxed	$90-$100
Outfits	$10-$15
Boxed outfits	$25
Julie	$35-$35

Doll Bodies, Inc.:
Mary Lu	$40-$50

Fortune Doll Co.:
Pam	$60-$65
Outfits	$10-$15
Boxed Outfits	$25
Pam Ballerina: (pointed toes)	$80-$85
Ninette	$40-$50

Hollywood Doll Mfg. Co.:
Girl	$40-$45
Rock-a-Bye Baby: boxed	$50-$60

Stashin Doll Co.:
Andrea: molded white strap shoes	$50-$60

Unidentified:
Black	$100-$125

Virga (Beehler Arts), molded white strap shoes:
Lolly-Pop: colored hair	$80-$90
Boxed	$125-$135
Lucy	$75-$80
Play-Mates	$75-$80
Boxed	$125-$135
Schiaparelli (GoGo)	$125-$135
Twinkle Ballerina: boxed	$150

*See separate entries for Cosmopolitan **Ginger,** Vogue **Ginny,** Nancy Ann Storybook **Muffie** and Alexander **Wendy.**

8in (20cm) *Andrea*, all original. *H & J Foulke, Inc.*

Girl Scout

Prices are for dolls in excellent overall condition with perfect hair and original clothes, including hat, scarf, belt, shoes and socks.

Georgene Novelties, Inc.: all-cloth, 1930s and 1940s.
Girl Scouts and Brownies:
Flat face: 15in (38cm)	**$350-$400**
Molded cloth face: 13in (33cm)	**$250-$275**
Molded plastic face: 13in (33cm)	**$100**

Terri Lee Sales Corp.: hard plastic, Ca. 1950.
Girl Scouts and Brownies:
Terri Lee: 16in (41cm)	**$400-$450**
Dress and hat only	**$125-$135**
Tiny Terri Lee: 10in (25cm)	**$200-$225**
Ginger: 8in (20cm)	**$175-$225**

Vogue Dolls, Inc.: hard plastic, Ca. 1956.
Girl Scouts and Brownies:
Ginny: painted eyelash walker, 8in (20cm)	**$275-$325**
Outfit only	**$125**
80th Anniversary, 8in (20cm):	
Boxed	**$75-$100**
Black, boxed	**$125**

Uneeda Doll Co.: vinyl head/hard plastic body, "U" on head, Ca. 1960.
Janie: 8in (20cm)	**$125-$150**
Carry Case	**$100**

Effanbee Doll Co.: vinyl, Ca. 1960 through 1970s.
Patsy Ann, 15in (38cm):	
Girl Scout	**$350-$400**
Brownie	**$500**
Blue Bird, Camp Fire	**$550****
Suzette, 15in (38cm):	
Girl Scout	**$500 up**
Brownie	**$500 up**
Blue Bird, Camp Fire	**$550****

Fluffy, 8in (20cm):
Girl Scout, Brownie	**$125-$150**
Boxed	**$175**
Camp Fire, Blue Bird	**$175**
Camp outfit or bathing suit sold separately	**$50-$75**

Punkin, 11in (28cm):
Girl Scout, Brownie	**$125-$135**
Camp Fire, Blue Bird	**$160-$175**

Jesco, Inc.: vinyl, Ca. 1985.
Katie: 9in (23cm)	**$75-$85**

Madame Alexander: hard plastic, 1992. 8in (20cm)
(blonde harder to find)	**$100-$125**

Pleasant Co.: 1999.
American Girl of Today Girl Scout	**$100-$125**
Outfit only	**$50-$60**
Brownie outfit only	**$50-$60**

Avon: Tender Memories, bisque,
14in (36cm) boxed	**$30-$40**

**Not enough price samples to compute a reliable range.

11in (28cm) Effanbee *Punkin* Brownie. *H & J Foulke, Inc.*

Godey's Little Lady Dolls

Ruth Gibbs Doll: Pink or white china head; cloth body with china limbs and painted slippers; original clothes; excellent condition.

7in (18cm)	**$90-$110**
Boxed	**$150-$165**
Little Women: set of five	**$850**
Trousseau: boxed set (four outfits)	**$575**
Fairy Tale: boxed set	**$575**
Williamsburg: boxed set (two outfits)	**$500**
Black, boxed	**$300-$350****
10in (25cm) skin wig	**$295**
12in (31cm)	**$145-$160**
12in (31cm) boxed	**$215-$235**

**Not enough price samples to compute a reliable range.

10in (25cm) *Godey's Little Lady* with skin wig. *H & J Foulke, Inc.*

FACTS
Ruth Gibbs, Flemington, NJ, U.S.A. 1946.
Designer: Herbert Johnson.
Mark: Paper label inside skirt "Godey's Little Lady Dolls;" "R.G." incised on back plate.

Hallmark

Tagged Hallmark Cloth doll: Printed on cloth with an article of separate clothing, usually a coat or skirt; stitch-jointed shoulders, hips and knees; shaped shoes and hats; all original and excellent.

6½-7½in (17-19cm)
1976 Bicentennial Commemorative Series:
 George Washington, Martha Washington, Betsy Ross, Benjamin Franklin: boxed $25-$35 each
1979 Series I:
 Amelia Earhart, Annie Oakley, G. W. Carver, Chief Joseph, Babe Ruth, Susan B. Anthony:
 boxed **$12-$15**
Babe Ruth: boxed **$125-$135**
Holiday Dolls:
 Little Drummer Boy, Santa Claus, Winifred Witch, Indian Maiden:
 boxed **$16-$18**
Series II:
 Davy Crockett, Molly Pitcher, Mark Twain, P. T. Barnum, Clara Barton: (never had boxes) **$6-$8**
 Juliette Low: (founder of the Girl Scouts) **$65-$75**

Hallmark *Babe Ruth* with original box. *Rae-Ellen Koenig, The Doll Express.*

FACTS
Hallmark Cards, Inc., Kansas City, MO. 1976-1979.
Mark: Cloth label on each doll.

Hard Plastic Dolls

Marked "Made in U.S.A." or with various letters: Ca. 1950s. All-hard plastic; sleep eyes, perfect wig; original clothes; all in excellent condition with very good coloring.

14in (36cm)	**$225-$250**
18in (46cm)	**$275-$300**
24in (61cm)	**$300-$325**

Miscellaneous Specific Dolls: All original clothes including underwear, shoes and socks; excellent condition with lovely complexion and perfect hair; unmarked except as indicated.

Answer Doll: 1951. Block Doll Corp., toddler with yes/no button:

10in (25cm)	**$75-$85**
Boy	**$140-$155**

Baby Walker: 1950s. Block Doll Corp., toddler, 10in (25cm) **$55-$65**

Duchess Doll Corp.: 1950s. Slender storybook and fashion dolls in various costumes:

Marked on back, 7-8in (18-20cm)	**$8-$10**
Boxed	**$15**

Walt Disney's Peter Pan and Tinker Bell **$20-$25 each**

Boxed	**$95-$100**

Gigi Perreau: 1952. Goldberger Doll Mfg. Co.; portrait doll of the movie star with smiling mouth and teeth, Dynel hair, vinyl head, excellent face color; hard plastic body.

20in (51cm)	**$600 up****

Haleoke: 1950s. Roberta Doll Co., 18in (46cm), with accessories and additional clothing **$450**

Heddi Stroller: 1952. Belle Doll & Toy Corp., walker, Saran braids,

20in (51cm)	**$165-$195**

Hollywood Doll Mfg. Co.: 1947 on. Storybook and fashion dolls in various costumes; marked on back:

4½-5½in (12-14cm), boxed	**$25-$35**
Ballerina: 5in (12cm) boxed	**$65-$75**
Rock-a-Bye Baby: boxed	**$50-$60**

Juliette: 1953. Eugenia Doll Co.,

21in (53cm)	**$400-$450**

LuAnn Simms: 1953. Roberta, Horsman & Valentine; **Mark:** "Made in U.S.A." or "180," walker:

14in (36cm)	**$275-$325**

14in (36cm) girl marked "Made in U.S.A." *H & J Foulke, Inc.*

21in (53cm) unmarked black girl. *H & J Foulke, Inc.*

13in (33cm) Furga, all original. *H & J Foulke, Inc.*

10in (25cm) Block *Answer Doll*, all original. *Kathy & Terri's Dolls.*

Marion: 1949. Monica Studios, rooted hair, sleep eyes, 18in (46cm)   **$400****
Mary Jane: 1955. G.H.&E. Freydberg, Inc., Terri Lee-type doll,
    17in (43cm)   **$275-$300**
Miss Gadabout: 1950s. Artisan Doll Co.
    Mark: "Heady Turny" label
    Walker, 20in (51cm)   **$165-$195**
Raving Beauty: 1953. Artisan Doll Co. Tag on some clothing: "Original Michelle//California;" separate clothing was available
    Open mouth, walker:
        19-20in (48-51cm)   **$325-$350**
Rita: 1952. Paris Doll Co.
    Walker, 29in (74cm)   **$250**
    Child Walker: 24in (61cm) boxed
                                     $175
Roxanne, Beat the Clock:
    16in (41cm) boxed   **$450**
Sandra Pla-Mate: Eugenia Doll Co.,
    16-18in (41-46cm)   **$300**
Susan Stroller: 1953, Goldberger Doll Mfg. Co., walker, Saran hair:
    Mark: "Eegee"
    23in (58cm)   **$165-$195**
Wanda the Walking Wonder: 1950s. Advance Doll Co., 17-19in (43-48cm)
                                 $150-$200

Italian Hard Plastic: Ca. 1950 on. Bonomi, Ottolini, Ratti, Furga, Magda and others. Heavy fine quality hard plastic; human hair wig, sleep eyes, sometimes flirty; original clothes; all in excellent condition.
Mark: Usually on head.
    12in (31cm)   **$125**
    15-17in (38-43cm)   **$150-$200**
    19-21in (48-53cm)   **$225-$250**
    25in (64cm) fashion   **$275**

English Black Hard Plastic Characters: 1950s. Pedigree and others. Curly black wig, sometimes over molded hair.
    16in (41cm)   **$150-$175**
    21in (53cm)   **$225-$275**

**Very few price samples available for comparison.

Hasbro

Little Miss No Name: 1965. Large round eyes, molded tear, forlorn expression; original ragged clothes; all in excellent condition, with tear.

15in (38cm)	**$90-$110**
Boxed	**200-$250**

Aimee: 1972, all-vinyl; original clothing; all in excellent condition **$45-$55**

Charlie's Angels: 1977. Gift Set,
boxed	**$250**

Jem Series: 1986-1987. All-vinyl fashion dolls; original clothing; all in excellent condition; in original box. Deduct one-third for an out-of-box doll. 12½in (32cm)

Jem	**$40-$45**
Kimber	**$45-$50**
Aja	**$50-$55**
Synergy	**$60-$70**
Roxy	**$60-$65**
Pizazz	**$65-$75**
Stormer	**$65-$75**
Rio	**$35-$40**
Boxed outfits	**$25-$35**

G.I. Joe: See pages 268-269.
Raggedy Ann: See page 169.

Charlie's Angels Gift Set, boxed. *Rosemary Kanizer.*

Himstedt, Annette

Marked Himstedt Doll: Hard vinyl head swivels on long shoulder plate, cloth lower torso, vinyl arms and curved legs; inset eyes with real eyelashes, painted feathered eyebrows, molded upper eyelids, open nose, human hair wig; original cotton clothing, bare feet; all in excellent condition with original box and certificate.

Barefoot Children: 1986. 26in (66cm):

Ellen	**$600-$700**
Kathe	**$600-$700**
Paula	**$550-$600**
Fatou	**$750-$850**
Lisa	**$550-$650**
Bastian	**$550-$600**

American Heartland Dolls: 1987. 19-20in (48-51cm):

Timi and Toni	**$250-$300 each**

The World Children Collection: 1988. 31in (79cm):

Kasimir	**$950-$1,150**
Malin	**$1,100-$1,200**
Michiko	**$950-$1,050**
Frederike	**$1,000-$1,100**
Makimura	**$750-$850**

Reflections of Youth: 1989. 26in (66cm):

Adrienne	**$600-$700**
Janka	**$600-$700**
Ayoka	**$650-$750**
Kai	**$550-$650**

FACTS
1986 on. Hard vinyl and cloth.
Designer: Annette Himstedt
Distributor: Mattel, Inc., Hawthorne, CA, U.S.A. Dolls made in Spain.
Mark: Wrist tag with doll's name; cloth signature label on clothes; signature on lower back plate and on back of doll's head under wig.

1990:

Fiene	$750-$850
Taki (baby)	$1,100-$1,300
Annchen (baby)	$550-$650

1991:

Liliane	$750-$850
Neblina	$650-$850
Tinka	$700-$800
Shireem	$450-$550
Freeke & Bibi (club doll)	
	$800-$900

1993:

Kima	$350-$400
Lona	$350-$400
Tara	$400-$500
Jule	$600-$650

1994:

Panchita, Pancho, Melvin, Elke	
	$250-$300

1998:

Baby Leischen (club doll)	
	$550-$600

1999:

Mia Yin	$950
Mirte & Little Mirte (club doll)	
	$600-$650

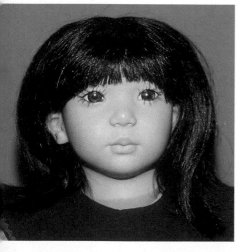

26in (66cm) *Shireem*, all original. *Emma Vann.*

Horsman

EARLY COMPOSITON DOLLS: Original or appropriate old clothes; all in good condition.

Billiken: 1909. Composition head, velvet or plush body. **Mark:** cloth label.
   12in (31cm)   **$350-$400**

"Can't Break 'Em" Characters: Ca. 1911. Character head; hard stuffed cloth body. **Mark:** "E.I.H. 1911."
   11-13in (28-33cm)   **$200 up**

Polly Pru:
   13in (33cm)   **$350-$375****

Little Mary Mix-Up:
   15in (31cm)   **$350-$375****

Cotton Joe: black,
   13in (33cm)   **$425-$475**

Uncle Sam's Kid: 1917, composition/cloth; all original,
   16in (41cm)   **$400-$450**

Baby Bumps   **$250**
   Black   **$300**

Puppy & Pussy Pippin: 1911. Grace G. Drayton. Plush body; composition head; cloth label.
   8in (20cm) sitting:

Puppy Pippin	$400-$450**
Pussy Pippin	$500-$600**

Peek-a-Boo: 1913-1915. Grace G. Drayton. Composition head, arms, legs and lower torso, cloth upper torso. **Mark:** cloth label on outfit.
   7½in (19cm)   **$150-$175**

Baby Butterfly: 1911-1913. Oriental doll; composition head; cloth body; original costume.
   13in (33cm)   **$500****

**Not enough price samples to compute a reliable range.

FACTS
E.I. Horsman Co., New York, NY. Manufacturer; also distributor of French and German dolls. 1878-on.

Peterkin: 1914-1930. All-composition; various boy and girl clothing or simply a large bow.

11in (28cm)	**$325-$375**
Boxed, at auction	**$500**

Gene Carr Characters: 1916. Composition/cloth. **Snowball** (black boy); **Mike** and **Jane** (eyes open); **Blink** and **Skinney** (eyes closed). Designed by Bernard Lipfert from Gene Carr's cartoon characters.

13-14in (33-36cm)	**$325-$375**
Black **Snowball**	**$450-$550**

Jackie Coogan: 1921. Composition/cloth; appropriate old clothes:

14in (36cm)	**$550-$600**

HEbee-SHEbee: 1925. All-composition; blue shoes indicate a **HEbee**; pink ones a **SHEbee.**

11in (28cm)	**$600-$650**
Fair condition, some peeling	**$325-$375**
Mint, all original	**$800-$900**

All-Bisque. See page 25.

Ella Cinders: 1925. Composition/cloth. From the comic strip by Bill Conselman and Charlie Plumb for Metropolitan Newspaper Service. **Mark:** "1925©MNS."

18in (46cm)	**$650-$750**

Baby Dimples: 1928. Composition/cloth; appropriate old clothes.

Mark:

"©
E.I.H. CO. INC."

16-18in (41-46cm)	**$300-$350**
22-24in (56-61cm)	**$400-$450**

Mama Dolls: late 1920s on. Composition/cloth.

Mark: "HORSMAN" or "E.I.H. CO. INC."

Babies, including **Brother** and **Sister:**

12-14in (31-36cm)	**$175-$200**
18-20in (46-51cm)	**$275-$300**

Girls, including **Rosebud** and **Peggy Ann:**

14-16in (36-41cm)	**$250-$275**
22-24in (56-61cm)	**$325-$375**

14cm (36cm) *Jackie Coogan,* all original with button. *H & J Foulke, Inc.*

10½in (26cm) composition *HE-bee*. *H & J Foulke, Inc.*

Tynie Baby: 1924. Slightly frowning face; cloth/composition; appropriate clothes. Designed by Bernard Lipfert. **Mark:**

> "© 1924
> E.I. Horsman Inc.
> Made in
> Germany"

Bisque head:
  8½–9½in (22-24cm) h.c.
                         $550-$650
  11-12in (28-31cm) h.c.**$750-$850**
Composition head:
  15in (38cm) long   **$300-$325**
  19in (48cm)   **$400-$425**
All-bisque: swivel neck, glass eyes, wigged or molded hair,
  8-10in (20-25cm)   **$2,200-$2,500**
Vinyl: 1950, 15in (38cm),
  boxed   **$90-$110**

ALL-COMPOSITION CHILD DOLLS: 1930s and 1940s. Original clothes; all in very good condition; may have "Gold Medal Doll" tag. **Mark: "HORSMAN"**
  13-14in (33-36cm)   **$225-$250**
  16-18in (41-46cm)   **$275-$325**
  15in (38cm) boxed   **$375**
Chubby toddler:
  16-18in (41-46cm)   **$300–$350**
Jo-Jo: 1937, 12in (31cm) **$275-$300**
Jeanne: 1937, 14in (36cm)   **$300**
Naughty Sue: 1937
  16in (41cm)   **$425-$475**
Roberta: 1937
  16in (41cm)   **$425-$475**
Bright Star: 1940
  17-20in (43-51cm)   **$450-$500**

ALL-HARD PLASTIC DOLLS: 1950s. Original clothing; perfect hair; good coloring; all in excellent condition.
Cindy: 1950-1955. Open mouth with teeth and tongue, synthetic wig; walker body. **Mark:** "160 [or "170" or "180"] Made in U.S.A."
  16-18in (41-46cm)   **$250-$ 300**
LuAnn Simms: Ca. 1953. Long brunette wig with front and side hair pulled to back, blue eyes; mold number **180** or **170:**
  18in (46cm)   **$350-$400**

17in (43cm) unmarked composition girl, probably Horsman, all original. *H & J Foulke, Inc.*

VINYL DOLLS: Original clothing; all in excellent condition with perfect hair and excellent color.

Rene Ballerina: 1957. Fully-jointed with high-heeled feet, rooted hair:

Mark: "82//HORSMAN"

19in (48cm)	**$150-$165**

Cindy: 1957, Fashion Doll,

19in (21cm)	**$200-$225**

Cindy Strutter: Child, 23in (58cm)

boxed	**$135**

Tweedie: 1958. Slender limbs, short hair:

Mark: "38 Horsman."

14½in (37cm)	**$50-$100**
Boxed	**$195**

Couturier Doll: 1958, Fashion doll with stuffed vinyl body, 20in (51cm)

boxed	**$225-$250**

Jackie Kennedy: 1961. Rooted black hair, blue sleep eyes; pearl jewelry:

Mark: "HORSMAN//19 © 61//JK25."

25in (64cm)	**$165-$185**

Poor Pitiful Pearl: 1963. Cartoon character:

Mark: "1963//Wm Steig//Horsman"

11-12in (28-31cm)	**$100-$115**
Boxed	**$200-$225**
16in (41cm)	**$165**
Boxed	**$250-$275**

Hansel & Gretel: 1963. Character faces:

Mark: "Michael Meyerberg, Inc."

15in (38cm)	**$200-$225**

Walt Disney's Cinderella Set: 1965. Extra head and costume for "poor" doll:.

Mark: "H"

11½in (29cm), boxed	**$150-$165**

Mary Poppins: 1964. Several different costumes:

12in (31cm)	**$30-$40**
Boxed set with 7in (18cm) **Jane** and **Michael**	**$150-$165**

Flying Nun: 1965, 12in (31cm) **$95**

Boxed	**$175-$185**

Patty Duke: 1965, Gray flannel pants, red sweater:

12in (31cm)	**$85**
Boxed	**$150-$175**

Elizabeth Taylor: 1976,

11½in (29cm)	**$55**

Angie Dickinson, Police Woman: 1970s, 9in (23cm) boxed **$45**

10½in (26cm) walking *Cindy*, all original. *Rosemary Kanizer.*

14½in (37cm) *Tweedie*, boxed. *H & J Foulke, Inc.*

Mary Hoyer

Ideal

Marked Mary Hoyer: Original tagged factory clothes or garments made at home from Mary Hoyer patterns; all in excellent condition.
Composition: 14in (36cm) **$350-$450**
Hard plastic:
14in (36cm):
   In knit outfit   **$400-$425**
   In tagged Hoyer outfit   **$425-$525**
   In tagged gown   **$500-$600**
14in (36cm) boy with caracul wig
               $500-$550
18in (46cm), **Gigi:**
   In tagged outfits   **$850-$1,250**
   Boxed   **$1,250-$1,650**
Vinyl Play doll: 14in (36cm) **$95-$110**

18in (46cm) Mary Hoyer *Gigi. Sidney Jeffrey Collection.*

Early Composition Dolls: 1910-1929. Composition heads; cloth bodies, composition lower arms; some with molded composition shoes; original or appropriate old clothes; all in good condition; some wear acceptable.
Head Mark:

Happy Hooligan: 1910, comic character, 21in (53cm)   **$500****
Snookums: 1910, plush body,
  14in (36cm)   **$600**
Ty Cobb: 1911, baseball outfit **$500****
Naughty Marietta (Coquette): 1912, molded hair with ribbon band
        $350-$400
Captain Jenks: 1912, khaki uniform
        $275-$325
Uneeda Kid: 1914-1919. Molded black boots; original bloomer suit, yellow slicker and rain hat, carrying a box of Uneeda Biscuits, showing some wear:
  16in (41cm)   **$475-$500**
Bronco Bill: 1915, cowboy outfit with gun and holster   **$325**
ZuZu Kid: 1916-1917, original clown suit, National Biscuit Co.,
  16in (41cm)   **$400-$450**
Liberty Boy: 1917, molded clothes, cloth hat, some wear,
  12in (31cm)   **$350-$375**
Soozie Smiles: 1923, two faces, crying and smiling   **$400-$425**
Flossie Flirt: 1924-1931. Eyes move side to side:
  14in (36cm)   **$225-$250**
  20in (51cm)   **$300-$350**

**Not enough price samples to compute a reliable range.

Buster Brown: 1929, red suit with hat, 17in (43cm) **$325-$375**

Peter Pan: 1929. Original felt suit and hat, 18in (46cm):

Excellent with label **$550-$600**
Good, some wear **$300-$400**

Early Children:
12-15in (31-38cm) **$225-$250**

Early Babies: Baby Mine, Prize Baby and others: 15-16in (38-41cm) **$225**

Composition Babies: 1930s and 1940s. Composition heads and lower limbs, cloth bodies; original or appropriate clothes; all in good condition with nice coloring; light crazing acceptable.

Tickletoes: 1930-1947, soft rubber arms and legs, flirty eyes, 16in (41cm) **$325-$375**

Baby Smiles: 1931, toddler with rubber arms, 17in (43cm) **$250-$275**

Snoozie: 1933. Designed by Bernard Lipfert. Yawning mouth, may have rubber arms.

Mark: "©

By B. LIPFERT"
16-20in (41-51cm) **$350-$400**

16in (41cm) early character girl. *H & J Foulke, Inc.*

20in (51cm) baby, all original. *H & J Foulke, Inc.*

16in (41cm) *Uneeda Kid*, original coat and hat with label. *H & J Foulke, Inc.*

12in (31cm) vinyl *Betsy Wetsy. Kathy & Terri's Dolls.*

Cuddles: 1933, rubber limbs,
22in (56cm)   **$350-$400**
Bathrobe Baby: 1933, rubber body,
12in (31cm)   **$100-$125**
Princess Beatrix: 1938. Magic eyes:
16in (41cm)   **$250-$300**
22in (56cm)   **$350-$400**

Betsy Wetsy: 1937-on. Drink-and-wet baby.
Head Mark: "IDEAL"
Composition or hard rubber head/rubber body: 14-16in (36-41cm)
                               $160-$185
Hard plastic head/rubber body:
12-14in (31-36cm)   **$110-$135**
Boxed with layette, early vinyl
body   **$475**
All-vinyl, 12in (31cm)   **$55-$65**

Composition Children: 1935-1947. All-composition in excellent condition with perfect hair and good cheek color; original clothes.
Shirley Temple: 1935. See page 301.
Snow White: 1937. Black wig, gown with rayon skirt showing figures of seven dwarfs.
Torso Mark: "SHIRLEY TEMPLE"
Dress tag: "An Ideal Doll"
11in (28cm) at auction   **$1,300**
18in (46cm)   **$650-$750**

All-cloth: 16in (41cm)   **$ 525-$575**
Mint-in-box   **$750**
With seven dwarfs, boxed,
at auction   **$3,800**

Deanna Durbin: 1938. Smiling mouth with teeth, metal button with picture.
Head Mark:
        "Deanna Durbin
        Ideal Doll, USA"
14in (36cm)   **$650-$750**
20-21in (51-53cm)   **$1,000-$1,200**
24in (61cm)   **$1,500-$1,600**
21in (53cm) mint-in-box   **$1,700**

Judy Garland as Dorothy from *The Wizard of Oz:* 1939.
Head Mark:
        "IDEAL DOLL
        MADE IN USA"
16in (41cm)   **$1,500-$1,650**
Replaced clothes   **$1,000-$1,100**
Strawman: cloth, 17in (43cm)
at auction   **$2,700**

Betty Jane, Little Princess, Pigtail Sally, Ginger, Cinderella, 1935-1947:
14in (36cm)   **$325-$375**
18in (46cm)   **$425-$475**
Soldier: Ca. 1942, character face; army uniform with jacket and hat,
13in (33cm)   **$325-$375**

21in (53cm) *Deanna Durbin,* all original with pin. *H & J Foulke, Inc.*

16in (41cm) *Judy Garland. H & J Foulke, Inc.*

13in (33cm) *Little Princess,* all original. *H & J Foulke, Inc.*

14in (36cm) *Magic Skin Baby,* all original. *H & J Foulke, Inc.*

Miss Curity: Ca. 1945. Nurse uniform:
  14in (36cm)   **$325-$375**
  All original, with nurse kit,
  at auction   **$725**
Miss Liberty: "Judy Garland" mold,
  21in (53cm) at auction   **$700**
Flexy Dolls: 1938 on, wire mesh torso, flexible metal cable arms and legs,
  12in (31cm):
  Baby Snooks (Fanny Brice)
                $250-$275
  Mortimer Snerd   **$250-$275**
  Soldier   **$200-$225**
  Children   **$200-$225**

Judy Garland from *Strike up the Band:* 1940. (For photograph, see *14th Blue Book,* page 283.)
Head Mark: "MADE IN U.S.A."
Body Mark:
      "IDEAL DOLL
      [backwards 21]"
  21in (53cm)   **$1,000-$1,200**
Composition and Wood Segmented Characters: 1940. Label on front torso:
  Pinocchio:
    10½in (27cm)   **$475-$525**
    20in (51cm)   **$800-$900**
  King Little: 14in (36cm) **$275-$325**
  Jiminy Cricket: 9in (23cm)
                $450-$500
  Gabby: 11in (28cm) **$375-$425**

Magic Skin Dolls: 1940-on. Stuffed latex rubber body in very good condition (subject to easy deterioration); original clothes; all in excellent condition. **Head Mark:** "IDEAL."
  Magic Skin Baby: 1940,
    14-15in (36-38cm) **$95-$110**
  Plassie, 1940:
    16in (41cm)   **$95-$110**
    Toddler: all-hard plastic,
    14in (36cm)   **$165-$195**
  Sparkle Plenty, 1947:
    15in (38cm) baby **$160-$185**
    Toddler   **$150-$175**

  Joan Palooka: 1953,
    14in (36cm)   **$125-$135**
  Baby Coos: 1948-1952, sounds like a baby when squeezed,
    14-16in (36-41cm) **$110-$135**
  Brother or Sister Coos: 25-30in (64-76cm), dressed like toddlers
                $200-$300

Howdy Doody: 1947-1955. Hard plastic head, movable jaw; stuffed body; all original:
  21in (53cm)   **$300-$325**
  25in (64cm)   **$400-$450**

Toni Family: 1948-on. Hard plastic "Toni" home permanent doll and derivatives; nylon wig, perfect hair, pretty cheek color; original clothes; all in excellent condition.
Head Mark: "IDEAL DOLL"
Body Mark:

"IDEAL DOLL
P-90
Made in USA"

Toni:

14-16in (36-41cm):	
P-90 & P-91	**$400**
Naked, untidy hair	**$70-$80**
Mint-in-box	**$550-$650**
19-21in (48-53cm) P-92 & P-93	**$600-$650**
22½in(57cm) P-94	**$950****
Playwave Box and contents	**$75**

Mary Hartline:

14in (36cm)	**$400**
22½in (57cm), mint, at auction	**$1,295**
Mint-in-box with accessories, 16in (41cm)	**$700**

Harriet Hubbard Ayer, vinyl head makeup doll:

14in (36cm)	**$200-$225**
21in (53cm)	**$400-$450****
Mint-in box with accessories	**$400-$450**

Miss Curity, Nurse:

14in (36cm)	**$400**
Mint-in-box with accessories	**$650**

Sara Ann, Saran hair:

14in (36cm)	**$400**
21in (53cm) Bride	**$600****

Saucy Walker: 1951-1955. All-hard plastic with walking mechanism; original clothes; excellent hair and cheek color.
Mark: "IDEAL DOLL"

16-17in (41-43cm)	**$150-$200**
20-22in (51-56cm)	**$225-$250**
Mint-in-box	**$350-$400**

Posie: 1954-1956, vinyl head,

17in (43cm)	**$185-$210**

Saralee: 1950. Black vinyl/cloth body. Designed by Sarah Lee Creech; modeled by Sheila Burlingame. Original clothes; excellent condition:

17-18in (43-46cm)	**$300-$350**
Undressed	**$125**

Bonny Braids: 1951. Vinyl character head; hard plastic body; original clothes; excellent condition:

13in (33cm)	**$150-$200**
Mint-in-comic strip-box	**$400**

**Not enough price samples to compute a reliable range.

Far Left: 14in (36cm) *Toni*, all original. *Kathy & Terri's Dolls.*

Left: *Miss Revlon,* all original and boxed. *Rosemary Kanizer.*

13in (33cm) *Bonny Braids*, all original with tag. *H & J Foulke, Inc.*

35in (89cm) *Patti Playpal. Helen Hargett.*

Revlon Dolls: 1955-1959. Vinyl head with rooted hair, perfect hair, bright cheek color; hard plastic body with jointed waist, high-heeled feet; original clothing; excellent condition.

Miss Revlon:	
18-20in (46-51cm)	**$225-$275**
Mint-in-box, dress	**$400 up**
Mint-in-box gown	**$475 up**
Little Miss Revlon:	
10½in (27cm)	**$135-$165**
Boxed	**$225-$250**

Patti Playpal Family: 1959-1962.

Patti: 35in (89cm)	**$425-$475**
Peter: 38in (97cm)	**$550-$650**
Daddy's Girl:	
42in (107cm)	**$1,000-$1,200**
Miss Ideal:	
29in (74cm)	**$400-$450**
25in (64cm)	**$375-$400**
Patti: 18in (46cm)	**$350-$450**
Bonnie & Johnny:	
24in (61cm) babies	**$225-$250**
Penny: 32in (81cm)	**$275-$300**
Saucy Walker:	
28in (71cm)	**$285**
30in (76cm)	**$325**

Patti: 1982, mint-in-box	**$125-$150**
Black: mint-in-box	**$225**

Tammy Family: 1962-1966. Mint-in-box; deduct 50% for an out-of-box doll:

Tammy: 12in (31cm)	**$85-$115**
Pos'n Tammy:	
12in (31cm)	**$125-$135**
Pos'n Misty & Telephone Booth	
	$175
Glamour Misty (Miss Clairol)	
	$95-$110
Ted (big brother):	
12½in (32cm)	**$150**
Mom: 12½in (32cm)	**$185**
Dad: 13in (33cm)	**$150**
Pepper (sister): 9in (23cm)	**$75-$85**
Pete (little brother):	
7¾in (20cm)	**$200 up**
Patti (Pepper's friend):	
9in (23cm)	**$250 up**
Dodi (Pepper's friend):	
9in (23cm)	**$85**
Salty (Pepper's friend):	
7¾in (20cm)	**$200**
Bud (Tammy's boyfriend):	
12½in (32cm)	**$200**
Boxed outfits	**$60-$85**

Miscellaneous Vinyl Dolls: All original; excellent coloring; perfect condition.

Lori Martin (National Velvet):
38in (97cm), 1961,   **$750-$800**

Magic Lips: 1955,
24in (61cm)   **$145-$165**

Thumbelina: 1961. Vinyl and cloth; wriggles like a real baby:
14in (36cm)   **$125-$165**
19in (48cm)   **$185-$225**
Mint-in-box, at auction   **$350**

Kissy: 1961-1964. Toddler,
22in (56cm)   **$90-$110**
Boxed   **$135-$150**

Bam Bam: 1963.
12in (31cm)   **$45-$50**
16in (41cm)   **$60-$75**

Pebbles: 1963.
8in (20cm)   **$25-$30**
12in (31cm)   **$45-$50**
15in (38cm) boxed   **$160-$175**

Betty Big Girl: 1968, 32in (81cm), boxed   **$350**

Little Lost Baby: 1968, three faces,
22in (56cm)   **$95-$110**

Flatsy: 1968-1970.
Each with accessory   **$20-$25**
Boxed   **$40-$50**
Boxed with frame   **$75-$95**

Joey Stivic: 1976, Archie Bunker's grandson, 15in (38cm)   **$65**

Dorothy Hammil: 1977,
11½in (29cm)   **$25**

Diana Ross:
17½in (45cm)   **$150-$175**
Giggles: 16in (41cm)   **$65-$75**
Hopalong Cassidy:
25in (63cm)   **$375**
Vicky Vanta: 9½in (24cm) baby with boxed layette, at auction   **$175**

Crissy and Family: 1968-1974. Growing hair dolls, all original and excellent:
Crissy, Beautiful Crissy   **$40-$50**
Black **Crissy**   **$100**
Velvet   **$30-$40**
Black **Velvet**   **$65**
Cinnamon   **$25-$35**
Black **Cinnamon**   **$40-$45**
Mia   **$40-$45**
Kerry   **$50-$60**
Tressy   **$60-$70**
Brandi   **$45-$50**
Dina   **$45-$50**
Cricket   **$175-$225**
Baby Crissy   **$65-$85**
Crissy Beauty Parlor:
boxed   **$40-$50**
Crissy Clothes Rack and Closet Set: boxed   **$65-$75**
Packaged clothes   **$15-$40**

Tiffany Taylor, 1974:
19in (48cm)   **$40-$45**
Boxed   **$55-$65**
Black   **$75**

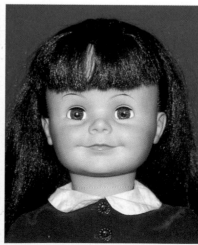

Far Left: *Pos'n Misty and her Telephone Booth. Rosemary Kanizer.*

Left: 29in (74cm) *Miss Ideal. Kathy & Terri's Dolls.*

Kenner

Dusty: 1974. Smiling face, freckles.
12in (31cm), boxed **$50-$60**
Outfits **$25**
Skye: 1974, black skin, 12in (31cm):
Boxed **$50-$60**
Outfits **$25**
Cover Girls: 1978-1980. Fashion dolls with bendable elbows and knees, jointed wrists; 12in (31cm):
Darci **$55-$65**
Erica (auburn) **$150-$175**
Dana (black skin) **$75-$85**
Outfits **$30-$40**
Hardy Boys: 1978. Mint-in-box dolls:
Shaun Cassidy, Parker Stevenson
$40-$50
Star Wars: 1974-1978. Mint-in-box dolls. For excellent out-of-box dolls, deduct 50%:
Darth Vader:
15in (38cm) **$150-$175**
Hans Solo: 12in (31cm) **$450-$475**
Luke Skywalker:
12in (31cm) **$250-$275**
Princess Leia:
11½in (29cm) **$175-$225**
Stormtrooper:
12in (31cm) **$200-$225**

Obi Wan Kenobi:
12in (31cm) **$125-$135**
R2D2: 7½in (19cm) **$165-$185**
C3PO: 12in (31cm) **$125-$135**
Boba Fett: 13in (33cm) **$250-$275**
Jawa: 8½in (22cm) **$90-$100**
IG88: 15in (38cm) **$550-$650**
Chewbacca: 15in (38cm) **$150-$160**
Yoda: 9in (23cm) **$85-$95**
Six Million Dollar Man: 1975-1978. 13in (33cm) boxed figures:
Bigfoot **$55-$65**
Steve Austin **$65-$85**
Jaime Sommers **$55-$65**
Bionic Man: at auction **$365**
Fembot **$165**
Bionic Woman Classroom Playset: at auction **$485**
Oscar Goldman **$60-$70**

Strawberry Shortcake, 1980-1986:
Vinyl doll with pet **$75-$100**
Boxed **$100-$200**
Cloth doll: 15in (38cm) **$80-$100**
Boxed **$150-$160**
Berry Happy Home Dollhouse with furniture **$250-$350**
Attic Playset: boxed **$200-$225**

Strawberry Shortcake Orange Blossom, boxed. *Rosemary Kanizer.*

Knickerbocker

Composition Snow White: 1937. All-composition; black mohair wig with hair ribbon; original clothing; all in very good condition:

15in (38cm)	**$425-$475**
20in (51cm)	**$550-$650**

With molded black hair and blue ribbon: 13-15in (33-38cm) **$350-$450**
Set: 15in (38cm) **Snow White** and seven 9in (23cm) **Dwarfs** **$2,750**

13in (33cm) *Snow White* with tag. *H & J Foulke, Inc.*

Composition Seven Dwarfs: All-composition; individual character faces; original velvet costumes and caps with identifying names: **Sneezy, Dopey, Grumpy, Doc, Happy, Sleepy** and **Bashful;** very good condition.

9in (23cm) **$250-$300 each**

Additional composition dolls:
Jiminy Cricket:
10in (25cm) **$450-$550**
Pinocchio:
14in (36cm) **$550-$650**
Figero the Cat **$500-$550**
Blondie: all original and boxed, at auction 11in (28cm) **$1680**
Dagwood: 13in (33cm) **$650-$750**
Alexander: 9in (23cm) **$400-$450**

Additional cloth dolls:
Seven Dwarfs:
14in (36cm) **$250-$275 each**
Snow White:
16in (41cm) **$375-$425**
Donald Duck **$500-$600**
Mickey Mouse: 1935 **$500-$650**
Two-Gun Mickey: Mint with tag, at auction **$3,900**
Minnie Mouse **$500 up**
Raggedy Ann & Andy: See page 168.
Little Lulu:
18in (46cm) **$400-$500****
Child Doll: 1935, mask face (washable), original clothes,
12-14in (31-36cm) **$125-$150**
Little Orphan Annie and Sandy: 1977, 16in (41cm) **$25-$35**

**Not enough price samples to compute a reliable range.

FACTS
Knickerbocker Doll & Toy Co.,
New York, NY, U.S.A. 1937.
Head Mark:
"WALT DISNEY
KNICKERBOCKER TOY CO."

Krueger

All-Cloth Doll: Ca. 1930. Mask face; oilcloth body with hinged shoulders and hips; original clothes; in excellent condition:

7in (18cm)	**$50-$60**
12in (31cm)	**$100-$125**
16in (41cm)	**$150-$165**
20in (51cm)	**$200-$225**

Pinocchio: Ca. 1940. Mask character face; cloth torso, wood jointed arms and legs; original clothes, all in good condition:

15in (38cm)	**$400-$450****

Kewpie: See page 132.

Dwarfs, Ca. 1937:

All-cloth, mask face:

12in (30cm)	**$175-$200**
Set of seven, with Snow White	**$2,200**

Scootles: 1935. Rose O'Neill. All-cloth, mask face, yarn hair:

10in (25cm)	**$450****
18in (46cm)	**$850****

**Not enough price samples to compute a reliable range.

13in (33cm) girl with mask face of the type made by Krueger, all original. *H & J Foulke, Inc.*

FACTS
Richard G. Krueger, Inc., New York, NY, U.S.A. 1917-on.
Mark: Cloth tag or label.

Mattel, Inc.

Condition: Unless otherwise indicated, all dolls should be in excellent unplayed-with condition, in original clothes with all accessories, perfect hair, excellent coloring.

Chatty Cathy Family: 1960-1965.

Chatty Cathy:

20in (51cm)	**$250-$275**
Boxed	**$375-$475**
Black	**$600-$800**
Canadian	**$350-$450**

Charmin' Chatty:

25in (64cm)	**$125-$135**

Chatty Baby:

18in (46cm)	**$95-$115**

Tiny Chatty Baby:

15in (38cm)	**$70-$75**
Black	**$100**

Tiny Chatty Brother:

15in (38cm)	**$70-$75**

Singing Chatty:

17in (43cm)	**$100-$125**

Buffy & Mrs. Beasley: 1967. All-vinyl Buffy, vinyl/cloth Mrs. Beasley:

6in (15cm) boxed	**$200**
10in (25cm) boxed	**$350**

Mrs. Beasley, vinyl and cloth, with glasses:

16in (40cm)	**$200-$300**
Boxed	**$400-$500**

Skediddles: 1966, mint-in-package **$65-$85**

Star-Spangled Dolls, 1976:
New England Girl, Pioneer Daughter, Southern Belle *$40-$45*

Sunshine Family: 1977, boxed set **$85-$95**

Guardian Goddesses: 1979.

11½in (29cm)	**$150-$175**

Toddlers and Babies: All original and excellent, unplayed-with, in working condition.

Baby Secret: 1966.

18in (46cm)	**$80-$90**

Baby First Step: 1966.

18in (46cm)	**$65-$75**

10in (25cm) *Buffy & Mrs. Beasley*, boxed. *Rosemary Kanizer*

8in (20cm) *Cheerful Tearful* with play case. *Rosemary Kanizer.*

Baby Pattaburp: 1964,
  16in (41cm)   **$40-$50**
Baby Tenderlove: 1970-1972,
  Newborn: 13in (33cm) **$45-$55**
  Living: 20in (51cm) **$65-$85**
  Brother (sexed):
    12in (31cm) **$35-$40**
Cheerful, Tearful: 1966,
  7in (17cm) with play case **$45-$50**
  13in (33cm) **$30-$40**
Dancerina: 1970,
  12in (31cm) **$30-$35**
  16in (41cm) **$60-$70**
  24in (61cm) **$125-$150**
Hi Dottie: 1969,
  17in (43cm) boxed **$50-$60**
Sister Belle: 1961,
  17in (43cm) **$65-$75**
Matty Mattel: 1961,
  17in (43cm) **$65-$75**
Timey Tell: 1964,
  17in (43cm) with watch **$45-$55**
  Boxed **$125**
Tippy Toes: 1967, 17in (43cm) with tricycle or horse, good face **$50-$60**

Dolls from Television Shows: All prices are for mint-in-box or package dolls.
  Charlie's Angels: 1978,
    11½in (29cm) **$50-$60**
  Debbie Boone: 1978,
    11½in (29cm) **$65**
  Dick Van Dyke: 1969, talks
    25in (64cm) **$125**

  Donny Osmond: 1978,
    12in (31cm) **$35-$40**
  Marie Osmond: 1978,
    12in (31cm) **$35-$40**
  Jimmy Osmond: 1979,
    10in (25cm) **$45-$50**
  Grizzly Adams: 1971,
    10in (25cm) **$40**
  Herman Munster, 1965:
    Hand puppet **$125**
    Full body **$200-$225**
  How the West Was Won: 1971,
    10in (25cm) **$25-$30 each**
  Welcome Back Kotter: 1973,
    9in (23cm) **$40-$50 each**

Little Kiddles: 1966. Mint-in-box or package; deduct 50% for an out-of-package doll with all accessories, in excellent condition.
Body Mark:
  "1965//Mattel, Inc.//Japan"
  Sleeping Biddle **$125**
  Liddle Biddle Peep **$165**
  Peter Pandiddle **$225**
  Liddle Middle Muffet **$185**
  Liddle Red Riding Hiddle **$185**
  Sizzly Friddle **$145**
  Freezy Sliddle **$135**
  Howard Biff Boodle **$135**
  Orange Ice Kone Kiddle **$60-$65**
  Kologne Kiddle **$50-$60**
  Locket Kiddle **$55-$65**
  Heart Pin Kiddle **$30-$35**
  Bracelet Kiddle **$65-$75**

Mego Corporation

Television, Movie and Entertainment Dolls: All prices are for mint-in-box or package dolls.

Batman: 1974, 8in (20cm) **$175-$200**
Penguin: 1974, 8in (20cm) **$85-$95**
Captain & Tenille: 1977,
  12½in (32cm) **$50-$60 each**
Cher, 1976: 12in (31cm) **$65-$75**
  Sonny **$40**
CHiPs: 1977, 8in (20cm)**$35-$40 each**
Diana Ross: 1977, 12½in (32cm) **$125**
Charlie's Angels: 1975,
  12½in (32cm) **$75-$85 each**
Happy Days: 1976,
  8in (20cm) **$40-$50 each**
KISS: 1978,
  12½in (32cm) **$125-$150 each**
Kojack: 1977, 9in (23cm) **$65-$70**
Laverne & Shirley: 1977,
  11½in (29cm) **$75-$85 each**
Joe Namath: 1971, 12in (31cm) **$85**
Our Gang: 1975,
  5in (13cm) **$25-$35 each**
Planet of the Apes: 1974,
  8in (20cm) **$100-$125 each**
Pirates: 1971,
  8in (20cm) **$70-$80 each**
Robin Hood Set: 1971,
  8in (20cm) **$50-$55 each**
Starsky & Hutch: 1976,
  8in (20cm) **$35-$40 each**
Suzanne Somers: 1978,
  12½in (32cm) **$50-$60**
The Waltons: 1975, 8in (20cm), two dolls in each box **$50-$60**
Wild West, 1974:
  Buffalo Bill, Cochise, Davy Crockett, Sitting Bull, Wild Bill Hickok, Wyatt Earp **$35-$40 each**
Wonder Woman: 1976,
  12½in (32cm) **$100-$115**
Wizard of Oz, 1974:
  Dorothy **$30-$35**
  Munchkins **$60-$65**
  Tin Man, Cowardly Lion **$30-$35**

Star Trek: 1975. Fully-jointed plastic; packaged on blister card. For unpackaged dolls, deduct 50%, 8in (20cm):

Captain Kirk	**$65-$75**
Mr. Spock	**$45-$50**
Dr. McCoy	**$110-$125**
Mr. Scott	**$135-$160**
Klingon	**$50-$60**
Lt. Uhura	**$85-$100**
Andorian	**$450-$500**
The Keeper	**$175-$200**
Romulan	**$700-$800**

Star Trek: 1979, mint-in-box,
  12½in (32cm):

Captain Kirk	**$75-$85**
Mr. Spock	**$75-$85**
Ilia	**$75-$85**

Star Trek Ilia, 1979. George Humphrey.

Molly-'es

Molly-'es Composition Dolls: Beautiful original outfits; all in good condition.

Babies: 15-18in (38-46cm)
$225-$250

Girls: 12-13in (31-33cm) **$175-$195**

Toddlers: 14-16in (36-41cm)
$275-$300

Ladies: 18-21in (46-53cm)
$500-$550

Internationals: All-cloth with mask faces; all original clothes; in excellent condition with wrist tag.

13in (33cm) **$95**

Mint-in-box **$125**

Raggedy Ann & Andy: See page 167.

Thief of Baghdad Series: 1939. Orange hang tag:

Sabu: composition, 15in (38cm)
$550-$600

Sultan: 19in (48cm) cloth
$650-$750

Princess: 15in (38cm) composition or 18in (46cm) cloth **$600-$650**

Prince: 23in (58cm) cloth **$750**

Hard Plastic: All original and excellent.

Stewardess: 14in (36cm) **$475**

Vinyl Dolls: All original and excellent.

Darling Little Women:

8in (20cm) **$50-$60****

12in (31cm) **$85-$95****

Internationals: 8in (20cm) **$40-$50**

Perky: 8in (20cm) **$50-$60**

**Not enough price samples to compute a reliable range.

FACTS
International Doll Co., Philadelphia, PA. Made clothing only. Purchased undressed dolls from various manufacturers. 1920s on.
Clothes Designer: Mollye Goldman.
Mark: A cardboard tag.

13in (33cm) international girl, all original. *H & J Foulke, Inc.*

15in (38cm) *Princess*, all original. *H & J Foulke, Inc.*

Nancy Ann Storybook Dolls

Painted Bisque Marked Storybook Doll: Mohair wig, painted eyes; one-piece body and head, jointed legs and arms; original clothes; excellent condition with sticker or wrist tag and box. Deduct 25-30% for out-of-box dolls. 5½–7in (13-19cm).

1936: Babies only. Gold sticker on dress; sunburst box.
Mark: "88 Made in Japan" or "87 Made in Japan"

3½-4½in (8-10cm)	**$450-$550**

1937-1938: Gold sticker on dress; sunburst box, gold label.
Mark: "Made in Japan 1146," "Made in Japan 1148," "Japan," "Made in Japan" or "AMERICA" **$600-$800**

1938-1939: Gold sticker on dress; sunburst transition to silver dot box.
Mark: "JUDY ANN USA" (crude mark), "STORYBOOK USA" (crude mark); molded socks/molded bangs.
Mark: "StoryBook Doll USA"

	$550-$750
Masquerade Series	**$800 each**
Topsy and **Eva**	**$1,200 pair**
Judy Ann	**$600**
Boxed, with wardrobe, at auction	
	$3,682
Oriental	**$1,700**
Gypsy	**$1,200**
Pirate	**$1,300**
Storybook Set	**$4,300**
Sports Series	**$1,200 each**

FACTS
Nancy Ann Storybook Dolls Co.,
South San Francisco, CA.
1936-on.

5in (12cm) "Made in Japan" 1146. *H & J Foulke, Inc.*

1940: Gold sticker on dress; colored box with white polka dots; molded socks.
Mark: "StoryBook Doll USA"

	$250 up
Margie Ann	**$325-$350**
"Pudgies"	**$250-$350**

1941-1942: Gold wrist tag; white box with colored polka dots; jointed legs.
Mark: "StoryBook Doll USA"

	$110-$125
White socks	**$135-$165**
"Pudgies"	**$250-$300**

1943-1947: Gold wrist tag; white box with colored polka dots; frozen legs.
Mark: "StoryBook Doll USA" (some later dolls with plastic arms) **$75-95**

Socket head	**$95-$115**
Operetta Series	**$175**
All Time Hit Parade Series	**$175**
Powder and Crinoline Series	
	$150-$175
Holiday inserts	**$100-$125**

Hard Plastic Marked Storybook Doll: Swivel head, mohair wig, painted eyes; jointed legs; original clothes; gold wrist tag; white box with colored polka dots, excellent condition.

Mark: "Story Book Doll USA"

5½-7in (13-19cm)	**$50-$60**
Topsy: (black)	**$125-$150**
Holiday inserts	**$75-$85**

Bent-limb Baby:

Star hand baby	**$175-$200**
Boxed twins, at auction	**$676**
Bisque with closed fist, open mouth	**$165-$185**
Painted bisque, hard plastic arms	**$100-$125**
Hard plastic	**$100**
Boxed furniture	**$300 up**

Muffie: all-hard plastic; wig, sleep eyes, 8in (12cm) tall.

Mark: "StoryBook Dolls USA" some with "Muffie"

1953: Straight-leg non-walker; painted eyelashes, no eyebrows, Dynel wig (side part with flip); 54 complete costumes; original clothes; excellent condition **$250-$300***

1954: Walker; molded eyelashes, eyebrows after 1955, side part flip or braided wig; 30 additional costumes; original clothes; excellent condition **$185-$225***

8in (20cm) *Muffie. Kathy & Terri's Dolls.*

1955-1956: Hard plastic walker or bent-knee walker; rooted Saran wig (ponytail, braids or side part flip); vinyl head and hard plastic body; molded or painted upper eyelashes **$150-$165**

1968, Muffie Around the World: reissued; unmarked; straight-leg walker; molded eyelashes, glued-on wig; 12 dolls in cellophane see-through boxes **$110-$125**

Nancy Ann Style Show:

18in (46cm) hard plastic	**$650-$850**
Boxed, at auction	**$1,691**

Miss Nancy Ann:

10½in (27cm) teenage body, high-heeled feet	**$100-$125**
Boxed	**$165**
Boxed outfits	**$85 up**

Debbie, hard plastic toddler:

10in (25cm)	**$160-$175**
Mint-in-box	**$350**

Little Miss Nancy Ann:

9in (23cm) boxed doll with two boxed outfits, at auction **$400**

5in (12cm) #57 *Southern Belle* with jointed legs. *H & J Foulke, Inc.*

*Allow extra for red hair.

Old Cottage

Old Cottage Doll: Rubber compound or hard plastic head with hand-painted features, wig; stuffed cloth body; original clothing; excellent condition.

8-9in (20-23cm):
Children and Storybook outfits **$165**
Scotch, Pearlies **$135**
12-13in (31-33cm), mint-in-box
$350**

Tweedledee & Tweedledum:
9in (23cm), at auction **$1,000 pair**

**Not enough price samples to compute a reliable range.

9in (23cm) Old Cottage Girl, all original.
H & J Foulke, Inc.

FACTS
Old Cottage Toys, Allargate, Rustington, Littlehampton, Sussex, Great Britain. 1948.
Designers: Greta Fleischmann and her daughter, Susi.
Mark: Paper label - "Old Cottage Toys - handmade in Great Britain"

House of Nisbet

Nisbet Portrait & Costume Doll: Historical personages and traditional characters of the United Kingdom. All-hard plastic; portrait face, painted eyes, styled wig; body jointed at arms only; painted shoes; original costume; excellent condition with box.

7½-8in (19-20cm) **$45-$65**
Teddy Roosevelt: with bear **$235**
Princess Anne:
Wedding Set **$165**
Royal Nanny: #LE 100 **$200**
Prince Albert: #LE 99 **$150**
Lady Jane Grey **$125**
Danny Kaye (Hans Christian Andersen) **$190**
Shah of Iran **$190**

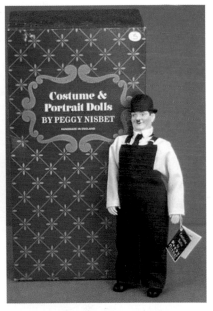

7½in (19cm) *Oliver Hardy*, #P/757, all original. *H & J Foulke, Inc.*

FACTS
House of Nisbet, Ltd., England.
1952-1995.
Designer: Peggy Nisbet
Mark: Black printed paper wrist tag.

Princess Diana Dolls

Dolls must be mint-in-box, complete with all accessories and have their certificates.

Madame Alexander: 1998, hard plastic, 10in (25cm)   **$100-$125**

Ashton-Drake: 1998. Porcelain. Designed by Titus Tomescu, in blue, red or green evening gown. Edition of 5,000.
18in (46cm)   **$125-$150**

Danbury Mint: 1982, porcelain, wedding gown, 19in (48cm) **$150-$175**
Royal Wardrobe Collection: doll with nine outfits   **$150-$200**

Effanbee: 1982, vinyl, wedding gown **$100-$125**

Franklin Mint: 1998, porcelain, beaded gown and others,
17in (43cm)   **$100-$125**
People's Princess: 1998, vinyl, blue suit, doll only
16in (41cm)   **$65-$80**
Boxed outfits   **$30-$40**

Millennium Princess: Limited Edition of 2000   **$185**

Gadco: 1998.
Young Diana: red coat and hat,
35in (89cm)   **$260-$310**
2001: Blue brocade gown,
16in (41cm)   **$120**

Royal Britannia Collection: 1997 reissue of 1982 doll, wedding gown,
12in (31cm) boxed   **$30-$40**

Royal Diana: Set of eight boxed dolls   **$100-$125**

Society for Preservation of History, Inc.: 1997, porcelain, blue satin gown
18in (46cm)   **$70**

Street Players Holding Corp.:
12in (31cm) vinyl:
1997, wedding gown   **$25**
1998, black dress   **$25**

Peggy Nisbet, 1982:
Wedding gown   **$65-$75**
Engagement dress   **$75**

Ashton-Drake Princess Diana, all original. *Rae-Ellen Koenig, The Doll Express.*

Raleigh

Ravca

Raleigh Doll: All heavy composition; appropriate clothes; all in good condition.
Child:
   11in (28cm) wigged   **$450-$500**
   13in (33cm) molded hair **$600-$650**
   18in (46cm) molded hair
                $950-$1,050
   22-24in (56-61cm) shoulder head
   on cloth body, composition arms
                $350-$450
Baby:
   12in (30cm)   **$400**
   18in (46cm)   **$600**

Bernard Ravca Doll: Paris, France, 1924-1939; New York, 1939 on. Stockinette face individually needles-culpted; cloth body and limbs; original clothes; all in excellent condition.
Mark: Paper label: "Original Ravca Fabrication Française"
   10in (25cm) French peasants
                $100-$125
   13in (33cm)   **$150-$165**
   21in (53cm)   **$350-$400**
American Historical Figures: **George Washington, Betsy Ross, Ben Franklin** and others,
   9in (23cm)   **$175-$225**
Crepe paper dolls, hand-painted faces:
   6½in (16cm)   **$10-$12**
Composition heads, bendable bodies:
   7½in (19cm)   **$35-$40**
Ravca-type fine quality peasant man or lady: 17in (43cm) **$225-$265 each**

Frances Diecks Ravca Doll: New York, 1935 on.
   Queen Elizabeth II and others:
   1952, 36in (91cm)   **$650-$850**
   "Easter Sunday:" 1973,
   12in (30cm) Black child   **$250**

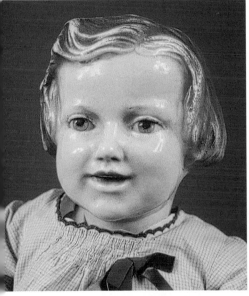

19in (48cm) Raleigh doll. *H & J Foulke, Inc.*

FACTS
Jessie McCutcheon Raleigh,
Chicago, IL. 1916-1920.
Designer: Jessie McCutcheon Raleigh.
Mark: None.

Right: 21in (53cm) Ravca lady with label. *H & J Foulke, Inc.*

Reliable Toy Co.

Remco Industries

Marked Reliable Doll: All-composition or composition shoulder head and lower arms, cloth torso and legs, sometimes composition legs; painted features; original clothes; all in good condition; some light crazing acceptable.

Barbara Ann Scott (Ice Skater):
15in (38cm) **$400-$500**
Canadian Mountie:
17in (43cm) **$300-$350**
Clicquot Club Soda Eskimo:
14in (36cm) **$250-$275**
Her Highness:
15in (38cm) **$350-$375**
Hiawatha or **Indian Maiden:**
13in (33cm) **$85-$110**
Military Man:
14in (36cm) **$225-$275**
Scots Girl or **Boy:**
14in (36cm) **$85-$110**
Shirley Temple: 22in (56cm)**$1,200**

14in (36cm) *Clicquot Club Soda Eskimo. H & J Foulke, Inc.*

FACTS
Reliable Toy Co.,
Toronto, Canada. 1920 on.
Mark: "RELIABLE//MADE IN//CANADA"

Littlechap Family: 1963. Basic doll, unplayed-with, in original box. Deduct 50% for out-of-box dolls.

Dr. John: 14½in (37cm) **$85-$95**
Lisa: 13½in (34cm) **$85-$95**
Judy: 12in (31cm) **$85-$95**
Libby: 10½in (27cm) **$85-$95**
Rooms **$300**
Office **$300**
Tagged clothes (packaged outfits)
$30-$75
Trunk **$75**

Television Programs & Personalities: All prices are for dolls that are mint, in original box.

Addams Family:
5½in (14cm) **$100-$125 each**
I Dream of Jeannie:
6in (15cm) **$50-$60**
Laurie Partridge (Susan Dey):
1973, 19in (48cm) **$85-$95**
Orphan Annie: 1967,
15in (38cm) **$45**
Beatles: 1964, set of four with guitars, 4½in (11cm) **$400**

13½ (34cm) *Lisa Littlechap*, all original. *Rosemary Kanizer.*

Santons

Sandra Sue

Santons: Figures representing the elderly people of Provence. Clay character heads, clay hands and legs, wire armature bodies; authentic costumes, many representing various occupations and activities; all original, excellent condition.

7in (18cm)	**$55**
10-12in (25-31cm)	**$100-$125**

7in (18cm) Santon. *H & J Foulke, Inc.*

Sandra Sue: 1952 on. All-hard plastic, slender; Saran wig, molded eyelashes; unmarked.

8in (20cm) basic doll: (camisole, panties, half-slip, shoes and socks)	**$125-$140**
Boxed	**$225-$250**
In street dresses	**$150-$175**
In gowns	**$200-$250**
Little Women	**$225**
Outfits, packaged	**$50-$100**
Bridal gown	**$125**
Communion dress	**$110**
Shoes	**$25**

Cindy Lou: 1951. All-hard plastic walker; Saran wig. Many outfits matched **Sandra Sue's.**

14in (36cm) basic doll: (camisole, panties, half-slip, shoes and socks)	**$275**
In street dresses	**$325**

14in (36cm) *Cindy Lou. Rosemary Kanizer.*

FACTS
1930s to present.
Simone Jouglas, J.P. Marinacei,
Syndicat de Satonniers de Provence
and others.
Provence, France.

FACTS
Richwood Toys, Inc., Annapolis, MD.
1952 on.
Designer: Ida H. Wood

Sasha

Götz "*Serie Sasha,*" all original. *H & J Foulke, Inc.*

Sasha: All-vinyl of exceptionally high quality long synthetic hair; original clothing, tiny circular wrist tag; excellent condition.

16in (41cm)	**$210-$225**
Boxed	**$250**
In cylinder package	**$350-$400**

Gregor (boy)	**$175-$200**
Boxed	**$225**
Cora (black girl), boxed	**$250-$275**
Caleb (black boy), boxed	**$250-$275**

Black baby, boxed	**$150**
White baby, boxed	**$125**
Sexed baby, pre-1979, boxed	**$165**
Packaged clothes	**$85**

Limited Edition Dolls, boxed:

1980 **Velvet Dress**	**$350-$375**
1982 **Pintucks Dress**	**$350-$375**
1983 **Kiltie**	**$350-$375**
1984 **Harlequin**	**$350-$375**
1985 **Prince Gregor**	**$350-$375**
1986 **Princess**	**$1,000-$1,500**
1986 **Sari**	**$725-$775**

"Serie Sasha:"
Götz model, 1965-1969:

All original,	
16in (41cm)	**$1,250-$1,650**
Boxed	**$2,200**
"No Nose"	**$1,500-$1,800**

Studio Model, 1950s-1960s:

20-21in (51-53cm) child	
	$7,500-$12,500
13in (33cm) baby, at auction	**$3,100**

Götz: 1995 on, boxed	**$200-$225**

FACTS
Trendon Toys, Ltd.,
Reddish, Stockport, England.
1965-1986.
Designer: Sasha Morgenthaler.

Shirley Temple

All-Composition Child: 1934 through late 1930s. Marked head and body; jointed composition body; all original including wig and clothes; entire doll in very good condition. Sizes 11-27in (28-69cm).

Mark: On body: **SHIRLEY TEMPLE 13**

On head: **13 SHIRLEY TEMPLE**

On cloth label:

> Genuine
> SHIRLEY TEMPLE
> DOLL
> REGISTERED U.S. PAT OFF
> IDEAL NOVELTY & TOY CO
> MADE IN U.S.A.

11in (28cm)	$900-$1,100*
13in (33cm)	$850-$900*
15-16in (38-41cm)	$850-$900*
18in (46cm)	$1,000-$1,100*
20-22in (51-56cm)	$1,200*
25in (64cm)	$1,400*
27in (69cm)	$1,800-$2,000*

*Allow 50-100% more for mint-in-box doll. Allow extra for **Texas Ranger, Captain January** and other unusual outfits.

FACTS
Ideal Novelty & Toy Corp., New York, NY. 1934 to present. **Designer:** Bernard Lipfert.

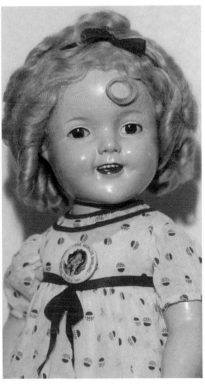

13in (33cm) composition *Shirley Temple,* all original. *H & J Foulke, Inc.*

22in (56cm) composition *Shirley Temple,* all original. *Mary Barnes Kelley Collection.*

18in (46cm) composition *Baby Shirley Temple*. *H & J Foulke, Inc.*

12in (30cm) vinyl *Shirley Temple*, all original and boxed. *H & J Foulke, Inc.*

16-18in (41-46cm) with trunk and wardrobe	**$1,700-$1,900**
Button	**$135**
Dress, tagged	**$175 up**
Shoes	**$75-$125**
Trunk	**$225-$250**
Carriage	**$600-$650**

Hawaiian Shirley:
18in (46cm)   **$900-$1,000**
Baby Shirley: Composition/cloth; original clothing; good condition,
16-18in (41-46cm)   **$1,250-$1,500**

Other Composition Shirley Temples:
Made in Japan:
7½in (19cm)   **$275-$325**
Reliable: (Canada), all original and boxed, 18-22in (46-56cm)   **$1,200**

Vinyl and Plastic: Excellent condition, original clothes.
1957:
12in (30cm)   **$225-$235**
Boxed   **$325-$425**
Boxed with 16 original outfits,
at auction   **$1,800**
15in (38cm)   **$300-$325**
17in (43cm)   **$375-$400**
19in (48cm)   **$425-$450**
36in (91cm)   **$1,500-$1,800**
Script name pin   **$40**
Name purse   **$25**
Tagged or boxed dress   **$65 up**
Black Plastic Curler Box   **$80**
1973:
16in (41cm) size only   **$100-$110**
Boxed   **$150-$$165**
Boxed dress   **$35**
1972, Montgomery Ward:
14in (36cm)   **$225-$250**
1982, 1983:
8in (20cm)   **$40-$50**
12in (30cm)   **$70-$80**
1984, Dolls, Dreams & Love:
36in (91cm)   **$250-$300**

Porcelain, all original and boxed:
1986, Danbury Mint:
14in (36cm)   **$75-$85**
18in (46cm) **Little Princess,**
at auction   **$300**

Skookum Indians

Skookum Indian Doll: Composition character face, black mohair wig; Indian blanket folded to represent arms; cotton print dress or shirt and felt trousers, headband with feathers; beads; suede boots; all very colorful; excellent unplayed-with condition.

Mailer	**$20-$30**
6in (15cm)	**$35-$45**
9-10in (23-25cm)	**$100-$150**
12in (31cm)	**$200-$250**
16in (41cm)	**$400-$450**
20in (51cm)	**$650-$750**
36in (91cm)	**$1,200-$1,500**

FACTS
Created and designed by Mary McAboy, Missoula, MT and Denver, CO. Dolls made by various companies including Arrow Novelty Co., New York and H.H. Tammen Co., New York, Denver and Los Angeles. 1913 on.
Mark: Sometimes a paper label on the sole of the foot.
Trademark: Skookum (Bully Good)

16in (41cm) *Skookum Squaw* with papoose, all original. *H & J Foulke, Inc.*

Sun Rubber Co.

Silly and **Popo:** 1937, comic characters with molded clothes, 10in (25cm)
$55-$65**

Minnie Mouse: 1937, in red-and-white polka dot sundress, 10½in (27cm)
$125-$150**

Bonnie Bear, Wiggy Wags, Happy Kappy, Rompy: 1940s. One-piece squeeze dolls with molded clothes and hats. Designed by Ruth E. Newton.
6-8in (15-20cm) **$15-$25****
So-Wee: 1941. Designed by Ruth E. Newton with painted or sleep eyes, molded hair, excellent,
10-12in (25-31cm) **$65-$75**

Sunbabe: 1950. Drink-and-wet baby with painted eyes and molded hair, excellent:
11-13in (28-33cm) **$45-$55**
In original box **$110-$125**
Sewing set, boxed **$150-$175**

Baby Bannister: 1954, all-vinyl drink-and-wet doll based on the famous baby photographs by Constance Bannister, excellent, 12in (31cm) in original box
$100-$125

Gerber Baby: 1955. All-rubber with inset eyes and molded hair, open/closed mouth, excellent:
11-13in (28-33cm) **$100-$125**
in original box **$275-$325**

**Not enough price samples to compute a reliable range.

> **FACTS**
> Barberton, OH. 1930s on.
> **Marks:** "Sun Rubber Co."
> with various numbers,
> names and dates

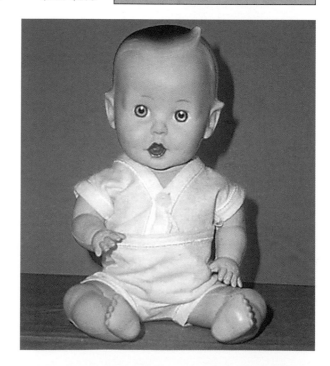

12in (31cm)
Gerber Baby.
Miriam
Blankman
Collection.

Terri Lee

Terri Lee Child Doll: Original wig, painted eyes; jointed at neck, shoulders and hips; all original tagged clothing and accessories; very good condition.

16in (41cm)

Composition, stiff hair	**$500-$600****
Hard Plastic:	
Pat. Pending	**$500-$600**
Terri Lee only	**$375-$475**
Mint-in-box	**$600-$650**
Talking Terri: boxed	**$700-$750**
Push walker: at auction	**$975**
Vinyl head: at auction	**$605**
Patty-Jo: (black)	**$900-$1,100**
Bonnie Lou: (black)	**$1,300**
Jerri Lee: 16in (41cm)	**$500-$600**
Benji: (black)	**$700-$800****
Clothing:	
School dress	**$125-$150**
Gown	**$125-$165**
Shoes	**$65**
Majorette outfit with boots	**$225**
Cowgirl outfit with hat	**$175**
Fur coat	**$150**
Clothes rack	**$125**
Tiny Terri Lee: inset eyes,	
10in (25cm)	**$165-$185**
Boxed	**$250-$265**
Tiny Jerri Lee: inset eyes,	
10in (25cm)	**$185-$210**
Connie Lynn	**$375-$425**
Gene Autry: at auction	**$1,800-$2,000**
Linda Baby: 10in (25cm)	**$165-$185**
Ginger Girl Scout:	
8in (20cm)	**$175-$225**

**Not enough price samples to compute a reliable range.

FACTS
TERRI LEE Sales Corp., V. Gradwohl, Pres. 1946-Lincoln, NE; then Apple Valley, CA, from 1952-Ca. 1962.
Mark: First dolls: "TERRI LEE PAT. PENDING" raised letters.
Later dolls: "TERRI LEE"

16in (41cm) *Terri Lee*, all original. *Courtesy of Susan Babkowski.*

10in (25cm) *Tiny Terri Lee*, all original. *H & J Foulke, Inc.*

Tiny Town Dolls

Uneeda Doll Co.

Tiny Town Dolls: Molded felt faces with painted eyes and mouths, mohair wigs of various styles and colors; wrapped cloth bodies over wire armatures, felt hands; weighted white metal shoes; original clothes; excellent condition.

4in (10cm)*	**$80-$85**
Boxed	**$125**

*Other known sizes are 5in (13cm) and 7¼in (19cm) but no prices are available.

Composition Dolls:
Lucky Lindy (Charles Lindbergh): 1927, composition/cloth, brown aviator suit, good condition, 14in (36cm)
$350-$450**

Rita Hayworth: 1939, all-composition, red mohair wig, all original clothes, excellent, 14in (36cm)
$450-$500

**Not enough price samples to compute a reliable range.

4in (10cm) Tiny Town *China Girl*, all original. *H & J Foulke, Inc.*

13in (33cm) composition toddler, all original. *H & J Foulke, Inc.*

FACTS
Alma LeBlane dba Lenna Lee's
Tiny Town Dolls,
San Francisco, CA.
Trademark registered
January 11, 1949.
Mark: Some have a gold octagonal wrist tag with "Tiny Town Dolls" on one side and name of doll on the other.

FACTS
New York. 1917 on.

Toddler: Ca. 1940, all-composition, all original clothes, very good condition, 13in (33cm) **$250-$275**

Hard Plastic and Vinyl Dolls: Excellent, unplayed-with condition with original clothes, perfect hair, rosy cheeks.

Dollikin: 1957. Fully-jointed hard plastic:
    8in (20cm) mint-in-box **$40-$45**
    11in (28cm) mint-in-box **$65-$75**
    19in (48cm) **$225-$275**

Baby Dollikin: 1958, jointed elbows and knees, 21in (53cm) **$150**
Saranade: 1962, with phonograph and record, 21in (53cm) **$150**
Pollyana: 1960. Haley Mills in pink-and-white checked outfit:
    10½in (27cm) **$35-$40**
    17in (43cm) **$50-$60**
    31in (79cm) **$200**

Wee Three: Mother, daughter and baby brother:
    Set **$125**
    Boxed set **$200**

Suzette: 1960, 12in (31cm) **$75-$85**
Bob: 1962, 12in (31cm) boxed **$90**
Annette Funicello: Ca. 1960,
    10in (26cm) **$75-$85**

10in (25cm)
*Annette
Funicello*,
all original.
*McMasters
Doll
Auctions.*

Vinyl Dolls

All dolls must be in excellent condition with perfect hair, excellent coloring, no discoloration and crisp original clothes.

14R Fashion Dolls: 1957-1965. All-vinyl, excellent quality ladies:
    19-20in (48-51cm) **$80-$90**
    Boxed **$135**

James Bond, Secret Agent 007: Gilbert Toys, movie character,
    12½in (31cm) boxed **$75-$100**

Angela Cartwright: 1961, Natural Doll Co., featured as Linda Williams on "The Danny Thomas Show," 14in (36cm) smiling character face **$75-$85**

Carol Channing: 1960, Nasco, all-vinyl, 11½in (29cm) costume from musical **$45-$55**

Dick Clark: 1958-1959, Juro Novelty Co., personality portrait doll, original clothes, 26in (66cm) at auction **$400-$500**

Debutante: Ca. 1960, Goldberger, high-heeled fashion doll, vinyl and hard plastic, 29in (74cm) **$90-$110**

Hello, Dolly: 1961, Kaysam, all-vinyl, 21in (53cm) costume from musical **$75-$100**

Honey West: 1965, Gilbert Toys, hard plastic and vinyl, painted eyes,
    11½in (29cm) **$125**

Lonely Lisa: 1964, Royal Doll Co., vinyl and cloth, large painted eyes,
    20in (51cm) **$90-$100**

Man from U.N.C.L.E.: 1965, Gilbert Toys, characters from television series,
    12½in (31cm) boxed **$100**

Miss America: 1957-1959. Sayco Doll Co., vinyl fashion doll:

10in (25cm)	**$55-$65**
18in (46cm)	**$90-$110**

Marilyn Monroe: 1983, World Doll Co., 18in (46cm) boxed, red dress
$65-$75

Puppetrina: 1963, Goldberger, vinyl head, cloth body, hand puppet doll, 22½in (57cm)   **$65**

Queen for a Day: 1957, Valentine, vinyl fashion doll, in taffeta gown and velvet cape, 20in (51cm)   **$90-$110**

Ginger Rogers: 1983, World Doll Co., 18in (46cm) boxed   **$75-$85**

Roxanne, Beat the Clock: 16in (41cm) boxed   **$450**

Sally Starr: 1960s, Philadelphia television personality, cowgirl outfit
10½in (26cm)   **$25-$35**

Left: 18in (46cm) H.J. Blumberg baby, all original; $45. *McMasters Doll Auctions.*

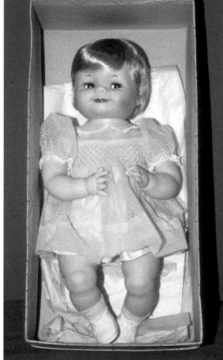

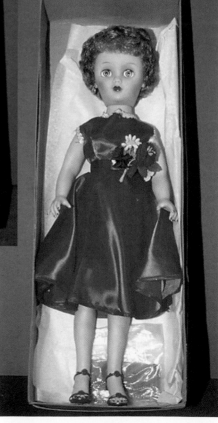

Right: 19in (48cm) 14R fashion lady, all original and boxed. *June & Norman Verro.*

Vogue

All-composition Girl: 1940s. Original clothes; all in good condition, with perfect hair.
Mark: None on doll; round silver sticker on front of outfit. May have name stamped on sole of shoe.

13in (33cm)	**$400-$450**
19in (48cm)	**$525-$575**

All-composition Toddles: 1937-1948. Painted eyes looking to side; original clothes; all in good condition.
Mark: "VOGUE" on head
"DOLL CO." on back
"TODDLES" stamped on sole of shoe

7-8in (18-20cm)	**$275-$325***
Boxed	**$400-$500**

Hard Plastic Ginny: Original wig and tagged clothes; all in excellent condition with perfect hair and pretty coloring. 7-8in (18-20cm)
Mark:
On strung dolls: "VOGUE DOLLS"
On walking dolls: "GINNY//VOGUE DOLLS"

1948-1949:

Painted eyes	**$375-$425***
Half-Century Series	**$1,000**
Crib Crowd Baby	**$800-$900**
Easter Bunny Baby	**$1,200-$1,400**

1950-1953:

Painted eyelashes, strung	**$400-$500***
Caracul wig, poodle cut	**$500-$600***
Beryl, Cheryl, Tiny Miss, Kindergarten: boxed	**$1,500**

FACTS
Vogue Dolls, Inc., Medford, MA.
Creator: Jennie Graves.
Clothes Designer:
Virginia Graves Carlson.
Clothes Label: "Vogue," "Vogue Dolls"
or "VOGUE DOLLS, INC.
MEDFORD, MASS. USA
® REG U.S. PAT OFF"

Queen Elizabeth II	**$900-$1,100**
Black **Ginny**	**$2,000-$2,500**

1954: Painted eyelashes, walks

	$300-$350*

1955-1957:
Molded eyelashes, walks

	$225-$275*
Davy Crockett	**$450-$500**
Girl Scout or **Brownie**	**$275-$325**
Bon Bon: boxed	**$400-$450**
Tiny Miss, Debs: boxed	**$350-$400**
Nun	**$350**

1957-1962:
Molded eyelashes, walks,

jointed knees	**$150-$200***

1962 on.
Vinyl head, hard plastic body with

jointed knees	**$90**

*Allow extra for unusual outfits, such as cowboy and **Uncle Sam.**
Allow extra for mint-in-box dolls and desirable outfits, such as **Tiny Miss Series and **Kindergarten Series.**

16in (41cm) composition *Southern Belle*, all original. *H & J Foulke, Inc.*

Accessories, All in excellent condition:

Ginny's Pup	**$225-$275**
Cardboard suitcase with contents	**$50**
Parasol	**$15-$18**
Gym set	**$450-$500**
Dresser, bed, rocking chair, wardrobe	**$55-$65 each**
Trousseau Tree	**$150-$175**
School bag	**$75-$85**
"Hi I'm Ginny" pin	**$75**
Ginny's First Secret book	**$125**
Swag bag, hat box, auto bag and garment bag	**$35 each**
Roller skates in cylinder	**$35**
Hats	**$15-$25**
Headband	**$8**
Dress and panties, tagged	**$35-$55**
Glasses	**$4-$5**

Shoes, center snap	**$75-$100**
Shoes, plastic	**$20-$25**
Boxed	**$30-$40**
Locket & chain	**$65**
Purse (Ginny)	**$6**
Christmas Stocking (no doll), at auction	**$900**
Boxed Clothing, 1950-1954	**$100-$200**

Vinyl Ginny: 1972.

Children and internationals	**$35-$40**
Gift Set	**$65-$75**

Vinyl Ginny: 1977 on.

8in (20cm) children	**$40-$50**
International costumes	**$35-$40**
Sasson	**$35**
Black **Ginnette**	**$15-$20**

Left: 8in (20cm) strung 1953 *Ginny "Nan,"* #32. *Kathy & Terri's Dolls.*

Below: 8in (20cm) *Ginnette,* all original and boxed. *Rosemary Kanizer.*

Other Dolls: All must be in excellent condition with perfect hair, excellent coloring and original clothes.

Jill: 1957, all-hard plastic, adult body,
| | |
10in (25cm) **$200-$225**
Boxed outfits **$75-$105**

Jeff: 1957. Vinyl head:
10in (25cm) **$75-$95**
Boxed **$150**

Jan: 1958.
All-vinyl **$95-$110**
Boxed **$150**

Ginnette: 1957. All-vinyl baby:
8in (20cm) boxed **$225-$275**
Ginnette Play Set, boxed **$400**
Baby Tender **$50**
Crib **$75**
Boxed outfits **$50-$85**

Jimmy: 1958.
8in (20cm) painted eyes **$135-$150**
Boxed **$175-$200**

Lil Imp: 1959-1960. Vinyl head, hard plastic body with bent knees:
11in (28cm) **$125-$150**
Boxed **$250-$300**

Wee Imp: 1960, all-hard plastic, red hair, 8in (20cm) **$275-$325**

Baby Dear: 1960-1964. Designed by Eloise Wilken. Vinyl head and limbs, cloth body:
12in (31cm) **$175-$195**
18in (46cm) **$275-$325**

Baby Dear One: 1962-1963,
25in (63cm) **$300-$350**

Baby Dear Two (toddler), 1963:
17in (43cm) **$225-$250**
23in (59cm) **$325-$375**

Miss Ginny: 1962, 16in (41cm)
$65-$75

Ginny: 1960, 36in (91cm)
$300-$500**

Brikette: 1961.
16in (41cm) **$125-$150**
22in (56cm) **$175-$185**

Love Me Linda: 1965, all-vinyl,
16in (41cm) **$65-$75**

Wright, R. John

Cloth Dolls: All boxed and in perfect condition.

Adult Characters (no boxes)
$1,200-$1,500
Father Christmas **$1,800**
Children **$750-$1,500**
Snow White & Seven Dwarfs:,
matching numbered set **$5,000**
Golliwog: 10in (25cm) **$425**
Hans & Gretel Brinker:
20in (51cm) **$950 each**
Pinocchio & Geppeto:
17in (43cm) **$2,000**
Christopher Robin & Winnie the Pooh:
12in (30cm) **$1,000**
17in (43cm) **$1,500-$2,000**
Christopher Robin Winter with sled: **$850**
Winnie the Pooh:
18in (46cm) **$1,200-$1,300**
14in (36cm) with honeypot **$700**
Piglet with Violets **$375-$425**
Kewpies **$450-$500**

R. John Wright *Father Christmas* with rare pink robe and hood. *Rae-Ellen Koenig, The Doll Express.*

Bibliography

Anderton, Johana.
Twentieth Century Dolls. North Kansas City,
Missouri: Trojan Press, 1971.
More Twentieth Century Dolls. North
Kansas City, Missouri: Athena Publishing
Co., 1974.

Angione, Genevieve. *All-Bisque & Half-
Bisque Dolls*. Exton, Pennsylvania: Schiffer
Publishing Ltd., 1969.

Borger, Mona. *Chinas, Dolls for Study and
Admiration*. San Francisco: Borger
Publications, 1983.

Cieslik, Jürgen and Marianne.
German Doll Encyclopedia 1800-1939.
Cumberland, Maryland: Hobby House
Press, Inc., 1985.

Coleman, Dorothy S., Elizabeth Ann and
Evelyn Jane. *The Collector's Book of Dolls'
Clothes*. New York: Crown Publishers,
Inc., 1975.
*The Collector's Encyclopedia of Dolls,
Volumes I & II*. New York: Crown
Publishers, Inc., 1968 & 1986.

Corson, Carol. *Schoenhut Dolls, A Collector's
Encyclopedia*. Cumberland, Maryland:
Hobby House Press, Inc., 1993.

Foulke, Jan.
*Blue Books of Dolls & Values, Volumes I-
XIII*. Cumberland, Maryland: Hobby House
Press, Inc., 1974-1997.
Doll Classics. Cumberland, Maryland:
Hobby House Press, Inc., 1987.
Focusing on Effanbee Composition Dolls.
Riverdale, Maryland: Hobby House Press,
1978.
Focusing on Gebrüder Heubach Dolls.
Cumberland, Maryland: Hobby House Press,
Inc., 1980.
Kestner, King of Dollmakers. Cumberland,
Maryland: Hobby House Press, Inc., 1982.
Simon & Halbig Dolls, The Artful Aspect.
Cumberland, Maryland: Hobby House Press,
Inc., 1984.
Treasury of Madame Alexander Dolls.
Riverdale, Maryland: Hobby House Press,
1979.
China Doll Collecting. Grantsville,
Maryland: Hobby House Press, Inc., 1995.
German 'Dolly' Collecting. Grantsville,
Maryland: Hobby House Press, Inc., 1995.
Doll Buying &Selling. Grantsville,
Maryland: Hobby House Press, Inc., 1995.

Gerken, Jo Elizabeth.
Wonderful Dolls of Papier-Mâché. Lincoln,
Nebraska: Doll Research Associates, 1970.

Hillier, Mary.
Dolls and Dollmakers. New York: G. P.
Putnam's Sons, 1968.

The History of Wax Dolls. Cumberland,
Maryland: Hobby House Press, Inc.;
London: Justin Knowles, 1985.

Izen, Judith.
Collector's Guide to Ideal Dolls. Paducah,
Kentucky: Collector Books, 1999.

Izen, Judith and Carol Stover.
Collector's Encyclopedia of Vogue Dolls.
Paducah, Kentucky: Collector Books. 1999.

Judd, Polly and Pam.
Hard Plastic Dolls. Cumberland, Maryland:
Hobby House Press, Inc., 1985.
Hard Plastic Dolls II. Cumberland,
Maryland: Hobby House Press, Inc., 1989.
Glamour Dolls of the 1950s &1960s.
Cumberland, Maryland: Hobby House Press,
Inc., 1988.
Compo Dolls 1928-1955. Cumberland,
Maryland: Hobby House Press, Inc., 1991.
Compo Dolls, Volume II. Cumberland,
Maryland: Hobby House Press, Inc., 1994.

Mathes, Ruth E. and **Robert C.**
Dolls, Toys and Childhood. Cumberland,
Maryland: Hobby House Press, Inc., 1987.

McGonagle, Dorothy A. *The Dolls of Jules
Nicolas Steiner*. Cumberland, Maryland:
Hobby House Press, Inc., 1988.

Merrill, Madeline O. *The Art of Dolls, 1700-
1940*. Cumberland, Maryland: Hobby House
Press, Inc., 1985.

Mertz, Ursula R.
*Collector's Encyclopedia fo American
Composition Dolls, 1900-1950*. Paducah,
Kentucky: Collector Books, 1999.

Pardella, Edward R. *Shirley Temple Dolls and
Fashions*. West Chester,
Pennsylvania: Schiffer Publishing, Ltd.,
1992.

Richter, Lydia. *Heubach Character Dolls and
Figurines*. Cumberland, Maryland:Hobby
House Press, Inc., 1992.

Schoonmaker, Patricia N.
*Effanbee Dolls: The Formative Years 1910-
1929*. Cumberland, Maryland: Hobby House
Press, Inc., 1984.
*Patsy Doll Family Encyclopedia, Volumes I
& II*. Cumberland, Maryland: Hobby House
Press, Inc., 1992.

Tabbat, Andrew.
*Collector's World of Raggedy Ann & Andy.
Volumes I & II*. Annapolis, Maryland: Gold
Horse Publishing, 1997.

Tarnowska, Maree. *Fashion Dolls*.
Cumberland, Maryland: Hobby House Press,
Inc., 1986.

About the Author

The name Jan Foulke is synonymous with accurate information. As the author of the *Blue Book of Dolls & Values®*, she is the most quoted source on doll information and the most respected and recognized authority on dolls and doll prices in the world.

Born in Burlington, New Jersey, Jan Foulke has always had a fondness for dolls. She recalls, "Many happy hours of my childhood were spent with dolls as companions, since we lived on a quiet county road, and until I was ten, I was an only child." Jan received a B.A. from Columbia Union College, where she was named to the *Who's Who in American Colleges & Universities* and was graduated with high honors. Jan taught for twelve years in the Montgomery County school system in Maryland and also supervised student teachers in English for the University of Maryland where she did graduate work.

Jan and her husband, Howard, who photographs the dolls presented in the *Blue Book*, were both fond of antiquing as a hobby, and in 1972, they decided to open a small antique shop of their own. Their daughter, Beth, was quite interested in dolls and this sparked their curiosity about the history of old dolls. The stock in their antique shop gradually changed and evolved into an antique doll shop.

Early in the development of their antique doll shop, Jan and Howard realized that there was a critical need for an accurate and reliable doll identification and price guide resource. In the early 1970s, the Foulkes teamed up with Hobby House Press to produce (along with Thelma Bateman) the first *Blue Book of Dolls & Values*, originally published in 1974. Since that time, the Foulkes have exclusively authored and illustrated the fourteen successive editions, and today the *Blue Book* is regarded by collectors and dealers as the definitive source for doll prices and values.

Jan and Howard Foulke now dedicate all of their professional time to the world

of dolls: writing and illustrating books and articles, appraising collections, lecturing on antique dolls, acting as consultants to museums, auction houses and major collectors, and selling dolls by mail order, the internet and exhibits at major shows throughout the United States. Mrs. Foulke is a member of the United Federation of Doll Clubs, Doll Collectors of America and an officer of the National Antique Doll Dealers Association. Her biography appears in *Who's Who in the East*.

Mrs. Foulke has appeared on numerous television talk shows and is often quoted in newspaper and magazine articles as the ultimate source for doll pricing and trends in collecting. Both *USA Today* and *The Washington Post* have stated that the *Blue Book of Dolls & Values* is "the bible of doll collecting."

In addition to her work on the fifteen editions of the *Blue Book of Dolls & Values*, Jan Foulke has also authored: *Focusing on Effanbee Composition Dolls; A Treasury of Madame Alexander Dolls; Kestner, King of Dollmakers; Simon & Halbig, The Artful Aspect; Focusing on Gebrüder Heubach Dolls; Doll Classics; Focusing on Dolls; China Doll Collecting; German 'Dolly' Collecting* and *Doll Buying and Selling*. She has been a regular contributor to *Doll Reader®* magazine for 29 years (since the beginning). Her current column is the popular *Antique Q&A*.

Glossary

Applied Ears: Ears molded independently and affixed to the head. (On most dolls the ear is included as part of the head mold.)

Bald Head: Head with no crown opening, could be covered by a wig or have painted hair.

Ball-jointed Body: Usually a body of composition or papier-mâché with wooden balls at knees, elbows, hips and shoulders to make swivel joints; some parts of the limbs may be wood.

Bébé: French child doll with "dolly face."

Belton-type: A bald head with one, two or three small holes for attaching wig.

Bent-limb Baby Body: Composition body of five pieces with chubby torso and curved arms and legs.

Biscaloid: Ceramic or composition substance for making dolls; also called imitation bisque.

Biskoline: Celluloid-type substance for making dolls.

Bisque: Unglazed porcelain, usually flesh tinted, used for dolls' heads or all-bisque dolls.

Breather: Doll with an actual opening in each nostril, also called open nostrils.

Breveté (or Bté): Used on French dolls to indicate that the patent is registered.

Character Doll: Dolls with bisque or composition heads, modeled to look lifelike, such as infants, young or older children, young ladies and so on.

China: Glazed porcelain used for dolls' heads and *Frozen Charlottes*.

Child Dolls: Dolls with a typical "dolly face," which represents a child.

Composition: A material used for dolls' heads and bodies, consisting of such items as wood pulp, glue, sawdust, flour, rags and sundry other substances.

Contemporary Clothes: Clothes not original to the doll, but dating from the same period when the doll would have been a plaything.

Crown Opening: The cut-away part of a doll head.

DEP: Abbreviation used on German and French dolls claiming registration.

D.R.G.M.: Abbreviation used on German dolls indicating a registered design or patent.

Dolly Face: Typical face used on bisque dolls before 1910 when the character face was developed; "dolly faces" were used also after 1910.

Embossed Mark: Raised letters, numbers or names on the backs of heads or bodies.

Feathered Eyebrows: Eyebrows composed of many tiny painted brush strokes to give a realistic look.

Fixed Eyes: Glass eyes that do not move or sleep.

Flange Neck: A doll's head with a ridge at the base of the neck which contains holes for sewing the head to a cloth body.

Flapper Dolls: Dolls of the 1920s period with bobbed wig or molded hair and slender arms and legs.

Flirting Eyes: Eyes which move from side to side as doll's head is tilted.

Frozen Charlotte: Doll molded all in one piece including arms and legs.

Ges. (Gesch.): Used on German dolls to indicate design is registered or patented.

Googly Eyes: Large, often round eyes looking to the side; also called roguish or goo goo eyes.

Hard Plastic: Hard material used for making dolls after 1948.

Ichimatsu: Japanese play doll. See page 159 for full description.

Incised Mark: Letters, numbers or names impressed into the bisque on the back of the head or on the shoulder plate.

Intaglio Eyes: Painted eyes with sunken pupil and iris.

JCB: Jointed composition body. See *ball-jointed body.*

Kid Body: Body of white or pink leather.

Lady Dolls: Dolls with an adult face and a body with adult proportions.

Mama Doll: American composition and cloth doll of the 1920s to 1940s with "mama" voice box.

Mohair: Goat's hair widely used in making doll wigs.

Molded Hair: Curls, waves and comb marks which are actually part of the mold and not merely painted onto the head.

Motschmann-type Body: Doll body with cloth midsection and upper limbs with floating joints; hard lower torso and lower limbs.

Open-Mouth: Lips parted with an actual opening in the bisque, usually has teeth either molded in the bisque or set in separately and sometimes a tongue.

Open/Closed Mouth: A mouth molded to appear open, but having no actual slit in the bisque.

Original Clothes: Clothes belonging to a doll during the childhood of the original owner, either commercial or homemade.

Painted Bisque: Bisque covered with a layer of flesh-colored paint which has not been baked in, so will easily rub or wash off.

Paperweight Eyes: Blown glass eyes which have depth and look real, usually found in French dolls.

Papier-mâché: A material used for dolls' heads and bodies, consisting of paper pulp, sizing, glue, clay or flour.

Parian: Very fine quality white bisque with no complexion tint, usually used to make molded hair dolls.

S.G.D.G.: Used on French dolls to indicate that the patent is registered "without guarantee of the government."

Shoulder Head: A doll's head and shoulders all in one piece.

Shoulder Plate: The actual shoulder portion sometimes molded in one with the head, sometimes a separate piece with a socket in which a head is inserted.

Socket Head: Head and neck which fit into an opening in the shoulder plate or the body.

Solid-dome Head: Head with no crown opening, could have painted hair or be covered by wig.

Stationary Eyes: Glass eyes which do not move or sleep.

Stone Bisque: Coarse white bisque of a lesser quality.

Toddler Body: Usually a chubby ball-jointed composition body with chunky, shorter thighs and a diagonal hip joint; sometimes has curved instead of jointed arms; sometimes is of five pieces with straight chubby legs.

Topsy Turvy: Doll with two heads, one usually concealed beneath a skirt.

Turned Shoulder Head: Head and shoulders are one piece, but the head is molded at an angle so that the doll is not looking straight ahead.

Vinyl: Soft plastic material used for making dolls after 1950s.

Watermelon Mouth: Closed line-type mouth curved up at each side in an impish expression.

Wax-Over: A doll with head and/or limbs of papier-mâché or composition covered with a layer of wax to give a natural lifelike finish.

Weighted Eyes: Eyes which can be made to sleep by means of a weight which is attached to the eyes.

Wire Eyes: Eyes that can be made to sleep by means of a wire which protrudes from doll's head.

Index

Mold Numbers

100: 35, 56, 116, 136
101: 53, 56, 117
102: 28, 117
103: 117
104: 50, 117
105: 117
106: 117, 135
107: 117
1000: 33
1008: 33
1009: 21, 56, 186-187
1010: 53, 187
1022: 33
1024: 33
1028: 33
1032: 34
1039: 186-187
1040: 187
1046: 33
1064: 33
1070: 126
10532: 104
10586: 104
10633: 104
10727: 156
1078: 186
1079: 186
108: 117
1080: 187
109: 96, 118-119, 142
1099: 158
1109: 186
110: 53
111: 53, 142
11173: 104
112: 92, 119
1123: 34
112x: 119
1139: 186
114: 118-119
1142: 33
115: 119
1159: 189
115A: 119
116: 119, 135
1160: 187
116A: 119
117: 119
117A: 119
117N: 14, 119
117X: 119

118A: 116
119: 96, 116
120: 28, 51, 187
121: 116, 170
1210: 33
122: 116
123: 120, 135
1235: 34
124: 120
1248: 187
1249: 56, 187
125: 35, 53, 97
1250: 187
1254: 33
126: 51, 56, 97, 116- 117, 170, 187
1260: 187
1266: 177
1267: 177
127: 98, 120, 170
1271: 177
1272: 56, 177
1276: 66
1279: 187
128: 53, 116-117, 124
1285: 177
1286: 177
1288: 33
129: 53, 124
1294: 170, 176, 188
1295: 177
1296: 177
1297: 56, 177
1299: 187
130: 97, 127
1303: 105, 189
1304: 33
1305: 189
1307: 189
1308: 189
131: 92, 94, 135
1310: 177
132: 51
1322: 35
1329: 35, 158-159
133: 124
1330: 150
1339: 188

134: 47, 98
1348: 80
1349: 56, 80
135: 120, 135
1352: 35
1357: 35
1358: 56
136: 51-52, 97
1361: 35
1362: 34
1369: 62
137: 15, 46
1373: 62
1377: 131
138: 133
1388: 188
139: 96
1398: 188
1407: 35, 42
141: 98
1415: 62
1418: 63
142: 97, 123
1428: 188
143: 124
1431: 35
144: 123
145: 123
1450: 35
146: 123
1468: 189
1469: 81, 189
147: 123
148: 123
1488: 188-189
1489: 188
149: 98, 124, 142
1498: 188-189
150: 29-30, 35, 97-98, 127, 156, 187
1500: 142
151: 97, 187
152: 97, 124, 189
153: 187
154: 98, 134, 154
155: 30, 124
156: 29-30, 188
158: 133
159: 53, 97, 142

160: 30, 124, 127, 133
161: 124
162: 128
163: 53, 93
164: 123, 158
165: 30, 93, 141
166: 94, 123, 133-134, 136
167: 123, 133
168: 124
169: 98, 121, 128, 134, 136, 186
170: 135
171: 120, 123-124
172: 93, 120, 128, 188
173: 94, 120, 124
174: 124, 187
175: 120
176: 135, 187
177: 127
178: 124, 127
179: 56, 92, 124
180: 94
182: 136
183: 46
184: 127
186: 135
188: 135
189: 92, 96, 135
1892: 148
1894: 56, 147-148
1896: 79, 148
1897: 148
190: 124, 136
1906: 179
1907: 104, 111, 170
1909: 170, 179
191: 111
192: 92, 111
1923: 56
1924: 170
195: 123
196: 124
198: 96

200: 44, 66, 93, 135
2000: 148
201: 64, 120
202: 154
2023: 176
2025: 176
203: 135
2033: 176
204: 44
2042: 176
2048: 175
206: 125
207: 64
208: 44, 64, 111, 125, 127
209: 44
2094: 175
2096: 175
2097: 176
210: 64, 92, 126
211: 126
212: 125
214: 53, 120, 123
215: 53, 124
217: 64, 92
22: 30, 116, 156, 170
220: 64, 125, 158
221: 94, 111
222: 30
224: 44-45
225: 35
226: 126, 173
227: 173
229: 173
23: 170
230: 111, 148, 173
231: 148
232: 195
233: 150, 173
234: 126, 173
235: 126, 173
236: 173
237: 126, 173
238: 127, 175, 177
239: 125, 173
240: 93
241: 93, 125

242: 173
243: 158
244: 105
245: 96, 127, 175
246: 44, 175
247: 127, 175, 199
248: 150-152, 175
249: 126
250: 101, 135, 151-152, 175
251: 101, 150-152, 175, 199
252: 94, 176-177
253: 8, 95
254: 136
255: 129
257: 5, 126
259: 151
260: 126-127
261: 101
262: 66, 101, 127
263: 66, 127
266: 175
267: 101, 127
269: 179
271: 101
272: 129
273: 44
275: 44, 101
277: 44, 55, 129
28: 141, 173
281: 129
282: 135
283: 99
289: 44
290: 116
293: 179
297: 44, 99
300: 44, 57, 102, 145, 154
301: 174-175, 199
302: 44
309: 44
31: 141-142, 173
310: 95
312: 101, 185
316: 57
32: 141, 173

320: 102
3200: 150
322: 95
323: 95
325: 44
326: 151
327: 151
329: 151
330: 94
338: 102
339: 102
34: 57, 141
340: 44, 102, 151
341: 57, 152-153
342: 102
347: 154
349: 102
350: 102
351: 57, 153
352: 154
36: 137
362: 57
370: 137, 150
371: 36
372: 137, 151
373: 137
377: 137
379: 44
38: 141
39: 53
390: 149
391: 27
394: 44
399: 57
400: 151, 154
4000: 182
401: 154
403: 116
405: 94
407: 101
408: 94
41: 142
410: 152
414: 57
418: 57
421: 99
425: 45, 179
426: 179
44: 142, 173
444: 53, 57
452: 57
458: 134
4600: 182
463: 57
47: 142
4711: 137

478: 53
497: 28
50: 52-53
500: 54, 151
5000: 182
501: 94
51: 52-53
513: 45
518: 152
520: 135
525: 134
526: 135
531: 134
536: 135
540: 190
546: 135
547: 135
548: 135
549: 135
550: 47, 151, 190
5500: 182
56: 142
560: 151
560A: 152
5636: 103
568: 135
5689: 103
570: 190
5700: 182
5730: 103
5777: 103
580: 153
5800: 182
585: 45
587: 45
590: 150-151, 153
60: 174-175, 199
600: 151, 190
602: 28
604: 45
609: 28
61: 137, 142
612: 47
619: 45
620: 45, 151
624: 45
630: 34
639: 34
640: 151
642: 45
660: 54
6692: 103
678: 45
680: 134
686: 95

6894: 103, 105
6898: 105
69: 98, 137
692: 179
6969: 103
697: 54
6970: 103
698: 34
700: 68, 151
701: 68
7054: 103
71: 137
717: 67-68
719: 188-189
720: 189
7246: 103-104
728: 67-68
7347: 103
739: 58, 189
740: 188-189
7407: 103
749: 188-189
759: 189
7602: 103, 105
7604: 103, 105
7622: 103
7661: 103
7663: 103
7665: 103
7671: 55
7679: 103
7684: 104
769: 183, 189
7711: 104
7759: 105
7764: 104
7788: 104
7820: 103
784: 33
7850: 104
7852: 104
7853: 104
7865: 104
7877: 105
790: 29
791: 29
7911: 104
792: 29
7920: 104
7925: 104
7926: 104
7959: 105
7977: 105
800: 54
8017: 103
8050: 104
809: 46, 58
8191: 104

8192: 104
820: 54
83: 34
830: 27
8381: 104
8413: 105
8420: 104-105
8457: 106
8550: 104
8556: 104
86: 53
8678: 96
8679: 84
886: 27, 36, 58, 187-188
89: 98
890: 27, 33, 188
894: 33
900: 151
905: 188-189
908: 188-189
9102: 104
911: 34
912: 34
9141: 104
916: 34
920: 153, 189
926: 33, 118
929: 188-189
93: 83
938: 34
939: 9, 188-189
940: 189
9467: 105-106
949: 58, 188-190
950: 96, 189
9573: 96
970: 58
971: 151
975: 220
979: 188-189
98: 137
980: 151
985: 151
99: 98, 137
990: 33
991: 151
995: 153
996: 151
X1: 122
X: 122

Other Titles by Author:

Blue Book of Dolls & Values®
2nd Blue Book of Dolls & Values®
3rd Blue Book of Dolls & Values®
4th Blue Book of Dolls & Values®
5th Blue Book of Dolls & Values®
6th Blue Book of Dolls & Values®
7th Blue Book of Dolls & Values®
8th Blue Book of Dolls & Values®
9th Blue Book of Dolls & Values®
10th Blue Book of Dolls & Values®
11th Blue Book of Dolls & Values®
12th Blue Book of Dolls & Values®
13th Blue Book of Dolls & Values®
14th Blue Book of Dolls & Values®

Focusing on Effanbee Composition Dolls
Focusing on Treasury of Mme. Alexander Dolls
Focusing on Gebrüder Heubach Dolls
Kestner: King of Dollmakers
Simon & Halbig Dolls: The Artful Aspect
Doll Classics
Focusing on Dolls
China Doll Collecting
Doll Buying & Selling
German 'Dolly' Collecting

Out-of-print editions of the *Blue Book® of Dolls & Values* have become collectors' items. Out-of-print books can be found at doll shows or auctions. The following prices are for clean books with light wear on covers and corners.

Blue Book® of Dolls & Values $135
2nd Blue Book® of Dolls & Values $110
3rd Blue Book® of Dolls & Values $75
4th Blue Book® of Dolls & Values $75
5th Blue Book® of Dolls & Values $50
6th Blue Book® of Dolls & Values $40
7th Blue Book® of Dolls & Values $40
8th Blue Book® of Dolls & Values $40
9th Blue Book® of Dolls & Values $30
10th Blue Book® of Dolls & Values $30